Hard Oiler!

Hard Oiler!
The Story of Early Canadians' Quest for Oil at Home and Abroad

Gary May

DUNDURN PRESS
TORONTO · OXFORD

Editor: Dennis Mills
Design: Scott Reid
Printer: Transcontinental Printing Inc.

Canadian Cataloguing in Publication Data

May, Gary, 1951-
    Hard oiler!

Includes bibliographical references and index.
ISBN 1-55002-316-0

1. Petroleum industry and trade — Canada — History.

HD9574.C32M39 1998   338.2'7282'0971   C98-931615-7

1 2 3 4 5 DM 02 01 00 99 98

We acknowledge the support of the **Canada Council for the Arts** for our publishing program. We also acknowledge the support of the **Ontario Arts Council** and the **Book Publishing Industry Development Program** of the **Department of Canadian Heritage.**

Printed and bound in Canada.

 Printed on recycled paper.

Dundurn Press	Dundurn Press	Dundurn Press
8 Market Street	73 Lime Walk	2250 Military Road
Suite 200	Headington, Oxford	Tonawanda, NY
Toronto, Ontario, Canada	England	U.S.A. 14150
M5E 1M6	OX3 7AD	

Contents

Acknowledgements

I offer my special thanks to Charles Whipp of Kincardine, Ontario, for helping me to work through the concept of the book, for pointing me in all the right directions and to all the right people, for critiquing my research and writing, and for all his encouragement and support. He knows more about this subject than any journalist anywhere, and I still think Charles should have been the one to write this book.

Thanks to Donna McGuire, curator of the Oil Museum of Canada in Oil Springs, Ontario, for opening up the museum's resources, finding and directing me to the appropriate materials, pointing me to the many people around the Lambton County with connections to the foreign drillers, for the photocopying, the hunting up of pictures, and for regularly offering coffee on those cold winter days.

To Helen Maddock of the Lambton Room at the Lambton County Library in Wyoming, Ontario, for guiding me through the acres of files and documents and peering through old microfilmed newspapers, and to her staff, for their patience, direction, and words of encouragement.

To Petrolia Discovery manager Betty Popelier for lending materials from her files, and to guide Don Wilde for the tours, for explaining the early oil technology, and for all those great stories.

To librarian/historian Edward Phelps of London, Ontario, for his guidance, wisdom and encyclopedic knowledge of the Hard Oilers' story, and for his suggestions and ideas.

To Charles Oliver Fairbank for sharing four generations of experiences in the petroleum business as well as his infectious enthusiasm for the story of the Hard Oilers.

To Paul Miller of the Lambton Heritage Museum in Grand Bend, Ontario, for searching for early pictures of the oil fields at home and abroad. To Bob Cochrane of Cairnlins Petroleum Services in Komoka, Ontario, for explaining and critiquing my description of oil's formation. To Terry Carter of the Ontario Oil, Gas, and Salt Resources Library, in London. And to Doug Gilbert, manager of the Ontario Petroleum Institute, in London.

In Austria, my thanks to Dr. Hermann F. Spoerker, managing director for Oil & Gas Tek International of Leoben, Austria, and Christian Hannesschlager of the Technisches Museum of Vienna, for helping to track down pieces of William McGarvey's story.

Thanks to all the people who contacted me with amazing anecdotes and information about their fantastic and daredevil relatives, including Maureen and Mildred Bradley of London, Murray Brown and Jim and

Bette Lackie of Petrolia, Jean Mearce of Corunna, and Fay Bertrand of Vancouver.

I'm grateful to those who answered my pleas for family histories and anecdotes, including Jane Day of Bury St. Edmunds, Suffolk, England; Lorna Mays of Mississauga, Ontario; and Pete McGarvey of Orillia, Ontario; as well as Lambton residents Dorothy and Charlie Stevenson, Laurence Oliver, Margaret Gregory Smith, Bertha Gleeson, Kathleen Gillespie, John McIntyre, Millicent Woods, Mary Wallen, Marion Berdan, and Gary Mater.

Thanks to Fritz Skeries of London, Ontario; Bill Wilson of Chicago, Illinois; and Arlene Gehmacher of Toronto for help in translating German-language documents.

And finally, thank you to all my friends and family, who endured listening to my regular updates without appearing visibly bored.

Introduction

A hard-luck Yankee fortune seeker. A Hamilton wagon maker hoping to sell cars to the new railways. And a howling swamp so isolated and foul that pioneer farmers had steered it a wide miss. An unlikely combination indeed. And yet this trio, seemingly unconnected, came together at just the right moment in time, to create one of the great but little known stories of Canada's early years.

It is the story of how the first commercial oil well in North America was dug into the heavy blue-clay soils of Lambton County in the far reaches of southwestern Ontario 140 years ago. That discovery set off a frenzy of land speculation and drilling that created both wealth and heartache. And it led to the training of a class of men who later introduced their expertise and equipment to new oil fields around the world, earning for Canadians a leading place among the pioneers of petroleum.

It is a story, too, about the invention of an industry, one that has changed our lives. Today, Canadians are the biggest consumers of energy of any people in the world. It seems only fitting, then, that the energy source that at the turn of a new century remains the world's most important — petroleum — was first captured and spun into a viable commercial enterprise in this country.

However, Canada's seminal part in opening up our modern-day oil industry has received little attention from historians and writers. Just what was that part? I began to ask that question back in the mid-1970s after being posted to a newspaper reporting job in Sarnia, Ontario. Why and how had that city become the petrochemical and oil-refining capital of Canada? After a preliminary search, I was astonished by what I found. Over time I became privy to one of the best kept secrets in Canadian history: the story of how oil had been discovered in Lambton County near Sarnia and how the subsequent exploitation of that oil gave birth to

8

what is arguably the world's most important industry today. It is the story of the men who to this day in Lambton are called the Hard Oilers.

After returning some twenty years later to continue the search, I unearthed an amazing chapter of Canadian history and accomplishment I had not even dreamed existed. I found that, contrary to American claims that Pennsylvania was the home of the modern oil industry, it was in Lambton County that James Miller Williams dug the first commercial oil well in North America — if not the world — and began refining and marketing his product as machine lubricant and lighting oil.

Williams thus set off a chain of events that resulted in the establishment of an industry on which our way of life today is so heavily dependent. What was the allure? Why would men leave their homes and travel, under very primitive conditions, into the stinking, mosquito-infested swamps of Lambton County, in search of oil? The search for adventure is as old as human existence. Something in the stories these men heard tapped into one of our species' most powerful emotions, the thrill of discovery and the quest for success. Like the early explorers who braved the uncharted oceans, trekked to the South Pole, or dared the fates in search of the fabled Northwest Passage, these early wildcatters, who came to be known as the Hard Oilers, were in search of the unknown.

The story, however, does not begin with Williams and it certainly does not end with him. It begins in the Paleozoic Era, and it continues through the gold-rush-like frenzy that sees the overnight rise and decline of the frontier town of Oil Springs, the creation of the much more permanent community of Petrolia, which still flashes its Victorian charm to this day, and then takes a more exotic twist. As early as 1873, Lambton oil drillers started to travel the globe and open up oil fields from Java to the Ukraine, from America to Venezuela, and in the Middle East.

It was said that during the latter part of the nineteenth and early twentieth centuries, no major oil field anywhere in the world was without its Lambton drillers — its Hard Oilers. I came across one account of a Petrolia man sitting in a park in Singapore in 1899 as he waited for the arrival of the steamship that would take him from the Asian field, where he had been a supervisor, back to his family in Canada. The man looked up to see a familiar face coming his way, another Petrolia driller who was on his way to the rain forests of Sumatra. Certainly these adventurers who came to be known in Lambton as the "foreign drillers" were among the best-travelled Canadians of their day. They, as well as their wives and children — both those left at home and those who travelled with the men to distant lands — could later recount fascinating stories of their escapades.

This book relates the astonishing story of the circumstances that

A forest of three-pole derricks rises over wells at Oil Springs.
Courtesy Lambton County Heritage Museum.

conspired for petroleum to be created and then discovered in the midst of southwestern Ontario's last wilderness, the establishment of a new industry, the men and women who are responsible for it, and the role they played in sharing the expertise and equipment they devised to open new fields around the world. It introduces hard-bitten pioneers who, against immense odds, carved out a place for themselves in the annals of Canadian history. It's a story about the entrepreneurs, the inventors, the fortune-seekers, the winners and losers, the dreamers, the hangers-on, and the charlatans, who all contributed to Canada's quest for oil.

There is a coarse romance to the story: The dingy little town of Oil Springs, beset with the pungent odour of petroleum sulphur; the building boom that saw one of the world's grandest hotels constructed and then closed down on the very day it was to officially open, when rumours of war frightened American drillers from the fields; the man who hauled open bottles of nitroglycerine through the streets of Petrolia; the woman who brewed nitro in her main-street apartment; and the row of nitro plants that, one by one, blew themselves off the face of the earth.

In foreign fields, the daring exploits continued: Drillers hiding for their lives in the mountains of Persia when First-World-War-era German troops and Ottoman-Empire Arabs blew up their rigs; surviving horrible accidents in medically primitive conditions; escaping Bolshevik troops in Russia after the murder of Czar Nicholas II and his family; and the Petrolia man who threw one of the grandest weddings during Vienna's most splendid era, then lived to watch his oil empire crumble under the boots and firepower of the Great War armies.

Icons in the world of petroleum are monuments to these Canadians' achievements: The first oil well drilled in Persia, which, at the time, was the world's largest; Canadian Hill in Borneo, where another "first" well was drilled; Canadian drillers bringing water to the parched outback of Australia and the drought-stricken villages of central India.

These simple men who became the foreign drillers often described themselves as living like kings. They were well paid, housed in the best of conditions and cared for by native servants, and ushered from home to the oil field at company expense. Had they stayed at home to farm or work in the Lambton oil fields, they could have scarcely imagined such a life. But having accepted the challenge, Lambton drillers and their families became far more worldly than most Canadians of their era, lured into a life of travel and adventure, and away from the unextraordinariness of small-town and rural life in the late nineteenth and early twentieth centuries.

Today, the historic Ontario oil fields remain. They are not the boiling pot of human activity they once were, but rather quiet, orderly places where the squeak and sigh of the jerker rods supplant the rush of the wind across the pancake landscape. There, old wells still pump small amounts of crude in the shadow of Sarnia's Chemical Valley, the maze of refineries and chemical plants that is their legacy, strung out like shiny pearls along the St. Clair River. The old wells of the historic field now produce, over the course of a year, only as much crude as the first Hibernia well pumps in less than two days. Yet they remain as statues to a more glorious past.

It's hard to imagine how such a fascinating story could go largely unknown. Fascinating, yes, but also important to the understanding of this significant Canadian contribution to the world. When we think of the discovery of oil, why do we think of Texas and Alberta and Saudi Arabia? How could these events have happened and we Canadians not know it?

Perhaps it is part of the cavalier attitude we have toward our own national saga, of how we really came to be here, and why we're the way we are. It's a sad commentary that many of the great tales of our nation go largely untold, or else told in so perfunctory a fashion that we don't bother to pay attention. Our neighbours to the south delight in the excitement, the mystery, and the romance of their past, in amplifying their heroes, and passing on the stories of their contributions to the world. We Canadians are fixated on the sterile institutions of our history, far too reticent to acknowledge the colourful characters who were our ancestors — and their exciting accomplishments.

The quest for oil, which began here so long ago, still goes on. Petroleum continues to be a highly prized commodity. We do everything with it. We eat food packaged in it and wear clothing made from it. We drive cars filled with parts manufactured from it and fuelled by it. We drive on streets and walk on sidewalks constructed from it. Our homes are built from and filled with materials and furniture produced from it. Our lives, our good health, our very being, depend on its capture, distilling, and conversion. We go to war for it.

When the Western democracies in 1991, became so agitated by Iraq's invasion of Kuwait, which so threatened their oil supplies that they launched Operation Desert Storm, it was not the first time Middle East oil had ignited the machinery of war. Oil was considered crucial in 1914 as well. At the outset of the First World War, Britain planted its stake on the supplies coming from Persia and went to war in that quarter of the globe to protect them.

While the world awaits a new energy source that will pace us through the twenty-first century, petroleum remains the life-blood of our society.

In Canada, two exciting new developments offer promise that this country will be a significant producer of petroleum as the twenty-first century dawns. Hibernia, off the coast of Newfoundland pumped its first barrel of crude on 17 November 1997, and estimates are that the underwater field's reserves amount to 750 million barrels or more. In the northern Alberta town of Fort McMurray, 440 kilometres northeast of Edmonton, the huge oil-sands project is flying into high gear. Advances in oil-sands technology can help make Canada more self-sufficient in the product that still drives the world economy.

These immense finds offer a prosperous future. As Canadians, however, we ought not forget where and how it all began and what part our ancestors played in this thrilling and significant story. It is a story too little known outside of Lambton County, Ontario, and perhaps only poorly understood within. But one of the great milestones of Canadian achievement can be traced back to one summer day in 1858, when James Miller Williams and the man who had led him to the site, Charles Nelson Tripp, struck oil at what was to be the world's first modern commercial petroleum operation. From the first tentative steps under the leadership of those early Hard Oilers, the petroleum industry we know today took root.

That industry has dominated the energy picture of our twentieth century, but that position will be challenged in the twenty-first. Powerful new batteries, electricity, nuclear fusion, solar, and perhaps some yet-unknown newcomer will crowd the energy market and, some day, muscle petroleum to the side. Before that day comes, Canadians should take stock of how the discoveries and experiences of our countrymen delivered us to this place.

This book tells of the discovery and the quest for oil. My hope is that it will, in some small part, convey to Canadians the importance of what happened in Lambton County those many years ago.

Part One
The Early Story of Oil

"Celebrated for its natural curing power. A natural medicine."
— Kier's advertisement for petroleum oil from Drake Well Museum,
Titusville, Pennsylvania; and Tower, Walter Sheldon, *The Story of Oil.*
[New York: D. Appleton & Co., 1909.]

Chapter One
Out of a Swamp

Picture a swamp. A hot, steamy, bug-infested, salt-water, tropical swamp. Gigantic fern-like trees, their roots sunk deep in a quagmire, their crowns reaching high into the heavens. Amphibians croaking and screeching their calls.

Now picture this swamp in southwestern Ontario — 320 kilometres southwest of where the metropolis of Toronto will rise, in four hundred million years or so.

It is in this swamp where the dying plant and animal life will fall, be covered in muck, and eventually, mysteriously, turned into a thick, dark substance that will some day make our modern society run the way it does.

It is oil.

Oil — petroleum — is taken from rocks that vary in age anywhere from 10 to 500 million years. It is not formed within the rock in which it is found, but rather migrates from its place of origin, a drop at a time, over great numbers of years.

Once, it was thought that petroleum was somehow associated with volcanic activity. Today, we know that petroleum comes into being when countless generations of organic material — plant and animal — die and fall into shallow seas. Petroleum can come from any organic material: fish, animals, land plants, and water plants. It is not the kind of organic material that is crucial to the creation of oil, but what happens to it after it dies.

Petroleum cannot be formed if these plants and animals and fish have been eaten by other creatures or if they rot in water with a high oxygen content. Petroleum is made in stagnant lagoons, where there is little oxygen, where these creatures and plants are simply buried in sediments. It can also be formed in deeper seas, where plankton sink to the seafloor and are buried by silt and clay. Bacterial action in the heavy sediment of plankton releases the oxygen and concentrates the hydrogen and carbon needed to produce petroleum. The conglomeration of materials "cooks" in high temperatures — but not too high — and under the pressure of the weight above.

The creation of petroleum is not just an old process that has, for some reason, stopped. Oil is being formed today. The problem is that it takes a long while for those individual drops of petroleum to make their way through rock that offers sufficient passageways so they can congregate in large enough quantities to be of interest to people. Petroleum occurs widely across the world, usually in very small quantities. Although it is the world's second most common liquid, petroleum is found in commercial quantities only in a very few places.

In southwestern Ontario, oil was formed because the area was once a shallow inland sea. Half a billion years ago, this sea stretched across the centre of the continent, from Newfoundland to Los Angeles. Slowly the water began to recede.

The sorts of plants and animals that inhabited the region changed drastically during the period of oil formation. From the small naked, simply branched vegetation without roots or leaves of the Devonian Period, to horsetails with their whorled appendages, and ferns, through to conifers and deciduous trees. From the simplest of marine animal life through to dinosaurs and early mammals.

Because of the diversity of materials that eventually turn into oil and the periods of time necessary for the transformation, petroleum varies widely in composition. Each concentration of oil bears its own "signature," based on its own unique blend of hydrocarbon.

Petroleum is constantly being formed somewhere on the earth. Its formation can begin almost as soon as the silt within which the organic material is contained becomes buried. Small quantities have been created synthetically, and carbon-14 dating of silt in the Gulf of Mexico shows some oil there as new as 500 years. Other traces in drill cores seem to be less than fifty years old. But that does not mean the supplies we are depleting will be magically replenished. Great quantities take many millions of years to form. In effect, oil is a non-renewable resource.

The important development that takes so long is not just the creation of petroleum, but also the pooling of sufficient amounts of petroleum to make its mining economical. Luckily for we humans, oil does not stay put after it is formed. When oil is found in the rocks in which it was actually created, the amounts are normally quite small. Large quantities of oil are only found in open sandstones and porous limestones that are generally adjacent to the source (or home rocks) where it was formed.

The oil, gas and ancient sea water are squeezed out like liquid from a

16

wet sponge when the source material is compacted into rock. The parts of this liquid separate according to how heavy they are, the heaviest water at the bottom, oil next, and the lighter gases at the top. Then these materials begin a voyage that will truly make the oil and gas valuable some day. Pushed by the heavier water, the oil and gas move through the pores of the sandstones and cracks of the limestones until they strike an impenetrable rock structure, or until they escape up fissures to the surface. When oil and gas reach the surface, the lighter gases disappear into the air. The remaining heavier oils harden into bitumen, a substance that looks like asphalt.

Sometimes the escaping gases are accidentally set on fire — from a lightning strike perhaps — and send out huge plumes of flame. And sometimes the oil is discovered as "gum beds," which consist of oil-saturated soil or clay.

For oil to be useful to humans, the rock encasing it also must be permeable, meaning the spaces in which the liquid is captured must be connected so that oil will flow through the rock when people drill a hole to seek it out. If it's not permeable rock, the oil cannot be captured. That is why, despite the frequency of its presence on our planet, few sources are worth the trouble and expense needed to search them out.

Five billion years ago, our earth raged angrily, a mass of fire and molten material. Then it cooled, hardened into rock, and water vaporized and gravitated to the holes and pits and canyons that pock-marked the surface.

Three and a half billion years ago, the first single-cell life appeared. Then this began to evolve into an incredible variety of creatures, like coral and mosses.

Half a billion years ago, our earliest ancestors appeared.

The region on earth that is now southwestern Ontario would have been quite unrecognizable. At one time, it was very tropical in character. It has been just during the past thirty million years — a short moment in the earth's history — that continental drift has seen that terrain become part of a cooler latitude. That set the stage for the past two million years, with the formation and sliding southward of the great glaciers that chiselled and sliced and scoured much of Canada into its current form.

And it was only in the past 9,000 years that southwestern Ontario has come to resemble its current self, its climate warming slightly again to something approaching that which we now know, and enabling the growth of the plants and animals that would be familiar to modern residents. The retreating glaciers left Ontario's southern peninsula surrounded on three sides by huge lakes, and left what people would name Lambton County covered by a heavy, blue clay and a smaller lake that would eventually contract into a swamp.

By the time all of this happened, the oil had formed and lay under that swampy, clay area, ready to be tapped by humans.

To be sure, it did not all remain buried. Since oil rises under pressure wherever it can find spaces through which to squeeze, it did just that in a couple of places in central Lambton. It followed fissures in the earth's crust and emerged at the surface to form beds of dried petroleum material — bitumen — or else saturated the clay to create gum beds. In another nearby spot, it bubbled up alongside the river that would one day be called the Thames.

Oil's Ancient Uses

Locations where petroleum and its constant companion, natural gas, made their way to the surface exist all over the globe. People have been making use of those escaped substances for at least six thousand years. And these substances have been dubbed with any number of names: pitch, gum, grease, bitumen, slime, burning stone, and tar. Where natural gas bubbled to the surface, it sometimes caught fire and was dubbed "burning waters."

In the Bible, pitch was used to coat Noah's Ark, and three friends of Daniel — Shadrach, Meshach, and Abednigo — were cast into a fiery furnace, which was probably burning gas escaping from gaps in the earth at a field in what is now northern Iraq. The Tower of Babel and Solomon's Temple were constructed using asphalt mortar.

The ancient Egyptians employed "slime" to embalm their dead. Pyramids as well as the Sphinx built as long ago as 3,000 years were waterproofed with asphalt. Asphalt was used, too, to waterproof the sides of pools built at the Hanging Gardens of Babylon.

Natural-gas fires burned at the shrine of the Oracle of Delphi and Baku. Marco Polo saw the Baku oil in the thirteenth century, and explained to his hometown audience it was used for medication and lighting oil.

In China and Burma, oil was hand-ladled from pools where it collected naturally, and used for medicinal purposes. There is some suggestion that the Chinese may have employed petroleum and gas for heat and light as early as two thousand years ago. The gas was transported from its source to its place of use by "pipelines" constructed from bamboo.

The first-century Roman historian Pliny said oil was burned in the lamps of the temple of Jupiter. A Roman general once coated pigs with oil, set them on fire, and then drove them through his enemy's ranks.

The Greeks poured oil onto the water and set it ablaze to keep an enemy fleet away. During the Second World War, the British were prepared to do the same in the event of a German invasion of their island.

By the early 1800s, workers skimmed and soaked up oil in large woollen blankets from surface deposits in Burma, Galicia in Austria-Hungary, and Baku in Azerbaijan, between Iran and Russia. In Burma and Baku, the supply was privately owned and closely guarded. Its use was deemed a hereditary right in the Yenangyoung field of the Irrawaddy Valley in Burma, and it was under the domain of the Khan of Baku in that land. In Galicia, labourers distilled oil found in shallow, hand-dug pits.

In North America, First Nations people used surface oil both internally and externally. The first written report of oil on this continent came from a French visitor[1] who crossed the Niagara River and arrived in what is now western New York state. There, the Franciscan missionary, Joseph de la Roche D'Allion, reported seeing bitumen "issuing" from Lake Ontario in 1627.

Its medicinal properties were widely valued before the mid-nineteenth century. In 1835, Andrew Lucas left Lanark County in eastern Ontario and settled in Lambton's Brooke Township. Lucas was a herbalist and doctor and became interested in stories of oil the Natives were said to use for medicinal purposes. He asked the Natives to lead him to the seeps, which were probably the gum beds near Oil Springs. There he spread an old woollen blanket over an area that was still gummy and had his guides tramp the blanket down into the oily substance. When the oil soaked into the wool, Lucas wrung it out into several containers. Family legend has it that after spending a few days in Lambton, Lucas went to Hamilton to seek lodging. But his clothing reeked so badly from the sulphurous petroleum, he was refused entry to a hotel.[2] It's not known just what use Lucas made of the substance.

Also in Lambton, there was a report of unrefined crude oil being smeared on oxen in the 1840s to protect them from flies.[3] At the same time, local Natives gave some oil to a white woman to help relieve her asthma attacks.

Meanwhile in Pittsburgh, Pennsylvania, a druggist, Samuel Kier, poured crude oil into bottles and slapped on this label:

Hard Oiler!

Kier's Petroleum or Rock Oil
Celebrated for its wonderful curing power
A natural Medicine
Pumped from a well in Allegheny County, Pennsylvania
400 feet below the surface of the ground[4]

Into the nineteenth century, whale oil was often utilized as an illuminating fuel, but it became increasingly expensive as the number of whales dwindled. The average sperm whale yielded 300 gallons of oil, called spermaceti or sperm oil, which was contained in the animal's head cavity. But for most early Americans and Europeans, tallow candles supplied their lighting needs, albeit in a very unsatisfactory manner.

People began to look for replacements for the dwindling whale oil. Camphene, a highly volatile mixture of turpentine and alcohol, was costly and dangerous. But coal, shales, asphalt, and petroleum oil all began to be talked of as potential sources for the creation of illuminating fluid.

Shale and coal were common enough materials, so experimentation soon began. The British naval commander at Halifax, the Earl of Dundonald, had patented (in 1813) a new lamp that would burn the oil obtained when Trinidad asphalt was boiled and distilled. And it just so happened that the commander was friends with a Canadian who was working on a process to make illuminating oil from coal and bitumen.

Abraham Gesner

That man, Abraham Gesner, was a geologist, author, chemist, and inventor. His work became crucial to the development of the petroleum industry in Canada and around the world. While he was not strictly speaking a Hard Oiler and never visited the home of the Canadian oil industry, Gesner's work nevertheless earns for him a title as a founder of that industry.[5]

As a geologist, he studied, described, and mapped rock formations in Britain's Maritime Canadian colonies. After graduating from British medical school, he returned to Nova Scotia and set up a medical practice. But geology remained Gesner's passion. He explored the colony on horseback, on foot, and by boat. In 1838 he moved to Saint John, New Brunswick, where his annual reports on the area's geology established him as the first government geologist in a British colony. While there, he went back to Albert County and took a second look at some bitumen deposits he had earlier found. He named these deposits "albertite" for the county in which they were discovered.

Chipping away some of these rock-hard oily secretions, Gesner took them home, threw them into a cauldron and melted them down. Through these early distilling experiments, he began, by 1846, to create a substance he later called kerosene. By 1853, he had perfected the substance into an oil that could be burned in lamps.

Gesner moved to the United States the following year, obtained patents, and established his North American Kerosene Gas and Light Company on Long Island, where he produced kerosene from coal. The term "coal oil" was thus born, and continued to be used even after the illuminating fluid began to be refined from petroleum.

Gesner became a successful businessman and news of his work was published in reports and books. He also authored numerous publications, the most important of which was his 1861 book, *A Practical Treatise on Coal, Petroleum and Other Distilled Oils*. But his findings had begun to be known by the late 1850s, and they became invaluable to those who worked in the field. Among those was a Hamilton man named James Miller Williams who would soon tramp into the swamps of Lambton County in search of petroleum. Gesner also invented a wood preservative, a process for paving highways with asphalt, and briquettes made from compressed coal dust.

Meanwhile, by 1850, the Scot, James H. Young, had taken out patents on a process to extract oil from coals and oil shales, to use for lighting, lubrication, and paraffin wax. The process became widely used in Britain, and whereas "coal oil" was becoming the popular term in America, "paraffin oil" was the preferred name in Britain.[6]

However, the incentive to refine petroleum was strong, according to Colonel R.B. Harkness, former oil and gas commissioner for Ontario and a petroleum historian. According to Harkness, chemists and geologists were in agreement as early as 1850 that crude oil would provide a far superior illuminating fuel to whale oil, and that it could be recovered from the bitumen deposits that seeped to the surface of the ground in many places.[7]

The demand for lighting fuels was growing: more people were becoming able to read, and the information explosion was offering increasing quantities of reading material. Urban areas were expanding, offering more cultural and social affairs to attend in the evenings. During the 1850s, newspapers printed countless advertisements for all kinds of oils: sperm whale and elephant oils, cod and fish oils, vegetable and animal oils, resins, and camphene.

Hard Oiler!

The Geological Survey of Canada

Even as these developments were being recorded, the government of the British province of Canada was setting up an agency called the Geological Survey to explore and locate natural resources that would help to boost the young colony's economy. It was 1841 when the legislature of the combined provinces of Canada East and Canada West approved the survey, and the next year, a geologist named William Edmond Logan was appointed its first director.

The following year, Logan headed out to Nova Scotia and New Brunswick to see what he might find. At the same time he sent an assistant, Alexander Murray, to look at lands in the southern peninsula of Canada West, between Lakes Erie and Huron.[8] Murray can be excused if he felt his boss had given him the raw end of that deal. While the Maritime provinces were well developed, with fairly good roads at the time, the lands in the western portion of the province of Canada between the lakes were relatively wild.

Still several years before the railroads would cross the Ontario plain, settlement hugged the lakefronts and rivers. There were the Lake Erie settlements of Colonel Thomas Talbot, once assistant to Upper Canada's first lieutenant-governor, John Graves Simcoe. At the southwestern tip of the province sat the military fortifications around Windsor. And on the Thames River, north of Talbot's settlements, was the tiny community of London, which became home, after the 1837 rebellion, to a British army regiment. In between were tiny, scattered settlements and Native communities. The Chippewa Indians had ceded to the Crown over two million acres of land north of the Talbot settlements and west of London in 1827.

Because of the great distances and poor communications, tiny self-sufficient communities sprang up across the territory wherever a handful of settlers gathered. Commerce grew up around a grist mill, saw mill, carding mill, general store, blacksmith shop, and a shop where a carpenter built furniture and wagons, and probably coffins. A tavern would arise to handle travellers' basic needs, a place with some tables that also offered shelter to newly arriving settlers until they had time to move in properly. The tavern's common room became the gathering place, the community centre, where ideas, news, and experiences were shared.

The least settled of this sparsely populated region was the centre of Lambton County, where Enniskillen Township was to be located, and where the first surveyor, in 1832, had noted water up to half a metre deep, and swamps that made things "altogether impassable."[9] He simply and swamps that made things "altogether impassable."[9] He simply abandoned his survey and returned to report how his men had to stand on guard each night against prowling bears and wolves. A year later, another surveyor declared the township's rivers and streams unsuitable for mills.

To these early surveyors, the township's waterlogged soils seemed totally inhospitable to farming. The centre of Lambton was looked on as nothing better than a breeding ground for malaria-carrying mosquitoes, a heavily wooded swamp land. None of these surveyors bothered to speak with the Natives who might, had they been asked, have told the visitors about the nearby oil seepages to which they soon would lead Andrew Lucas.

Consequently, the discovery of the bitumen by those who would do something about it would have to await another event. Colonel Harkness believed that event was the arrival on Sir William Logan's desk, about 1850, of a sample of Lambton bitumen. From whom had the samples come? That is not known. Perhaps from Andrew Lucas, or perhaps it was Alexander Murray who, after all, had been sent to the district earlier in the 1840s. Logan had seen similar material during his travels to Quebec's Gaspé. He handed the samples over to a chemist in his employ, Thomas Sterry Hunt, who described the material's properties in the Geological Survey report of 1849/50.

Now with that report in hand, Logan would turn to the man he had sent to explore the district some years earlier, Murray, for a closer evaluation. Murray left his Woodstock-area farm and ventured westward, past London, into the wilds of Lambton, to visit the deposits from which the samples had been sent. He compiled a full report on his findings for the Geological Survey in 1852/53. In it, he confirmed Hunt's findings, and declared the material suitable for the production of illuminating gas, paints, varnishes, and tars.

Murray's report contained another piece of intriguing information. He found that the gum beds and bitumen deposits were no longer being ignored. He told Logan that he had come across a test pit of some nine metres deep, dug into the clay.[10] The signs of activity were already there. An early entrepreneur had left his mark. The era of the Hard Oilers had commenced.

Part Two
Discovery

"Upon running out to ascertain the nature of the disturbance,
he perceived a huge fountain of what seemed to be black mud
bursting with great violence from the hole ..."
— J.T. Henry, *The Early and Late History of Petroleum.*
[New York: Augustus M. Kelley,1970; original publication 1873.]

Chapter Two
The First of the Hard Oilers

"Hard Oiler" is a name that is still worn proudly in central Lambton County by descendants of the pioneers of the region's oil industry. One version of its origins has it that in the heyday of the foreign drillers, Petrolia and Oil Springs men would saunter into a saloon in far-away locales such as London, England, which was known for a time as the oil men's Gateway to the Foreign Fields. The visitor would shout, "Hard Oiler!" at the top of his lungs. More often than not, there would be a like reply, and, having thus identified themselves, two or more Canadian oil men would sit down to hoist a couple of brews, swap tales of their adventures in foreign lands, and pass along the latest news from home.

True or not, it's a good story. A twist on that story has it that two foreign drillers once used the term as a greeting when they happened upon one another in a Middle East desert.[11]

Others contend the phrase originated at a football game in the early 1900s. "We're going to beat them to a hard oil finish," was the way long-time Petrolia resident Bertha Gleeson says her late husband, sports columnist Lew Gleeson, recounted it to her. After that, Gleeson and other area residents took up the cause and applied the term Hard Oil to everything related to petroleum. "When the foreign drillers went away, that's the way they'd identify themselves," says Bertha Gleeson. "Everything was Hard Oil. If you were born here, you were Hard Oil. If you came here from away, you were a Johnny-come-lately."[12]

Purists will still tell you the term applies only to Petrolians, and not to those from Oil Springs. But for the most part, those from central Lambton are all recognized as Hard Oilers.

Hard Oiler!

Charles Nelson Tripp

Charles Nelson Tripp was a man with a dream he was certain would make him rich. He followed his vision to the Lambton oil lands, perhaps a bit ahead of his time, or at least ahead of the railroad's time. Rather than achieve his dream, Tripp languished in debt and died penniless, success always tantalizingly close. Yet his crucial part in opening the way into the oil lands makes him the first of those who can now truly be consecrated with the title Hard Oiler.

Like many of the early Hard Oilers, he was not native to this country, but rather came from Schenectady, New York. Unlike many others, he never actually adopted Canada as his own land, but merely passed through on his petroleum pursuit. While Tripp fell victim to the double-edged curse of hard luck and short finances, his efforts assured him a place in history as "the original oil man of Canada."[13]

Just how and why Tripp made his way from the United States to the village of Bath in eastern Ontario is not known, but records show that is where he lived, age twenty-seven, in 1850, the foreman of John Counter's stove foundry. His younger brother, Henry, lived just east of London, Ontario, in Woodstock. On Woodstock's edge, too, sat the farm of Alexander Murray, the young geologist who had been employed by the Geological Survey of Canada and who would soon be sent to check out the Lambton gum beds.[14]

Undoubtedly through his brother in Woodstock, Charles Nelson Tripp learned of the report of the gum beds chronicled by Thomas Sterry Hunt, a chemist for the Geological Survey. Having tried unsuccessfully in Bath to turn minerals into money, Tripp became enthralled with the prospects of producing asphalt from the gum-bed materials, and around 1850 decided to go to Lambton in search of the substance that bubbled to the surface.[15]

It would not have been an easy journey. Steamships carted passengers and mail across the Great Lakes and up newly built canals and the larger rivers of Canada West. But overland passage was still painfully slow and uncomfortable. Citizens complained about the condition of the roads, which were often mere muddy tracks through dense forests. The colony's poor roads severely hindered its early development and limited settlement to the regions that hugged the waterways. And the railway through southwestern Ontario to Sarnia was still a few years away. So it was no minor adventure when Charles Tripp journeyed into the wilds of Lambton County to check out the bitumen and gum beds.

What he found must have impressed him, though, because, during

1851 and 1852, Tripp and his brother, Henry, as well as some other men from Woodstock, Hamilton, and New York, formed what must have been the world's first oil company, predating the Pennsylvania Rock Oil Company of New York. Or at least they instigated proceedings about this time that would lead to the granting of the company's charter. It took until 18 December 1854 to actually incorporate the International Mining and Manufacturing Company.[16]

During the intervening years, the group started work at the site, and it appears that buildings were erected there by 1852 to manufacture asphalt from the gum beds. The charter gave the partners the right to explore for asphalt beds, oil and salt springs, and to manufacture products from those sources for various uses. Meanwhile, records show that Tripp made a series of land purchases in the Oil Springs and Petrolia area.[17] He was beginning to accumulate what he hoped would be his empire.

The process they devised for exploiting the gum beds was simple. The men used pick and shovel to break up the hard bitumen that sat on the surface. In other places, they came across a softer oily muck that consisted of clay mixed with petroleum. Then they built what was, in effect, a still from a big pot or cauldron, and lit a fire under it. Into the cauldron went the bitumen or muck, to be boiled down into a thick tar. The tar was poured out and formed into blocks that cooled into molds of asphalt.[18]

Tripp had already taken a sample of this asphalt to two different men: Dr. Thomas Antisell, a New York chemist, and Thomas McIlwraith, manager of the Hamilton Gas Company in Hamilton, Ontario. Antisell reported enthusiastically in 1853 that the asphalt was highly suitable for paints, mastics or adhesive products, waterproofing materials and, if distilled, even lighting oil.[19]

McIlwraith added that when they gasified the asphalt, instead of coal, the product was suitable for lighting oil.

Commercially, things should have been promising for the young enterprise. But the company now began to fail even before it could get off the ground.[20] Tripp did not take full advantage of what he had discovered. Whether that was because he did not fully comprehend the possibilities, or because he felt the isolation of the region would defeat his efforts, the result was the same.

If he didn't appreciate the potential, we should not judge him too harshly. Experimentation with gasifying and liquefying coal and bitumen was in its infancy, and word of Gesner's work was only beginning to be reported at a time when communications were poor by today's standards. The world was developing a powerful thirst for lighting oil, and yet Tripp and his partners seem to have paid little attention to the prospects of using the bitumen for that purpose, despite the words of encouragement from Antisell and McIlwraith.

Tripp could not have produced asphalt from the gum beds without also producing lighter oil by-products, and yet he did not try to market them. He may simply have decided the trouble and expense were too great to bother, and that the best he could hope for was to turn a quick dollar on the asphalt.

After all, he was dealing with the unimaginably poor transportation system in Canada West. It is hard to comprehend in this day of excellent roads — paved with asphalt, it should be noted — just how horrific transportation was in what is now southwestern Ontario. Experienced travellers were known to curse the roads of Canada West as the worst they had ever experienced. When they came to Lambton, they could claim to have seen the worst of the worst.

In four successive periods fairly recent in geological terms, vast walls of ice moved across southern Ontario. In Lambton they left behind a clay bed and shallow lakes with few gravel deposits. The land was impermeable, forcing water to pool on the surface rather than drain away. The resulting swamps made central Lambton the last area of southwestern Ontario to be settled, and only the discovery of oil spurred even that late development.

While railroads were expanding, it would not be until 1858 that the Great Western Railway would arrive, and even then it only came as far as Wyoming, which was sixteen kilometres north of the gum beds. Those sixteen kilometres must have seemed like a hundred and sixteen. There was no passageway that rightly deserved the term "road," and when it rained, the clay soils turned to a terrible grey-black quagmire so immense that it threatened to swallow wagons, horses, cargo, and all. The best time to move the asphalt was the winter when horse-drawn sleighs could carry it the thirty or so kilometres to Port Sarnia for loading onto ships.

Tripp's company began to sink into debt. Yet even then, its product was gaining widespread recognition and accolades. Tripp sent a sample of asphalt to the Universal Exhibition in Paris in 1855 and it won an honourable mention.[21] At the same time as the exhibit, the city of Paris sent Tripp an order for asphalt to pave its streets. Europeans were coming to appreciate the advantages of asphalt-paved streets and sidewalks, and the demand for the product was growing.

But fame could not keep the wolf from the door. Tripp was hobbled by personal financial problems, and in late 1855 he sold two hundred acres to his brother, Henry, for four hundred pounds. Charles Tripp owed money to the Bank of Canada[22] as well as to several Sarnia area business people from whom he had purchased goods and services. That's probably why he now began to look east for help rather than west to Sarnia. He soon found himself in Hamilton looking for equipment to cart his asphalt out of the Lambton wilderness.

James Miller Williams

James Miller Williams, the Hamilton wagon maker, began the first large-scale commercial petroleum enterprise in Canada, if not the world.
Courtesy Oil Museum of Canada.

It required someone with greater resources than Tripp to take advantage of the opportunities that lay buried beneath the Lambton swamps. That man was James Miller Williams, who in quick order fashioned a fully integrated petroleum corporation exploring, recovering, transporting, refining, and marketing oil. No one on the face of the earth had ever achieved that on such a scale before.

31

Williams was another of those American-born pioneers of Canada's oil industry, but one who took eagerly to the citizenship of British North America. Born in Camden, New Jersey, in 1818, his family had emigrated to the United States from Wales.[23] Williams learned the carriage trade, then, lured north by his love for his British heritage, moved to London in 1840. He went into business with a carriage maker named M. Holmes, whom he soon bought out. In 1842, Williams married Melinda Clarissa Jackson.

London was still a small community on the edge of civilization, and Williams ascertained there were better business opportunities in Hamilton. In 1846, he moved his carriage operation to that city and teamed up with Henry G. Cooper, who was already running the Hamilton Coach Factory. For a decade, the partnership thrived.

Hamilton was the second largest city in Canada West, which later became Ontario, with a population of more than 10,000. It was a thriving community where some of the most prosperous citizens had begun to put down roots and erect solid, large homes of limestone quarried from the Niagara Escarpment, homes designed in the Italianate manner, classical revival, or Georgian. One of the grandest of the new homes was built by Sir Allan MacNab — Dundurn Castle, on the northwest edge of the town. Williams purchased a piece of property on Queen Street South and built a somewhat grim-looking mansion he dubbed Mapleside.

Hamilton was beginning to enjoy the trappings of a respectable nineteenth century town of some significance and longevity. Its proud citizens set up a private lending library in 1849, and an orphans' home was erected soon afterwards. The community's success was founded upon the hard work and good fortune of a strong business class.

Williams was one of the most successful of Hamilton's entrepreneurs. The Williams and Cooper Carriage Factory employed forty people. In the 1850s, he and Cooper had high hopes for supplying rail cars for the quickly expanding railway business. By 1855 the Great Western Railway extended from Toronto to Niagara Falls and westward to Windsor where it was connected to the thriving American city of Detroit. Hamilton was happily situated at the join of the Niagara and Windsor lines, and the city's future looked golden.

Williams must have talked with Charles Nelson Tripp when the latter came to the carriage shop looking to place orders, and was apparently intrigued by what he heard. One account of their first meeting is that Tripp owed Williams's company for a wagon he had purchased and offered some of his oil lands as payment. When Tripp sold 400 acres of his International Petroleum and Mining Company land to a group from

Hamilton, Williams was one of the buyers. Williams had begun to suspect that the Great Western Railway intended to build its own cars rather than purchase them from outside contractors so he sold his share of the business. Williams must have thought that, with Tripp's arrival, fate was handing him a gold-embossed invitation to a new career. He was right.

Williams was interested not in asphalt but in illuminating oil. By the latter part of the 1850s, scientific journals were reporting on the findings of men like Gesner and Young. Whale oil grew increasingly rare, and new sources were in high demand.

Ever the shrewd businessman, Williams no doubt recognized Tripp's value to his new enterprise. The Hamilton wagon maker hired Tripp and the two set off into the swampy lands of Canada West's frontier. Rather than head directly to the gum beds, however, they initially travelled a bit farther south to the village of Bothwell.[24] Why they chose this location is unclear, although certainly it had been known for years there was a seepage of oil there. Upper Canada's first lieutenant-governor, John Graves Simcoe, reported a petroleum spring along the Thames River at Bothwell when he passed through in February 1793.[25] Simcoe was told by Natives that they used it as a liniment to alleviate rheumatism.

Williams may have been in search of a cleaner source than Tripp's petroleum gumbo, a dirty stew of oil mixed with leaves, soil and twigs. Regardless, the first attempt by Williams and Tripp to find flowing oil at Bothwell proved unsuccessful. Having dug down by hand to a depth of about eight metres, they found the hole filling up with little more than oily water. They drove in a pipe, which broke off, and abandoned the effort.[26]

Then Williams made a decision that would change his life. He went back with Tripp to the gum beds in which he was part owner, thanks to the deal he had penned in Hamilton. Several unsuccessful attempts were made to find oil before they hit the thick, dark green, pay dirt. One report of the day had it that they were actually digging a water well to supply the workers at the gumbeds when oil was struck.[27] It's equally likely that Williams had suspected there was a clean flow of oil beneath the surface that fed the gum beds and it was that flow he was seeking.

Regardless of what he was looking for, in the early summer of 1858, fifteen and a half metres below the surface of the ground, Williams struck oil. Amid the black-walnut trees that thrived in the waterlogged clay soils of central Lambton, Williams's heart must have skipped a beat or two as he watched the oil ooze up into the hole he had dug. The overpowering rotten-eggs-like aroma of the sulphur-charged oil must have seemed like the sweetest scent in the world to him as he stood in the dark forest contemplating his rosy future.

The First-Well Controversy

The first wells in Lambton were dug by hand, and those that remain suggest they were generally about two metres by three metres across. As they dug, the men fit wooden cribbing along the sides to keep the blue clay soil from breaking and falling into the well. Williams brought in a steam-powered engine to work a couple pumps to haul the petroleum out of the ground. He was now in business as the world's first oil man.

Popular American belief is that this title belongs to Edwin L. Drake for his find at Titusville, Pennsylvania on 27 August 1859. Certainly, the displays at the Drake Well Museum in Titusville, Pennsylvania, make that claim. However, as early as June 1860 the American book, *Oil In Pennsylvania and Elsewhere*, acknowledged Williams's earlier discovery. That book indicated at the time of publication that Williams's well had been in operation for two years, a full year before Titusville began producing.

Other sources contemporary to the discovery are equally convincing. As early as August 1858, newspapers were reporting on a dug well and oil flowing from it. In Sarnia, the *Canadian Observer*[28] of 26 August 1858 referred to oils from Lambton being "barrelled up and sent to Hamilton to be prepared there," an obvious reference to Williams's oil works. The owner, according to the newspaper article, was preparing to make the product available for lighting fuel and other purposes.

The oil, it said, "seems to abound over a considerable tract of the land where it was discovered; in fact, the earth is thoroughly saturated by it, so that a hole dug eight or ten feet in width, and about the same depth, will collect from 200 to 250 gallons a day."

By the time Drake struck oil in Pennsylvania, the Ontario industry had sufficiently matured, according to Dr. J.J. Talman, former chief librarian at the University of Western Ontario in London, to have experienced its first consumer complaints. Talman said customers were already angry about high prices,[29] a protest that will strike a certain resonance with today's motorists.

The honour of the claim to the continent's first oil well has nearly always been good natured, and sometimes has taken on humourous tones. At times, the battle has raged furiously between those who favour Pennsylvania's claim and those who side with Ontario. In 1960 a series of letters passed between Colonel R.B. Harkness, then Ontario oil commissioner and one of this country's great petroleum historians, and Ernest C. Miller, vice-president of West Penn Oil Company of Warren, Pennsylvania.[30]

Often the dispute hinged on whether Williams's hand-dug well really counted when compared to the drilled well sunk by Colonel Drake. If a mere "dug pit" constituted an oil well, sniffed Miller, then the United States could still lay claim to the first well by virtue of dug pits in what is now West Virginia that predated Williams's find by three decades.

This was too much for Harkness, who grew a little heated and accused the American of jingoist poppycock. Some pit, Harkness countered. Some pit indeed, having initially been dug to the depth of fifteen and a half metres and then later deepened to forty-five metres. Against immense odds, Williams had dug the well, distilled the oil, hauled it out of the middle of a stinking swamp and over a trail through the wilderness to the railhead some sixteen kilometres away, carted it by train another 170 kilometres to Hamilton, then marketed it. Williams had a fully operational petroleum company, mining, refining, and marketing its product, all before Drake had "drilled" his well.

Harkness noted that if Williams had so desired, he could have "drilled" his well rather than dug it with pick and shovel, since a water drill was in existence at St. Catharines. But he must have decided that, given the trouble he would face having to haul the rig through the wilds of Lambton, it would be a lot easier just to dig it by hand.

Today, the staff at the Drake Well Museum in Titusville, Pennsylvania, will acknowledge, when pressed, that the Oil Springs "dug" well came first, but cling to their claim of having the first "drilled" well. However, their insistence on claiming to be the birthplace of the modern petroleum industry is far more suspect when you look at the facts surrounding Williams's exploits.

Williams's discovery demonstrated that timing is everything. He was considerably luckier than the hapless Tripp in that the London-to-Sarnia branch of the Great Western Railway opened the very year he struck oil. That meant that, if he could get it to Wyoming, he could send it out by train.

As word of the Lambton find spread, men began to tramp into the region in search of riches. Others looked in the dozens of other locations across the continent where seepages similar to the Lambton gum beds and Bothwell springs had been known of over the years. The first tentative steps in North America's oil boom had commenced. A full-blown rush would soon follow.

A Primitive Business Begins

So, in 1858, Williams was in the business of digging for crude and turning it into lighting oil and lubricants. An advertisement in his hometown newspaper indicated illuminating oil was available at 70 cents a gallon, and that machinery oil could be had for 60 cents.[31] Williams also sold crude oil.

Besides sales in Sarnia, London, Hamilton, and Toronto, Williams unloaded 180 barrels of lamp oil to a New York City businessman, A.C. Ferris.[32] If oil had been available in Pennsylvania by that time, surely he would have bought it there instead.

Williams first "refined" his oil right at the site. Tripp had set up a primitive refinery, which consisted of some buildings and a cauldron in which he boiled the bitumen.[33] It's quite possible that Williams used that facility for some test runs, but must have soon decided Hamilton was better suited to the large-scale refining that would be necessary, and a lot closer to the major population centres where the oil would be marketed.

Williams formed a partnership with the Fisher brothers — John, William, and Nathaniel — and Isaac Jameson to create the Rock Oil Company. At the base of Hamilton's Wentworth Street, at Coal Oil Inlet on Burlington Bay, the partners opened their refinery in early 1860, about the time the firm was renamed the Canadian Oil Company. The company advertised its Canada Earth Oil as being superior to coal oil. One of its most famous and best-selling products was a lamp fuel called Victoria Oil. In the coming years the product would also be sold in Europe, South America, and China.

But collecting and refining oil was a tricky business. On 6 April 1860, The *Hamilton Times* noted that a large vat had burst at the local refinery and a sheet of flame had engulfed the establishment, causing $6,000 worth of damage. That was the second loss in six weeks, said the *Times*, fire having taken its toll on the Lambton works where the oil was collected, and causing $3,000 to $4,000 in damages. And on June 20 of that year, the *London Free Press* quoted a Sarnia report that Williams's still at "the Oil Springs" had burned down on June 12. Despite such setbacks, Williams became a successful Hard Oiler and the true father of the modern oil industry. Yet he remained restless and eager to tackle new challenges.

For a time in the 1850s, he served as a Hamilton alderman. With Confederation in 1867, Williams was elected a Liberal member of the Ontario legislature for Hamilton and served in that capacity for twelve years. In the 1870s, he slipped away from the oil business and set up a pressed tinware company. He became a director for several corporations, including the Bank of Hamilton, several railways, a loan society, and an insurance company. After he retired from politics he was chosen registrar for Wentworth County, in which capacity he served for the rest of his life. When he died in 1890 at his Mapleside mansion, Williams was a very successful — and very wealthy — man, a true pioneer of Canadian oil.

Charles Tripp's life turned out less happy. Records show a sheriff's sale of his lands on 28 March 1857, and innumerable lawsuits and judgments against him between 1855 and 1858.[34] Soon after he and Williams struck oil, Tripp was off again, this time to the southern United States where his quest for wealth in the mineral business continued. Perhaps he could not bear to watch another man benefit from his hard work. A newspaper obituary that ran on 2 November 1866 reported that "the original oil man of Canada" had died in New Orleans on 30 September from "congestion of the brain."[35]

Up to the time of his death, Tripp, still pursuing the elusive success, had been organizing companies to develop minerals, oil, copper, lead, zinc, and iron in Louisiana and Texas. Who knows, maybe that last time Tripp might actually have struck it rich. Instead, he died with only his dreams intact.

But while Tripp and Williams are almost certainly the first to have appreciated the commercial value of the oil that oozed from its underground vault to the surface, some residents argue they don't deserve a special dose of credit. An Oil Springs native who went on to become Ontario's education director, Frank W. Merchant, wrote in the 1930s: "I cannot think that there is any evidence to show that he [Tripp] was the original discoverer of oil."[36]

Merchant lived in Oil Springs during the village's most boisterous and exciting era. He was born in what was then referred to only as Black Creek, about 1854, and lived there until leaving for university in 1872. In May 1932, Merchant replied by letter to a series of questions posed by Mrs. James Miller, who was compiling a history of the village.

"The fact is that most of the early pioneers of this district knew of places where the oil oozed through the ground or trickled away into the streams," he wrote. "One of these places was beside the creek [Black Creek], not far above the present bridge on the main street of the village. The pioneers secured oil here by soaking it up with flannel cloths and wringing it out into vessels. The oil was used mainly as a dressing for cuts and sores, especially on their cattle. This oil was secured years before Williams came to the district. Evidently he did not know of this practice."[37]

As mentioned earlier, Merchant also leant credence to the story that

Williams was in search of water when he struck his first oil. The water was to supply workmen labouring at the nearby gum beds, Merchant believed. The gum would then be melted down in a cauldron and turned into lamp oil. "He had not gone very far with his water well when he struck surface oil. He then gave up on the notion of utilizing the gum, and used his still for preparing distillate from the oil."

That Touch of Genius

Regardless of how common the use of petroleum was for such home remedies, Tripp and Williams undoubtedly deserve credit for recognizing the commercial value and doing something about it. There is a kind of arrogance in the nature of any true pioneer, a cockiness built on the premise that regardless of the odds, they can be overcome, that success lies just beyond the next bend in the river. Tripp and Williams were guilty of such cockiness, certain that they could harness the forces of nature for their own, and mankind's, benefit. The genius lies not in being the first to observe a natural occurrence, but in being sufficiently far-sighted to visualize the prospects.

Tripp saw a portion of that picture but was unable to take full advantage of it. Williams benefited from Tripp's early experience, from the opening of the railroad to Wyoming in 1858, and from having the financial means to overcome the obstacles that stood in the path of getting the petroleum out of the bush and back to civilization in Hamilton. But both could truly lay claim to the title of Hard Oilers.

Outside circumstances seemed to play as important a part in the oil field's development, however, as the oil itself and the vision of those two men. For a time oil was overshadowed by the discovery, in 1859, of gold in British Columbia. For sheer drawing power, the lure of gold had it all over the evil-smelling dark crude. Nevertheless, the population of Lambton grew steadily, and a fair-sized town began to take shape along Black Creek. Between 1851 and 1861 the population of Lambton grew from 10,800 to 24,900;[38] in that time Black Creek, which was also coming to be known by the names of Oil Springs, Olicia, and sometimes just "the city of grease" grew from a couple of log cabins to a village of several hundred.

Newspaper reports and real estate records show that a steady trickle of oil-seekers was drawn to the area after word of Williams's discovery began circulating. Farmland in central Lambton had never been very highly valued, partly because the heavy clay made drainage difficult and partly because of poor transportation. Now, landowners were making a good price by selling their land or leasing it for oil exploration. In 1860, drillers began searching northwest of the Oil Springs site along Bear Creek, while others looked farther south in Kent County, around Bothwell. Small quantities of petroleum were found but nothing to rival Oil Springs.

To turn the trickle into a full-scale oil rush, for the city of grease, it would take the coming of an itinerant photographer, who came to be known locally as "that insane Yankee." When Hugh Nixon Shaw arrived on the scene, the oil fields of Lambton were turned on their ear and the fuse was lit that would open the way to boom time.

Chapter Three
The Man Who Made Boom-Town Boom

In the early 1860s, getting to the oil country on Black Creek took a titanic effort. And once you were there, you might well wonder to what you had come.

Horse-drawn coach trips from Wyoming to the place that was coming to be called Oil Springs were so bone-jarring, passengers would be heaped together in a pile — tossed perhaps on the seat, perhaps to the floor. Early settlers all agreed that Black Creek was well named: the water soiled regularly by the oil runoff, and the grime from laundered work clothes. And ladies dared not even consider the consequences of tumbling from the crowded sidewalks built of logs, into the substance of which the main street consisted: a congealed amalgam of blue clay, oil, sawdust, and animal droppings.

It was not a pretty picture that was painted by the early inhabitants of the rough-and-tumble pioneer settlement. And yet increasing numbers of wildcatters — oil seekers — were drawn to it, their dreams filled with images of adventure and quick riches.

Skeptics stopped laughing at the man they called "that insane Yankee" when Hugh Nixon Shaw struck Canada's first gusher at Oil Springs in 1862.
Courtesy Oil Museum of Canada.

Hard Oiler!

Hugh Nixon Shaw

Among those who dared fate was a Bible-thumping Methodist whose odd ways earned him the nick name, "that insane Yankee."[39] Yet in his short career as a wildcatter, Hugh Nixon Shaw struck the immense gusher that would forever stamp the "Oil" on Oil Springs and put the "Boom" in Boom-Town.

Shaw was a tall, lanky, Irishman.[40] When he left his home on the emerald isle, his mother pressed a Bible into his eager hand, a book the man would frequently turn to for solace. He first went to the United States and then on to Cooksville, near Toronto, where he ran a general store. On the side, he was a lithographer and itinerant photographer.

Frank W. Merchant, son of an early Oil Springs pioneer family, recalled Shaw in his letters to the local historian, Mrs. John Miller. "He was a photographer with a movable enclosed van, which he used as a dark room and studio," Merchant wrote. "He did a thriving business for a time, but soon became interested, as all others were, in making his fortune through oil."

It was probably 1860 when Shaw travelled to the Petrolia area where he set aside his photographer's business and went into partnership with two other men eager to strike oil. The three apparently had a falling-out — Shaw probably spent too much time preaching to them from his mother's Bible — and it was agreed the other two would get rid of Shaw by giving him his own piece of property at Oil Springs.

The first Lambton wells, such as that of James Miller Williams, were shallow and dug entirely by hand.[41] Soon, as people began looking for better and faster methods, they borrowed from the experience of artesian well drillers. Thus was the spring-pole method introduced to the oil fields, around 1860.

Initially, a well hole was dug or drilled, with an auger, through the clay to the rock. Then the spring-pole rig was used. This consisted of a long sturdy pole, usually the trunk of an ash tree, placed parallel to the ground. The pole was fastened to the ground at one end, creating a bow in it. From the other end, a heavy drilling bit was suspended by a chain down into the hole. A treadle was constructed at the top of the hole and attached to the spring pole. A man, or men, would step onto the treadle and the spring action of the tree trunk would lift and lower the iron bit. Each step would thrust the bit further into the rock. After the bit "punched" a hole down a certain distance, another link was added to the chain and the punching process would continue.[42]

Over the hole, a three-pole derrick was erected. This was used to support a winch, to help the men lift the heavy drilling tools and equipment in and out of the hole.

Once he had obtained his property at Black Creek, Shaw hired two men to help him dig his well, Hugh Smiley on the treadle, which was also called a kick board, and John Coryell, who was in charge of the drilling tools.[43] Coryell was also responsible for guiding the drill bit, turning it occasionally to ensure it bored a round hole.

Shaw and his crew drilled through the winter months of 1861/62. As time went by and no oil was found, his money dwindled. But he refused to quit as long as he could obtain credit.

Shaw later told his story to a visiting correspondent from the *London Free Press*. "Means were exhausted; hope almost extinguished; credit gone; he was on the eve of utter despair," wrote the journalist. "He resolved on one more day's effort before he would utterly abandon hope."[44]

Shaw worked on, the drill bit occasionally becoming dulled from its regular pounding on the rock as it chipped, slowly, deeper. He had become increasingly disheartened, the brunt of many jokes by his fellow Hard Oilers. To them he was "the insane Yankee" who was going deeper, deeper than anyone had dug for oil before. No one could possibly expect to find oil at such great depths was the prevailing wisdom of the day.

Shaw showed them otherwise. At ten o'clock in the morning on 16 January 1862, Shaw's drill having gone beyond sixty metres, Canada's first oil gusher was struck. Whether Shaw was actually present or whether Coryell and Smiley were working when the gusher came in, is not now known for sure. But an American report published a few years later said that Shaw was eating nearby when the quiet was shattered by a loud crack like an explosion, and the earth shook. J.T. Henry described it this way in his book, *The Early and Late History of Petroleum*, published in 1873:

> Upon running out to ascertain the nature of the disturbance, he perceived a huge fountain of what seemed to be black mud bursting with great violence from the hole where he had been digging. The mud emitted a very offensive smell. The jet, when he first cast eyes upon it, was, as nearly as he could judge, about a foot in diameter, and it every moment increased in volume, frequently shooting high up in to the air ... The well continued to flow with occasional brief cessations for upwards of sixty-seven hours.[45]

Henry's picture seems complete and certainly plausible. But it should be noted he got many things confused in his account of oil's discovery in Canada. For example, Henry credits Shaw with making the first discovery, rather than Tripp and Williams, and places Shaw's work back in the 1850s.

The crude from Shaw's well gushed, unchecked, shooting up to tree-top height, at least six metres into the air. From the well's untamed fury, oil flooded the hollow in which it was situated, flowed into Black Creek, and fouled the Sydenham River all the way downstream to Lake St. Clair. Thousands of barrels were lost each day for at least four days. The roar could be heard for miles.

Several attempts to shut off the flow failed, until two men drilling nearby, who had experience in dealing with gushers in the Pennsylvania fields — J.H. Johnston and a man named Winters — gave it a go. According to Johnston's son, Arthur B. Johnston, whose memories were compiled in a booklet, *Recollections of Oil Drilling at Oil Springs Ontario*, a packing material made from green calfskin and filled with flax seed, which expands when wet, was used to stop the flow. The packer was tapered and forced into the five-centimetre well pipe, but an opening had to be left to vent the gas pressure.[46]

"The gas was so strong that the men were blinded and had to be taken away," said the younger Johnston. The packing material was forced into the opening and several attempts were made before the flow was halted, he said.

Hope Morritt, in her book, *Rivers of Oil*, says Shaw later explained his find by quoting from his favourite book, the Bible, from Job 24:6: "When I washed my steps with butter, and the rock poured out rivers of oil."[47]

Shaw told the *Free Press* correspondent the rushing oil filled the entire well cavity within fifteen minutes on that Friday morning and that it was not until the following Monday morning that attempts to bring it under control succeeded.

Days later, when the journalist visited, "I measured the depth of oil on the creek in several places, and found a varying deposit of from three to four inches [eight or ten centimetres], just as pure as when it flowed from the well," he wrote.

All of a sudden the man chided as "that insane Yankee" had become "that gentleman." The *Free Press* correspondent described him as "intelligent, courteous and frank, easy of access and really a gentleman in his deportment." Everyone called him a gentleman by then, continued the sharp-tongued journalist, "though many failed to discover the attributes of the gentleman … until Providence rewarded his indomitable energy with a fortune of which no one can tell the extent."

Just before the *Free Press* reporter arrived, another visitor wrote to a Chatham newspaper, the *Planet*, that oil lay on the ice of Black Creek to a depth of a foot as far downstream as a mile. In a passage dated 4 February 1862, the writer continued that oil flowed from the well at a rate of 1,500 barrels a day, and "everyone who is not a well owner and can get barrels, is gathering it up and barrelling it, and selling it for what they can get."

With snow still covering the ground, curiosity seekers were arriving by sleigh at the rate of 100 a day, the Chatham writer continued. Five hundred barrels of oil were leaving for Wyoming station each day, and there would be more if enough barrels could be found, he wrote.

"To parties thinking of coming to this place to invest or settle, I must say that now is the time for better chances than there ever will be again."

Challenging popular belief of the day, Shaw had succeeded in drilling beyond the shallow sand and gravel beds from where the first surface oil had seeped, and into the limestone below. That second horizon of porous limestone was itself tapped out by about 1866. Fifteen years later, a third and deeper level of oil would be struck.

But for the time, Oil Springs was the centre of mad speculation, of dreams turned to both riches and nightmares. People who had gone farther afield, to Petrolia and Bothwell, returned to Oil Springs, and in quick succession, new gushers came in. Probably the biggest was the Black and Mathieson well, which is reputed to have given up 7,500 barrels a day for several months before receding.[48] For weeks it defied efforts to control, and flooded the surrounding country to a depth of a metre. It was said that men worked around the well by jumping from log to log that floated on top of the crude, making their way with the help of long poles.

In the United States, the Civil War raged, cutting off, from the Confederate states, the trade in turpentine which was required to produce camphene for oil lamps. Everything was conspiring to open up the market to the Canadian product, and American drillers hurried across the border into Canada West to take advantage of the opportunities they perceived. For a short time in history, Canada led the world in terms of the petroleum industry. The *Oil Springs Chronicle* of 22 January 1863 claimed that the oil-bearing rocks had been more attentively studied in Canada than in any other country.

Hard Oiler!

The Canal

In the summer of 1861, a few months before Shaw's find, business in the Lambton oil patch had settled in for a good stay. Prospectors were flowing into the region and on 29 August 1861, the *Daily Globe* reported that just three years after James Miller Williams struck oil on Black Creek, there were four hundred wells in operation. Yet it was not yet certain there were sufficient buyers to sustain that amount of activity.

Transportation had improved somewhat from the days when Charles Nelson Tripp first ventured through. At least the railway now went through Wyoming, some sixteen kilometres north of where men drilled and prayed for oil.

Thomas Sterry Hunt, the man who had been sent by the Geological Survey to report on the potential of the gum beds, again visited central Lambton that summer and in a private letter now on file at the Lambton County Library he offered these observations:

> There is no market for the oil and many thousands of barrels are stowed up in tanks and pits awaiting purchasers. A plank road is being made to Wyoming station on the Great Western Railway ... It is hoped from recent information from England that a good market for the oil will be opened there. The results of the last ten days in this region have surpassed the dreams of the most sanguine as to the supply of oil, and judging from present appearances the wells of Enniskillen [Township] will rival those of Burma and Persia which have for centuries supplied the east with petroleum.[49]

From the first oil sold by Williams in 1858, up to 1861, just 50,000 barrels had been shipped northward to Wyoming. Some went in its crude form, as pumped out of the ground; some was refined at primitive refineries, which were really just big cast-iron kettles, which were popping up right in the oil fields.[50]

But the potential was there for much more, and the small amount of oil that was moving up the road to the train station did not reflect any lack of the substance. New discoveries had been made after Williams and Tripp, including a huge find by Leonard Baldwin Vaughn, who would later make his name in banking. The oil industry was being hampered by the lack of means to move crude and refined oil to market. The route was simply incapable of accommodating any more traffic. This horrible stretch of mud had come to be known as "the canal," a slick, glistening swath cut through the dense forests that connected the wells on Black Creek to Wyoming.

In the best of conditions, a team of oxen was able to drag a flat-bottomed wooden "stone boat" or barge up the canal of mud, loaded down with two thirty-five-gallon barrels. The oxen, straining against the suction created by the mud, sometimes sank to their bellies in the dreadful muck. Ironically, rain made the trek a bit easier. At least when it rained, water would lay on top of the packed clay surface, which was about half a metre below the surrounding grade, and the barges would actually float, easing the terrible burden on the straining animals. One can imagine the scene, mud coating men, beasts, barrels, and barges as they made their appearance at the Wyoming train station. An estimated 500 or more teams of oxen regularly worked the canal.[51]

So the canal was actually a ditch, about one and a half metres wide, which ran next to the Black Creek Road. The road itself was not a great deal better than the canal, however, and passengers in farm wagons and stage coaches would be bounced, bumped, and pummelled along its rutted length.

One traveller of the era, a correspondent for the *London Free Press,* described the experience in that newspaper's edition of 31 August 1861: "We arrived at Wyoming on the morning train — I took one of the half dozen stages that run to the oil regions. Thirty-five or forty passengers went out the same day to the [Black] Creek. The road for the first six miles was tolerably good. The road is cut and cleared most of the way and is partially ditched. At a distance of four miles we came to a store and tavern. This is Petrolia."

Years later, an early Oil Springs resident, Annie Adamson Gale, recalled the coach rides of those pioneer days. After a few particularly jarring bumps, she said, sometimes all the passengers found themselves piled on top of one another in the middle of the coach.[52]

James Miller Williams had already proved himself a shrewd businessman, and certainly realized his business was not growing as fast as it could be, due to the limitations of the canal. In late 1860 Williams and two other men, W.E. Sanborne and Andrew Elliott, formed the Black Creek Plank Road Company and began to sell stock. In the winter of 1861/62, work began on the area's first plank toll road.[53]

Jealousy and fear of competition inspired a group of businessmen in nearby Port Sarnia to form their own plank road company. The two competing companies stepped up work on felling trees and sawing the wood into planks to construct toll roads to the oil wells. The Sarnia group was never able to catch up with the Williams group, however, whose work was well under way during 1862, and by early '63 they had completed the entire route between Black Creek and Wyoming. The Sarnia road was not opened for another two years.

The huge new finds and improved transportation to the railhead at Wyoming meant that crude was more plentiful and the price dropped sharply, from $2.50 to as low as 10 cents a barrel.[54]

Price aside, the product was receiving international accolades. In 1862, Williams's Canadian Oil Company walked away with top honours for petroleum at the International Exhibition in London, England, taking a gold medal for being the first to produce crude oil and a second gold for being the first to refine oils in Canada.[55]

For the animals and teamsters who drove them, the return trip south to Black Creek along the canal was no easier than the run north. From Wyoming, the teams would cart back food, building supplies, and the machinery needed to drill new wells and pump the dark, stinky crude from the ground.

City of Grease and Oil

Wyoming represented some link from the oil fields to civilization. It must have been a welcome link for the City of Grease that was rising along the banks of Black Creek. The community itself was agonizingly primitive. One anonymous eye-witness account from the 1860s found in the Lambton Library files described it this way:

> Close by the principal hotel there runs a small sluggish flowing stream. In it diggers covered with oil washed their dirty selves after the day's work, swilled the mud off their boots and quenched the thirst of their horses. From this ditch also was regularly procured the water of which the tea and coffee were made and in which the salt pork, the staple article of food for many long months, was boiled.[56]

There was so much oil on the creek that it often caught fire. Mrs. A. J. Yates, who came to Oil Springs as a child in 1861, recalled one particularly large conflagration:

> The oil on the creek took fire one day by someone

carelessly placing hot coke from a small refinery too near the creek. For a time, the fire which made a terrific blaze, the smoke which could be seen in London, threatened to run all the way [down river] to Wilkesport. But after many trees were felled, fresh sods cut and used with clay to make a barricade, it was put out. Many amusing stories were told of geese, pigs, cattle and sheep that went to the [burning] river to bathe.[57]

(Fires on Black and then nearby Bear Creek were common although few reached the size described by Mrs. Yates. Longtime Petrolia resident and newspaper editor Charles Whipp recalled the fire department being called out to smaller blazes on Bear Creek even up into the 1960s.)[58]

The community on the banks of Black Creek mushroomed. In late 1861 it had finally been determined its official name would be Oil Springs.[59] On the eve of Shaw's discovery, the population had swelled to over five hundred, a far cry from the couple of little shacks that stood there when James Miller Williams first arrived.

In the aftermath of the huge new discoveries, hotels and boarding houses were slapped up, stores and suppliers of equipment for the drilling of oil thrived. And the population shot up — to 2,000 and then 4,000 by 1866.

Quickly erected hotels helped to accommodate the 4,000 people who rushed to Oil Springs between the first commercial exploitation of oil in 1858 and 1866 when the first boom ended. Beds were in such short supply, hotel tenants slept in shifts.
Courtesy Oil Museum of Canada.

Mrs. A.J. Yates recalled the crude shelters and shanties made of bark that were quickly erected to help accommodate the influx of fortune seekers. "Oil Springs had several banks, stores, bakeries, butcher shops, refineries, and it was indeed a great showplace, with stages constantly on the move, night and day, bringing in prospectors, spectators and whatnot, each one of whom expected to see at least one flowing well in action."

The sidewalks were big logs laid adjacent on the mud. A broad axe was used to flatten them for walking. Cracks were filled with sawdust. "The street was so crowded I almost got pushed off," Annie Adamson Gale said. "And that would have been a serious thing, as most of the sidewalks were high. The mud was dreadful clay that left a stain ... some people said there was oil in it."

Workmen laboured night and day, changing shifts at noon and midnight. Fresh water was scarce, and a man who carted it around in a horse-drawn wagon charged two cents a pail. "Many people put down wells hoping to get water," said Annie Adamson Gale. "Dusty Fletcher put down one quite close to his kitchen door and got a good oil well. He had to board up that door and I remember so well that part of the house was black with oil. My father put down a well back of our house, but did not get either water or oil."

Women were few, liquor was plentiful, and the community had grown so rapidly there was little time to set up proper policing, just one constable for the whole town. Nevertheless, reports of lawlessness were infrequent.

Labour and Racial Strife

There was one incident of note, however. On a Saturday night in mid-March, 1863, a mob of some 100 white oil men congregated at the east end of the main street.[60] A black driller had committed some perceived slight on a white woman of some standing, and the drillers intended to avenge her honour. Hard feelings already existed toward the blacks, who had showed themselves willing to work for less money than the whites felt fair. On this evening, the whites, probably emboldened by generous amounts of liquor, determined to rid the town of all blacks by burning down the small community they had formed.

Some of what the *Observer* later termed "the more orderly and law-abiding citizens" tried to talk the men out of their plan but were threatened with like treatment if they didn't get out of the way. The would-be peacemakers retreated.

The men, armed with clubs fashioned from tree branches and iron pipes, advanced on the homes of four or five black families, who were pulled from their shanties and beaten. The buildings were set on fire and the occupants driven into the nearby woods.

The town's lone constable immediately swore in several special assistants, and nine of the riot's ringleaders were arrested the following Monday. The newspaper account must leave the reader suspicious of what happened next. Of the nine arrested, three or four escaped on the way to the lockup, and on the way back to jail, after appearing before the justice of the peace, two others slipped off their handcuffs and escaped. The obvious question is just how the constable and his assistants could have been so lax. Could there have been collusion? While the *Observer* editor blamed the actions on recent immigrants from the United States, the actions of the authorities provided British justice with little of which to be proud.

The No-Surprise Hotels

Meanwhile visitors to Oil Springs returned home with tales of life on Canada's oil frontier. There were accounts of the shortage of lodging. The Michigan Exchange Hotel offered lodging in one room consisting of fifty or so beds arranged like a ship's berths, one above the other, and of course two to a bed. Boots served as pillows and many were turned away at the door.[61]

Other hotels double-sold their valuable beds, taking advantage of the regular twelve-hour work shifts. One group of patrons was awakened at midnight to allow for the second to take over. We can only imagine just how clean the sheets would have been after a few such shifts. When one American who had gone to bed with his boots on was scolded by the innkeeper, the client said not to worry, that his boots were old and wouldn't be adversely affected by the experience.

In March 1862, a group of curiosity seekers from Toronto went down to take a look at what all the fuss was about in the oil country. The last leg of the trip from Wyoming was done by sleigh and luckily there was sufficient snow or they'd probably have never made it. In the *Daily Globe,* one of the Toronto visitors described the scene coming into Oil Springs: "Many shanties have been erected since last summer and portions of the forest cleared." But the road was dreary, the forests impenetrable, except for where large numbers of trees had been felled, presumably to provide lumber for the plank road.[62]

Unprepared for the crude living conditions that met them in Oil Springs, each Torontonian insisted that the innkeeper provide them with a room to themselves. The innkeeper was equally insistent that he would not turn out the regulars. A chambermaid explained the situation to one of the visitors: "They are ile (oil) men, sir, nice men, sir, and rich men, sir."[63]

Belden's Illustrated Historical Atlas of the County of Lambton, Ontario, 1880, described the Oil Springs of the mid-1860s. It said the main street was planked for a distance of a mile and a half with double-width and a double thickness of white oak. This was "justly called the finest paved street in Canada." A line of horse-drawn buses ran from one end of town to the other, every five minutes during the day, less frequently throughout the night. The streets were brilliantly lighted with ornamental lamps set on handsome posts.

The rough-and-tumble town of Oil Springs never shook its pioneer beginnings.
Courtesy Oil Museum of Canada.

A regular line of stage coaches connected Oil Springs with Sarnia once the plank road to that town was completed. Traffic on the plank road was so heavy "that two continuous streams of vehicles poured over it in opposite directions day in and day out," said Belden's Atlas.

The Currency of Oil

In the early days of British rule in Canada, the pound sterling system of money was used. In the by-now independent United States, a new currency sprang up based on the decimal system, and centred around the dollar. The American decimal currency began to creep into use in British North America by 1856 where people took quickly to its far simpler basis. Perhaps spurred on by increasing north-south trade, the final transition from sterling to the dollar-decimal system had taken place by the time Tripp led Williams to oil in 1858.

In Lambton, oil was the most important currency. Its buying, selling, and trading became the most significant order of commerce. Discussion of its future was the overriding concern of everyone, including the fourth estate.

The inaugural edition of the Oil Springs *Chronicle* was published on 23 April 1862 by two Americans named Hudson and Solice. On the front-page banner, beneath the publication's title, Hugh Nixon Shaw's words were immortalized: "And the Rock poured me out Rivers of Oil."

In that first edition, Professor J.Y. Hind of Toronto made an interesting prediction: "From its cheapness, petroleum will necessarily supersede alcohol, which is commonly used for fuel for cooking purposes during the summer months, and we may look for its adoption as fuel for the generation of steam in our ocean steamers when economy in bulk and weight is so great a desideratum ... the question of its adoption as a steam generator is dependent on the abundance of the supply."

Shaw rejected an offer of $10,000 for his well.[64] He should have taken it. In February 1863, Shaw was working with some other men on his well when something went wrong. He asked them to lower him into the cavity. According to the obituary that ran on 20 February 1963 in the *Daily Globe:* "His death was occasioned by suffocation, from inhaling obnoxious gases while in an oil well, into which he had descended for the purpose of pulling up a piece of gas pipe." Shaw was reportedly within four metres of the surface and the other men heard him breathing heavily. He fell back into the well and disappeared, although his body was later found. Shaw was fifty-one years old.

His career as a Hard Oiler was brief, but in that short time, Shaw exerted a huge influence on the oil business. He had proved flowing oil existed far deeper than had earlier been suspected. And the frenzied development that followed was almost all on account of his find.

The boom slackened somewhat in late 1862 and early '63, before new discoveries gave it a fresh injection of vitality. Oil prices rose and fell with the decrease and then increase of supplies. From a high of $11 a barrel in 1865, new discoveries the next year resulted in the price of crude dropping to 50 cents.

Various people tried to do something to bring some stability to this highly volatile industry, to fix prices and guarantee supplies. But oil remained an industry dominated by individualistic entrepreneurs who distrusted such endeavours as needless meddling and veiled attempts to gain the upper hand in a highly competitive business.

The *Chronicle* built a reputation for a high degree of sophistication and knowledge of the oil industry. During the period when oil production temporarily slackened, an editorial on 22 January 1863 urged a concerted effort to shore up the business's future. One of the hindrances to the development of the oil trade, said the editorial, was the great caution exercised by capitalists in investing in either the production or manufacture of oil. The sudden failure of so many flowing wells shook their confidence. The *Chronicle* did not regard the stoppage of the flowing wells as an indication of an exhaustion of the oil. Instead, it urged an experiment.

> The oil men of Enniskillen [Township] have thus far laboured in the dark; they have extended their capital in developing a trade, and have laid the foundation of an immense traffic without knowing whether that foundation was one of rock or of sand. It is time that question was definitely solved, and the sooner steps are taken to settle it, the better. The only way in which that can be done is to sink a well to a greater depth than has yet been penetrated — if necessary to a depth of 2,000 or more feet, and reaching, if possible, what is by many confidently believed to exist, a great reservoir of petroleum ... It is an experiment ... which will be an expensive one — too expensive for any one individual to bear alone; but, as all are equally interested in the result, let all contribute towards it, put the matter in proper hands and let a test well be put down to a depth which will satisfy the minds of all as to what we have to depend upon.

The newspaper went on to urge a joint stock company or one formed under the limited partnerships act with shares issued at perhaps $10. "In this way only can the question be determined as to the real extent and permanency of our resources."

The day of the two-thousand-foot (six-hundred-metre) well was not to be realized for more than fifty years. Despite the urgings of such far-sighted analysts, oil remained a business of independent-minded individuals in which petty jealousies and greed stood in the way of common sense. It took the threat of the American industrialist, John D. Rockefeller, to change the climate and force the major producers into an alliance that created Imperial Oil, but not until 1880.

Meanwhile, with new petroleum discovered and Oil Springs's renewed vitality, the town decided to incorporate, and a special census was held in early 1866 to prove the case. The census found a population of 3,046 where a few years earlier only a few cabins had stood. Later in the same year, population estimates came closer to 4,000. The town boasted twelve large general stores, many smaller shops, the *Chronicle*, nine large hotels and saloons. And an estimated 1,500 wells pumped oil from the ground.[65]

Land speculation was rampant at Oil Springs during the first half of the 1860s as the quest for oil led to thousands of oil wells dotting the landscape.
Courtesy Oil Museum of Canada.

Land speculation was rampant. The west half of Lot 17, Concession One, sold for $22,000, and no oil was found on it.[66] Lot 21, Concession One, was purchased for $80,000 by a man who ended up selling it for $1,200. The Chicago and Oil Springs Company paid $14,000 in gold for 8.5 acres of property and offered $20,000 for another piece of equal size adjacent, but was refused. An American businessman's offer of $9,000 in gold for the Oxford House Hotel and half an acre of property was refused.

Seventy kilometres to the east, the city of London was also enjoying the boom. A deal with the railway enticed oil operators to spend time in the city, and favourable shipping rates encouraged related businesses to locate there. Oil had helped lift the city out of the depression of the late 1850s, and now in the 1860s, all talk on the streets turned to oil.[67] The fortune hunters formed joint stock companies by the dozens, and test wells were sunk.

Even in London itself, a well was drilled at the forks of the Thames River, right in the city, in 1865. While it failed to offer up petroleum, the sulphur water allowed promoter Charles Dunnett to open a health spa. The Ontario White Sulphur Springs, an oil derrick for its symbol, remained in business until 1906, offering clients waters that it claimed were beneficial if taken internally or bathed in.[68]

London's first refinery was probably the one built in 1863 by William Spencer and Herman Waterman[69], and at one time there were up to a dozen different refineries operating in the city, as well as several secondary industries that produced chemicals. The city remained a significant refining centre until about 1883, and families made wealthy in the boom built sturdy mansions along its most-fashionable tree-lined streets.

The Boom Goes Bust

Back in Oil Springs, a Chicago company was building an extensive hotel in anticipation of the oil boom's continuance.[70] With 108 bedrooms, it was said to be the largest wooden building in Ontario. Its completion ironically marked the end of boom times.

Several things happened at about the same time to end Oil Springs' rule: In nearby Petrolia, John King had, in 1865, made a big new discovery in an area where it was previously thought oil did not exist — some distance away from water. A rail spur was completed to Petrolia in 1866, making crude from that region a lot cheaper to transport than that from Oil Springs. In the United States, the Civil War had ended, America was turning its attention back to industrial expansion, and exploration was uncovering huge new sources of petroleum in Pennsylvania. And finally, the Fenians were threatening.

The Fenians were radical Irish-American patriots who believed that if they captured Canada and held it ransom, they could convince the British to vacate Ireland. Their threat to invade Canada from their American bases caused a panic in 1866 through the Lambton oil fields where Americans constituted a large percentage of the drillers. Although the Fenian threat proved to be far less than it was believed, the American oil men feared that war between British North America and the United States was imminent. Many of them fled, heading back across the border.[71]

(While the Fenian threat proved exaggerated, it was taken seriously by the military authorities of the day. One of the young men counted on to defend British North America, John H. Rowe, recounted the circumstances. As a young man, Rowe joined the militia in the village of Vienna, Ontario, and entered the fife and drum band. When the Fenians threatened, his unit was sent to Sarnia. While the attack never came, Rowe recalled in later years it was not unusual for the young men of his unit to go to bed in full uniform, rifles at their side.)[72]

On the very day the plasterers finished work on what would be Oil Springs' grandest hotel, word of the Fenian threat came. The new hotel was reportedly never even swept out for the grand opening. Part of it was torn down and the materials reused. For a time, the dining room remained and was used for balls and socials. As of 1880, when *Belden's Atlas* was published, a significant portion of the building remained, having become a haven for bats, rat, and owls rather than Hard Oilers.

In short order, the booming town of Oil Springs was largely abandoned. According to *Belden's Atlas,* "among the many instances of rapid growth and subsequent decay, no place in Canada that we are aware of stands out so prominently … in a remarkably short space of time it rose from the forest, and ranked as a leading centre of trade and commerce; in a still shorter, it tumbled from its zenith of prosperity to a counterpart of the deserted village."

The town's population quickly plummeted to below three hundred. *Belden's Atlas* described the scene in 1880:

> The town has … a most dilapidated and forlorn appearance; houses in all stages of ruin and decay, and general inactivity, being the chief features presenting themselves … The place bears no evidence of having been an oil centre, the derricks and machinery having been all either destroyed or removed to Petrolia; nought but hundreds of dry holes remaining as evidence of the character of the industry which gave the town its existence.

From a high (in 1862) of some 271,000 barrels of oil coming out of Lambton, mostly from Oil Springs, production began to slide until the Petrolia wells commenced serious production in 1865.[73] In Oil Springs there would be a revival of sorts in the 1880s, when deeper wells released new petroleum deposits. But not even the peak of 180,000 barrels reached in mid-decade could match the fantastic production of '62. Oil Springs would never be the same, and Petrolia would begin to take its dominant place.

Chapter Four
John Henry Fairbank: Putting Down Roots

Oil Springs lived its short existence rowdy and brash as capital of the petroleum patch. By contrast, Petrolia would grow stylish and cultured, but certainly not without a wayward youth that threatened its very existence. In its early days, Petrolia was known as smelly and oil-smeared, loud and uncouth. But as the young Canadian oil business began to mature, so did Petrolia. Soon it had shed its veneer of transience, its odour of impermanence, and unlike its predecessor to the south, often known in contempt as Grease City or the city of grease, Petrolia began to take on the aura of a community that would stay. At its zenith in the 1890s, it would be known as the most significant manufacturing town in the Dominion.

The Arrival of J.H. Fairbank

No family is more connected to the transition in the Lambton oil industry than the Fairbanks. From his arrival in Oil Springs in 1861, John Henry Fairbank built an empire, the jewel of which would be the longest surviving oil company in the world.

Through the nearly five decades following his coming to Lambton, Fairbank typified the maturing of the Canadian oil industry. To this day, more than eight decades after his death, the Fairbank family remains, one foot in Oil Springs and another in Petrolia, acutely aware of their place in Canada's story of oil. In 1998, Charles Oliver Fairbank III continues to operate Charles Fairbank Oil Properties Ltd., more than 130 years after its founding.

It was the grandfather of John Henry Fairbank who left his English home and settled in the Massachusetts Bay Colony, later fighting with the

When John Henry Fairbank arrived in Lambton County in 1861, he gave birth to an oil company that remains in the hands of his descendants today.
Courtesy Oil Museum of Canada.

colonial rebels and spending the winter of 1777/78 with General George Washington at Valley Forge.[74] After the revolution, he went to New York state and settled his family at Rouse's Point.

There, John Henry's father, Asa, was born. And it was there that John Henry himself was born, in 1831. Then, at the age of twenty-one, John Henry left for Niagara Falls, in the British colony of Upper Canada, where he met Edna Crysler. John Henry always said Edna was responsible for his being "annexed" by Canada.

A surveyor, John Henry procured a job with the Great Western Railway in 1855, the same year he married Edna. He farmed and surveyed, and two sons, Henry Addington and Charles Oliver, were born. Three years later, Mrs. Julia Macklem, a wealthy Niagara landowner, bought some land in the oil patch of Lambton County which the cash-strapped Charles Tripp was unloading, and she hired J.H. Fairbank to survey it. This he did, dividing the hundred-acre tract into 198 plots suitable for resale to wildcatters. And while he was there, J.H. Fairbank, like so many others of his era, was bitten by the oil bug.

Setting Up Business

In 1861, seventy kilometres east of Oil Springs, the city of London was the business centre of the oil trade. London too was bitten with the bug and for a while, oil was the staple talk on the streets. London was the centre of speculation, *The Illustrated Historical Atlas of the County of Middlesex* reported in 1878, the place where oil lands were bought and sold.

So it was to London that John Henry Fairbank went, and paid $10 down for a plot of land in Lambton. Back in Oil Springs, he built a log-and-mud shack, about 3.5 by 4.5 metres. Edna, happy with the comforts of her family's life in the relatively genteel Niagara, refused to join John Henry on the rough-and-tumble frontier.

Near his new home, Fairbank dug a surface well and struck oil. He and a partner then travelled between London and St. Thomas selling machine lubricating oil. At 25 cents a gallon, they cleared $8 to $10 apiece on ten barrels. And while Edna still refused to venture into the wilds of Lambton County, Fairbank's mother agreed to come from Rouse's Point, New York, later bringing his younger son, Charles, then four years old, to share Fairbank's cabin.

While transportation was certainly easier than in Charles Nelson Tripp's day, it remained a problem. However, Fairbank demonstrated a genius for innovation early in his career as a Hard Oiler. He got some men together and hauled 3,000 or 4,000 barrels of oil to the banks of Black Creek. With "the road nature had given" him, Fairbank decided it was possible to float the oil down Black Creek to the Sydenham River, which flowed into Lake St. Clair. There, the barrels would be loaded onto a ship for export.

The problem was that Black Creek was quickly freezing. But the men followed J.H. Fairbank, sometimes up to their armpits in the frigid water. Using hand pikes, they maneuvered the barrels to the lake for loading. Unfortunately, the ship they loaded the petroleum onto was lost at sea. Eventually the crude oil, safe in its barrels, was recovered from the sea and returned to Sarnia for refining.

The good news, though, was that in 1862 seventeen ships left Montreal for Europe, British Guiana, and Australia, carrying 35,000 barrels of crude[75] and refined oil. Canada's oil export business had commenced.

New Developments in Oil

Oil prices fluctuated widely in those days, and in 1862, in an attempt to fix prices, Fairbank joined about 300 other oil men in forming the Canada Oil Association of Oil Springs. It was to be the first of many such attempts to control the business, yet prices still varied from $1 to $2 a barrel during the single year of the association's existence.[76]

According to his biographer Edward Phelps, Fairbank's fortunes began to show signs of a rosy future in 1863: in one single day he netted $150 profit from Old Fairbank, his first well, and he said he never expected to see that kind of money again. He would.

Fairbank was an innovator, and it was about that time he introduced what was to become a significant new development in oil patch technology. Up to then, each well was powered independently. That meant that poorly producing wells were often decommissioned because it wasn't worth maintaining all those power sources. Fairbank hitched several wells up to one power source.

A four-armed spider or field wheel, set horizontal to the ground, supplied power to the wells connected to each string of what came to be named jerker rods. By attaching the wells in this way, Fairbank could run eighty or ninety wells from one boiler and two engines, he told the 1890 Ontario Royal Commission on Mineral Resources. The system is still used by some, including his great-grandson Charles III, in the historic Lambton oil field.

It was during the early 1860s that larger, centralized refineries began to replace the rudimentary refining units that were often set up right out in the fields. The typical field refinery of the day consisted of two sugar kettles placed, one atop the other, to form a globe. From the top of the globe, a pipe was connected. Vapour was passed up the pipe, through a fine iron screen and a brass-wire mesh, to remove impurities. From the iron pipe attached to a worm pipe, another small iron pipe passed through the roof to the open air and allowed benzole to escape.[77]

The remaining vapor condensed in the worm and drained into a collecting tank. The valuable illuminating oil was transferred to another tank and agitated in a sulphuric acid bath, then neutralized by washing in caustic soda to remove at least some of the smelly sulphur. In effect, these early refineries were simply stills, and highly dangerous ones to boot. Many blew up, and people were often injured or killed.

Even when William Spencer and Herman Waterman built the first refinery in London in 1863, the process remained dangerous. While London quickly became an important refining centre, and for a while the petroleum capital of Canada, the city fathers were never happy to have this volatile and odoriferous industry in their proximity. Eventually they forced the refineries to locate east of the city, and a new industrial community, East London, grew up around them.[78]

Captain Bernard King Finds Oil in Petrolia

About the time Fairbank was surveying Mrs. Macklem's property, oil was first discovered in the vicinity of Bear Creek to the north. The man who found it proved to the young industry that petroleum existed where no one had, to that point, ever considered it possible.

In the early 1860s, the community known as Petrolea — spelled with an "ea" instead of the modern "ia" — consisted of a boarding house, a refinery, a few scattered log homes, and the faint smell of crude.[79] One of the few early settlers was Samuel Eveland, who arrived in 1838. But the isolation of the farmland around him and the fact oil was first discovered farther south at Oil Springs, had meant Petrolea would remain undeveloped for a few years longer.

In the early '60s, a bit of oil was found at Petrolea, but nothing to rival Oil Springs in the heady days of Hugh Nixon Shaw's discovery. Andrew Thompson came from Sarnia to open the first store, and William Coutlee built the first tavern on the Oil Springs-to-Wyoming Road. Patrick Barclay, who had settled in the Bear Creek region in 1853, became the first postmaster and is credited, along with four friends, for naming Petrolea, or "Petrolia" as it later became, due to a government clerk's error.

It would take a surprise discovery far to the west of Bear Creek to light a fire under the settlement's feet, however, and the man who was to light that fire was a Great Lakes ship's captain, Bernard King.

When King arrived from St. Catharines and began to drill a well in the swampy woods on the heights west of Bear Creek, it was commonly believed oil could only be found near water. King proved them wrong. In 1865 he struck oil on what would later be named Eureka Street, in honour of the happy discovery, and within a few years, that roadway was lined with the skeletal framework of dozens of tripod oil derricks constructed from black ash poles.

About the time of King's discovery, a correspondent for the *London Advertiser* visited the young community on Bear Creek, and in the paper's 22 December 1865 edition offered this friendly advice to prospective entrepreneurs:

> Parties who would start a good boarding house in Petrolia would make money. At present there is but one small shanty as a tavern; it certainly does not deserve to be dignified with the name "hotel." It is impossible to get a bed or a good meal. The person who runs this

arrangement knows (and knows no more) how to charge exorbitant prices for value not received. The majority of those who go there prospecting or speculating are under necessity of returning to Wyoming or Oil Springs for the evening, by stage over a corduroy [plank] road. At either of these places the charges are higher than at a first-class hotel in this city. A line of stages in addition to those now running is an absolute necessity, and would pay well. From five to seven dollars a trip is now made, and not more than one half the travellers can be accommodated. Any enterprising party who would keep a good stock of horses at Wyoming, would coin money; the demand for livery is at present not half supplied, and the charges are exorbitant.

A view of Petrolia's main street about 1874. The community would soon grow into a stable, sophisticated Victorian town.
Courtesy Oil Museum of Canada.

With the King discovery and quick demise of the Fenian threat, the American invasion of the Black Creek fields soon was replicated at Bear Creek. Construction couldn't keep up with demand as more and more fortune-seekers surged in. Boarding house and hotel guests occupied beds in relays, with fifteen-minute intervals to shake out the sheets. The names of the hotels — United States, American, Saginaw, and New York — reflected the tremendous American influence on the community.

Fairbank joined the rush to Petrolia, obtained some land in late 1865, and built a white frame home. The following May, Edna finally agreed to join her husband and younger son, bringing their elder son with her.

Setting Up Business

One might almost feel John Henry Fairbank could sense that here in Petrolia stood an opportunity to create a more permanent presence. Rather than rely totally on drilling oil for his livelihood, Fairbank began to expand his influence throughout the community.

No sooner had he arrived in 1865 than he set up a grocery and liquor business in partnership with Benjamin Van Tuyl. This, in turn, expanded into hardware and oil-well supplies in the late '60s. Fairbank bought and sold real estate and traded in lumber. In 1869 he joined with Leonard Vaughn to set up the town's first bank, and thirteen years later hooked up with Jacob Englehart and others in creating the Crown Savings and Loan Company. Fairbank also entered politics, was elected three times to council, and served as reeve 1868/70, and once as the federal Liberal member of Parliament for East Lambton in 1882. He was defeated five years later.

If Fairbank believed Petrolia had a brighter future than the flash-in-the-pan existence of Oil Springs, he proved to be correct. And it didn't take long after King's discovery for the town to begin to blossom. Over the following year, Petrolia swelled from a dozen houses to a population of 2,300. But the rapid growth came at a price, and the early appearance of Petrolia left much to be desired according to this 1866 account from a gazetteer and directory for the counties of Kent, Lambton, and Essex:

> The rapid rise of Petrolia and the unparalleled success of the wells which have been sunk since oil was first discovered here, have prevented in a great measure, the several improvements requisite in a village of its size; in fact, the early gold seeker to California or to Pike's Peak will be reminded of his experience in those Pacific-found localities at the time of their first discovery. Situated in the midst of a woody country, with hill, dale, and swamp in abundance, it will be some time before the village of Petrolia will present the appearance of an old established settlement.
>
> The retail business of the village is confined to one street, which presents quite an animated appearance. There are several large and well-stocked stores, and others are being rapidly built. The hotels are numerous and capable of affording all the accommodation usually found in a city. The number

of wells sunk in the locality is beyond computation. Some of them are very successful.[80]

The local oil producers began to clamber for a railway, and in 1866 a group led by John Henry Fairbank built an eight-kilometre spur line from the Great Western depot at Wyoming. Great Western took the line over soon after. Previously, Great Western had been induced by London business interests to charge more for shipping refined oil from Petrolia and less for crude, thus encouraging crude to be sent to London and hurting Petrolia refiners. The spur line helped the local economy, but complaints about unfair freight rates continued until 1877 when a spur from the Canada Southern was built to Petrolia and provided competition. Fairbank would again be instrumental.

John D. Noble and the Great Fire Inspiration

From the ashes of disaster, often rises the phoenix of inspiration. And from a disastrous fire that threatened the very existence of the new oil town of Petrolia grew the brain wave of John D'Oyley Noble, himself a victim of that fire, which would revolutionize the storage of crude.

Fire was a constant threat in the oil fields and surrounding area. The air reeked of oil. It coated the buildings and streets. After the devastating fire of 1867, Petrolia's town leaders were forced to take steps to make sure it never happened again.

Noble lived an adventurous life. He left his native Ireland and came to New York in 1854.[81] He was jailed by Texas Rangers as a Yankee sympathizer in Missouri during the American Civil War and later went to live with his uncle in Kingston, Ontario. There he got into the business of shipping lumber. Noble was down at Kingston harbour inspecting one of his ships one day when he noticed to his horror that its former white hull was smeared in a terrible black muck. He turned to his captain and demanded to know what had happened.

When Noble learned the hull had become coated in the oil that flowed from the Lambton oil lands and into Lake St. Clair, he decided he was in the wrong business. He immediately began to make plans to join in the oil hunt, and in 1866 he arrived in Petrolia and drilled his first well.

The following year, two fires struck the Petrolia fields. The most devastating one began at the King wells on August 23, a Saturday night. The blaze broke out on a rig — some say a night watchman became careless with a lantern. By the time men began arriving to put out the flames, it had spread to a nearby oil holding tank.

The men attacked the fire in the traditional way — by emptying the tank of its oil. Normally that worked. In the Pennsylvania fields, a cannon sometimes was used to blast a hole near the base of the tank, allowing the oil to flow out and be pumped away, thus reducing the intensity of the fire.[82]

But in this case it proved too little, too late. The tank's staves, saturated in crude, caught fire, and the tank collapsed before the men could get rid of it. The oil, now flaming, gushed forth in all directions, igniting tank after tank. Flames were reported to have leaped thirty metres high, and for two weeks the fire raged, consuming ten acres. The fire could be seen for kilometres, and vegetation was scorched in all directions. When the inferno exhausted itself, it left ashes and charred earth two-thirds of a metre deep.

Soon the wells were restored, and the business of oil continued. The silver lining to the terrible cloud at least was that the fire took care of the over-supply that had depressed prices, and crude prices rose.

As an immediate consequence of the fire, the Hard Oilers began constructing the tanks of iron. But it soon became evident that lightning strikes could also cause fires. Then John Noble got together with fellow oil man Charles Jenkins and devised an ingenious solution: they would build a vast network of underground pipelines connecting the wells and the refineries.

The holding tanks were changed, too. Rather than being built above ground, Noble and Jenkins took advantage of the clay soil's natural imperviousness to water. They dug out huge pits in the clay and lined them, from bottom up, with wooden rings to keep the clay from caving in. The clay was leakproof. A typical tank was nine metres in diameter, eighteen metres deep, and held 8,000 barrels of crude.[83] Out of disaster had come an innovation and Noble, drawn to the oil fields by the oily grime that coated the hull of his ship, had made a name for himself as a Hard Oiler.

Nathaniel Boswell, Hotelier

By 1867 Petrolia's building craze was in full swing, and it was in that year that the Englishman, Nathaniel Boswell, arrived and built the American Hotel.

Boswell, too, had been an adventurer, and at a very early age. In England, at the age of nine, he had walked one hundred kilometres to get a job on the docks of London. He served as a teamster in the Crimean War, then came to America where he laid track for a series of railway companies. When the Civil War broke out, he bought a river steamer and ran the Union blockade carrying cotton, sugar, and molasses before being captured. His vessel was turned into a hospital ship on which he was forced to serve.[84]

After the war, he went to Oil Springs where he built his first of three hotels, conducted a livery, and ran a stage coach to Petrolia and Wyoming. Later, Boswell bought an oil well, founded the village of Brigden, and established mills, shops, and two more hotels.

Producers' Associations

Early Lambton Hard Oilers near Bothwell in Kent County load barrels of crude onto a wagon for the trip to the railhead, about 1866.
Courtesy Oil Museum of Canada.

Fluctuating oil prices continued to imperil the producers. But just as in Oil Springs, attempts to band the producers together for a common purpose failed. Jealousy, suspicion, greed, and sheer independence thwarted three attempts, in quick order, to establish organizations that would fix prices to the benefit of the producers.

First, in the fall of 1867, a committee of oil men recommended the wells be shut down to force a shortage that would boost prices.[85] It wasn't long, though, before the first member broke ranks and began selling independently. Then early the following year, John Henry Fairbank was instrumental in organizing the Petroleum Amalgamation Company, a union of producers. The producers were to lease their properties to the union for one or two years, but again in-fighting arose, several members broke ranks, and the idea collapsed.

But the organizers didn't give up. In 1868 the major producers, including Fairbank, created the Crude Oil Association, fashioned on the Canada Oil Association that had existed at Oil Springs eight years earlier. This time oil prices rose.

Later that year the refiners formed an association to regulate prices and promote trade, but it failed because of the same lack of single-mindedness that so often afflicted the producers. It was a telling tale, though: while the still independent-minded producers clearly respected John Henry Fairbank's leadership sufficiently to set aside their differences for a time, the refiners did not yet have a leader of similar stature. Some day they would, and Imperial Oil would be formed.

Partnerships

The oil business continued to spin off related industries. In 1868 the blacksmith and ironworker James Joyce left drilling behind and decided to go into the business of supplying it instead, making pumping and drilling equipment. It was the beginning of a company that eventually, through amalgamation with the McKenzie firm and with the opening up of oil fields in distant lands, became internationally known.[86]

Throughout his years in Petrolia, Fairbank enjoyed two long-lasting business partnerships. One was with Leonard Vaughn, who had, in 1860, started a small lending business in Oil Springs. Vaughn was also the first man in Canada to use steam to power his drilling equipment.[87] He also was a neighbour of Fairbank's, and the two became friends. They decided to open Petrolia's first banking institution, and in 1869 they hauled a building from Oil Springs up the road to Petrolia.[88]

The building came to be known as the Little Red Bank. The partners hired Edwin Kerby as their first accountant. Kerby proved to be a dedicated employee. He took a room upstairs above the vault from where he could keep vigil on the money through a slot in the floor. Vaughn worked behind the counter. Ten years later he built the Vaughn Block, the first major brick-business block in the town, and he operated a dry-goods store in it.

But banking was not the only thing for which Vaughn was known. One of his antecedents had been a physician, and Vaughn practised homeopathy, sometimes during banking hours. Visitors to the Little Red Bank sometimes came away with a free sample of chamomile or a suggestion that they try a dose of belladonna or arsenic, courtesy of the ministering banker.

Fairbank's other long-time partner, Benjamin Van Tuyl, was a college teacher of business who became a major for the Union army in the United States Civil War. After the war he came to Petrolia and entered the water-and oil-drilling business.

Education was important to Fairbank and other important Hard Oiler families. As Petrolia's first decade was coming to a close, the wealthier families were beginning to send their children to better schools outside the area. In southwestern Ontario that often meant the London Collegiate Institute, later renamed Hellmuth College. Henry and then Charles Fairbank were both enrolled. Young Charles and subsequently his son, also named Charles, rose to positions of influence and leadership in Petrolia. Both were eventually elected reeve of the town.

The Roberts Torpedo

Technological change made inroads into the oil patch in those early days, but none caused more of a bang than the return to Petrolia in the early 1870s of Richard Isaiah Bradley with his Roberts Torpedoes.

Bradley had left Petrolia at the age of seventeen, about 1865, and had spent several years as a foreman in the Pennsylvania fields.[89] There he observed the tremendous success of the Roberts Torpedo. It had been 1862 when an officer in the volunteer services in the Army of the Potomac, Colonel E.A.L. Roberts, conceived the idea of dropping explosives into wells to "fracture" the well and increase production. Roberts obtained a patent two years later, and the following January visited Titusville, Pennsylvania, with his first six "torpedoes."[90] Well operators were sceptical, but Roberts's amazing success in increasing production soon convinced them.

In 1872 Richard Isaiah Bradley returned to Petrolia with the marvelous new discovery. Bradley explained the process: a tin can filled with nitroglycerine was lowered into the well. A second tin can, called a squib, was filled with gravel, a few drops of nitro, and a lit fuse. The men who put the nitro down the well were called "shooters." The shooters dropped the squib from the ground into the well. If the shock of the two cans striking one another didn't cause an explosion, the fuse in the squib usually did.

R.I. Bradley introduced the American-originated Roberts Torpedo nitroglycerine "shooter" to the Lambton oil fields as a way of "fracing" a well to increase production.
Courtesy Oil Museum of Canada.

With his savings, Bradley bought a few gallons of nitro and tried to convince the Hard Oilers of the soundness of his plan. When he finally talked one well owner into letting him give it a try, and production rose from ten barrels to one hundred barrels a day, R.I. knew he was about to make his fortune. Initially he had to ship the nitro in from Pennsylvania, but when the railway discovered what he was doing, they refused to carry his cargo. An undaunted R.I. simply hired a mule and brought the goods in by foot. Soon after, Bradley built the first of a long succession of nitro plants in Petrolia. (More on the story of nitroglycerine in Chapter 5.)

In this early postcard, the effects of torpedoing or fracing a well are demonstrated at Petrolia. A plume of crude and mud jets upwards from the cavity.
Courtesy Lambton County Heritage Museum.

Hard Oiler!

The Petroleum Roller Coaster

The 1870s proved to be a roller-coaster decade for the young petroleum industry. It dawned promising enough, hundreds of oil wells pumping, and sufficient money, apparently, for producers and refiners alike. Before it was over, however, a deep depression would rock Canada, and the oil patch would prove it was not immune.

In 1871 Fairbank took the lead again in organizing a producers' group, the Lambton Crude Oil Partnership.[91] Things looked good, temporarily at least, when the following year the Pennsylvania producers shut down operations as a way of forcing up prices there. The shutdown of the American industry opened new opportunities for the Canadians and throughout that year Canadian refiners expanded their capacity to new levels, well beyond the needs of the domestic market.

In 1873 Canadian oil exports hit a record six million gallons or 170,000 barrels.[92] But while crude started the year at nearly $2 a barrel, the price fell throughout the coming months in the face of new discoveries in Pennsylvania. By year's end crude stood at just 70 cents a barrel.

The Canadian industry was thrown into depression. Wells were shut down and refiners forced to close. The Vaughn & Fairbank bank was hurt when Carbon Oil Company of Hamilton went under, leaving them with an outstanding $30,000 loan.[93] Throughout 1873, workers left the oil fields in droves.[94] Many went to Manitoba, where farmland was being opened up.

Fairbank led another attempt to increase producer leverage by forming the Home Oil Company in 1873. The company erected its own refinery in Petrolia despite the overcapacity that already existed, and it survived for eight years, with Fairbank as president. Hard Oil pioneer James Miller Williams of Hamilton was a shareholder.

By May 1874 only Home Oil and F.A. Fitzgerald of London were still refining. Then in September the London companies joined to form the London Oil Refining Company cartel. The producers not connected to Home Oil formed the rival Petrolia Crude Oil and Tanking Company, acting as a third major force in the industry. When the three agreed to a working arrangement, prices rose to everyone's benefit — except consumers'.

In 1877 the London Oil Refining Company was dissolved, and the producers in that city began a new round of combinations that would eventually result in the formation of the Imperial Oil Company Limited.

Quality Hill, Pithole, and Brooklyn

Back in the oil patch, the little town of Petrolia continued to grow despite the depression, but not always in an attractive fashion. Here is one account dated 4 July 1873:

> What a contrast between Pithole and the aristocratic quarter of Petrolia, designated "Quality Hill," where are the residences of some of the magnates of the town. Prodigious iron tanks are in Pithole, some connected by pipes of 1 1/2-inch diameter, directly from the wells at various distances ranging from one to two miles. The total number of wells that have been sunk from time to time in or around Petrolia since the oil operations first began there ten or twelve years ago is computed about 2,000, but of these not more than 250, or 300 at the most, are now producing oil in sufficient quantity to warrant them being worked.[95]

Oil Rigs and labourers' shanties sat side by side in the west Petrolia community of Pithole.
Courtesy Lambton County Heritage Museum.

Each section of town boasted its own name. The older working-class area east of Bear Creek came to be known as Brooklyn, a name it maintained for many years. At the top of the west hill was a collection of statelier homes built by the town's wealthy Hard Oilers, an area that came to be known as Crescent Park and — perhaps somewhat cheekily —

Quality Hill. Clear distinctions were beginning to appear among the town's various residential areas.

Fairbank was certainly one of the "magnates" of the town. However, always fiercely independent, he continued to live relatively modestly, in his white frame home, not in "Quality Hill" but at its edge on Petrolia's main street. It was perhaps a sign of what Edward Phelps referred to in his unpublished thesis on John Henry Fairbank, whom he says never lost his common touch. As an example, Phelps pointed out that Fairbank proudly accepted an appointment as fire chief in the 1870s, always heading out like all the other firemen when duty called. He retained the title until 1889 when, at the age of fifty-eight, he decided he was a little too old to keep running to fires.

A Man of Many Means

Fairbank even dabbled in the railway business. With most of the rails running east to west across Ontario, it was felt the oil region would be well served with a north-south line. Fairbank took over a bid by the Erie and Huron Railway, but the whole plan was abandoned over financing. Meanwhile the Sarnia, Chatham, and Erie charter was secured, and in late 1877 rail was laid from Oil City to Petrolia, finally freeing the local oil producers from the grasp of Great Western and its tariffs, which had always benefited the London refiners. While the spur from the Canada Southern line was never much used, Great Western recognized the potential competition and cut its rates.

Fairbank's rail interests turned westward as well. John W. Sifton of Oil Springs moved to Manitoba in 1870. Through his friend Sifton, Fairbank became involved in the financing of the Canadian Pacific rail line west of the Lakehead and Fairbank actually travelled to northwestern Ontario to oversee part of the construction in 1875/76.

(Oil Springs' Sifton family became nationally famous. One of John Sifton's sons, Clifford, became a cabinet minister in the government of Wilfrid Laurier; the other, Arthur, became premier of Alberta.)

The tussle between producers and refiners over oil prices and control of the industry continued. In the fall of 1877 the producers took advantage of disorganization among the refiners to form the Mutual Oil Association. It proved to be the most successful organizing bid to date. Members sold crude through the managers, and for a year Petrolia thrived on higher crude prices. New wells were drilled and old ones were restored to production.

In 1878 the refiners struck back and reactivated the London Oil Refining Company. The Mutual died on 1 May 1879 — the day named "black Friday" by the *Petrolia Advertiser*.[96] Crude prices fell to 40 cents a barrel, then recovered somewhat, struggling back to $1.40 through 1880.

From its beginning, Canada's oil business had been marked by the pioneer spirit of discovery, of independent-minded enterprise, and of struggle between producers and refiners. It had been a time when John Henry Fairbank was the undisputed leader of the oil producers, with several refiners such as Jacob "Jake" Englehart and A.C. Edward competing to take a leading role in that side of the business. Both those men would make their mark on Lambton's oil patch.

Jake Englehart arrived in London from the United States in the 1860s and at the age of nineteen set up a refinery there. Later he moved to Petrolia and was instrumental in the creation of Imperial Oil. Eventually Englehart and Fairbank would set aside their business differences and, together with several others, form a partnership in the Crown Savings and Loan Company (1882). Before he was done, Englehart and his wife, Charlotte Eleanor, would live to be among the most respected and beloved citizens of the town.

Alexander Clark Edward was born in Scotland in 1853[97] and arrived in Petrolia at the age of twenty in the employ of a London, England, accounting firm with interests in oil. Edward quickly switched careers and launched his own oil company. Then when the Mutual Oil Association was formed, he was selected to manage it. In later years Edward would rack up a string of successes in politics (he was elected Petrolia mayor three times) as well as in foreign oil fields.

Despite its amazing creation, its rising out of the swamps in such a few short years, Petrolia wasn't gaining much respect in its first decade or so of existence. *Belden's Atlas* reported that in 1879 the town had forty-nine stores, ten hotels, a large number of saloons, billiard halls, and the regular array of shops and liveries. "The general character of the buildings of Petrolea [note spelling] is inferior, there being very few which are really good, the majority being of wood material ... The Vaughn block, completed last year, was the first really fine business block ... though there are already quite a number of very good private residences."

Petrolia was an oil town, continued *Belden's*. "The alpha and omega of Petrolia is oil, oil, oil. Everything smells of oil; everything tastes of oil; everything is covered and smeared with oil ... You hear nothing but oil spoken of in the cars, in the hotels, in the public offices."

Certainly that would have seemed the case to anyone searching the newspapers of the era. For it didn't take long after Captain Bernard King's discovery for the Fourth Estate to leave its mark. Richard Owen Herring arrived in town in 1869 from Oil Springs where he once operated the *Chronicle*, Canada's first "oil" newspaper. In his new home he published the *Advertiser*, operating it in the fine, rollicking old style of nineteenth-century Canadian newspapering for many years. For instance, as a Conservative, he frequently engaged in dust-ups with the Liberal entrepreneur, Fairbank, whose views were more closely associated with the *Petrolia Topic*, founded in 1879. Herring also used his publication to campaign strongly for local projects in which he believed, including a waterworks, a town hall, a farmer's market, and improved sewers and streets.

The newspapers reflected the sense that Petrolia was there to stay. Unlike Oil Springs, it would remain strong and healthy. In the coming years the newspapers would diligently report on significant developments in the business of petroleum, at home and abroad. They would keep an eye on Pennsylvania and the dozens of other locations oil was being found in the United States. And when Lambton Hard Oilers began to spread out across the globe in search of new fields, the Petrolia newspapers would chronicle their progress and diarize their adventures.

Drawing oil from a Gusher, Petrolia, Ont.

Oil was the "alpha and omega" of Petrolia according to Belden's county atlas of 1880. Here a group of Hard Oilers hauls oil away from a well by horse-drawn tank wagon.
Courtesy Lambton County Heritage Museum.

Chapter Five
Rascals, Heroes, Blasts, and Blazes

Given the potential for wealth in the oil lands of Lambton, there was surprisingly little crime, yet certainly there was a bit of lawlessness. With the potential for disaster that must have existed within the oil-sodden landscape, with the preponderance of explosive and highly combustible materials that were used, there were surprisingly few disasters, yet terrible accidents did occur.

Amid it all, an occasional hero would be thrust into the limelight, or someone would live to tell of a narrow escape from death. And of course the high spirits of the fun-seekers and the jokesters added a sense of frivolity to the bleak scene.

From the biggest con artist of the day, to the man who brought peace and order to Petrolia; from those who risked their lives to save others, to the danger and pain the workers often faced; the early oil fields were witness to vagabonds, risk-takers, and the just plain strange.

The Prince of the Shady Deal

Many suspicious transactions cast a pall over the Lambton oil lands. That was not surprising, given the huge amounts of money that passed among the businessmen of the day, beckoning to the region those who were all too eager to make the most of the folly and greed of others. Men speculated in land, buying, selling and leasing real estate; others salivated at the thought of striking a rich pool of oil beneath the heavy clay soils of Lambton County. Often, those who engaged in these transactions were more successful in making their fortunes than those who drilled for oil.

Occasionally some would take speculation a step too far and venture wholeheartedly into the realm of dishonesty. The most famous rascal of the era was Harry Prince, whose colourful story was told for the first time in *Belden's Atlas*.[98] Prince was the son of the notorious Colonel John Prince, who in 1838 ordered four American "patriot" raiders summarily shot when they crossed the border at Detroit in support of the Upper Canada rebellion. Harry Prince had been a conductor on the Great Western Railway, and somehow, on what would have been a fairly modest wage, he managed to save $30,000, a great deal of money for the era.

In the Petrolia of the early oil days, Harry Prince became well known for his lavish life-style and dinner entertainments. Securing several thousand acres of oil lands he claimed to be of a very high quality and level of production, Prince formed the Western of Canada Oil Works Land Company. The smooth-talking Prince somehow persuaded a number of highly respected and influential men of the region to lend their names to his enterprise. Among them were Hard Oilers John Henry Fairbank and Hugh W. Lancey of Petrolia, London businessman John Carling of the beer-making family, the Kent riding MP Rufus Stephenson, and even Elgin County's sheriff. It was a highly respectable list.

Then Prince turned to England, where excitement was growing over the Canadian oil business. He offered shares in the company and invited the prospective British investors over to take a look at what they would be buying. Suspicions should have arisen when Prince went to the extreme lengths he did to keep the visitors away from the locals, but apparently no one cottoned on to what was happening. Prince even went so far as to "salt" some worthless oil wells — temporarily connecting them to good wells — for the edification of the buyers.

The British investors were wined and dined and entertained in Harry Prince's patented exquisite style. He bowled the visitors over with visions of lavish profits. They went away happy men, confident that their Canadian investments would be returned many times over.

The lands proved to be of poor quality, and the investors lost their money. Harry Prince fled to Chicago with an estimated $200,000, leaving the hapless local "names" to explain and clean up the mess. Some faced personal law suits from the unamused Englishmen. The only justice to come from the affair was that Prince could not bear to pass up the opportunity to parlay his ill-gotten funds into something much bigger. He invested the money in speculations in Chicago, lost everything, and in October 1878, died a pauper.[99]

The Man in Blue

1134 Andes Fire Co., 1876, Petrolia, Canada

Thomas Jackson, second from the left, front row, served both on the Petrolia West End Fire Department and later as the town's police chief. The town, its wooden buildings smeared in oil, boasted two fire departments which often raced one another to the scene to fight Petrolia's frequent fires.
Courtesy Oil Museum of Canada.

Thomas Jackson was a big man. Over six feet tall and weighing a good 230 pounds, he came to Petrolia in 1866, and in the early 1870s was appointed to the fire department. Soon he was also was named chief of police, a post he held until 1900, for the princely sum of $53 a month.[100]

At about the same time Jackson arrived, Petrolia bought its first set of handcuffs, which it awarded to its two constables for safekeeping. Most of the infractions the police had to deal with consisted of a few drunken fist-fights, and the cuffs were just the thing to calm a man down long enough to get him to the town jail, which had just been opened. The lockup was in the back of the ground floor of the municipal building where the fire department was also located. Upstairs were the mayor's and clerk's offices, council chamber, and courtroom.

Now, despite all the saloons Oil Springs and then Petrolia boasted in their youthful days, despite the air of frontier crudeness, and the fact that a lot of young men who worked in the oil fields were single and pretty well off, there was surprising little violence in the region. Oh, the drillers were a boisterous bunch, and they loved to whoop it up whenever they got the chance, but serious violence rarely broke out.

Perhaps it was because so many of the Hard Oilers had just come from the American Civil War and had seen more than a lifetime's worth of violence in a few short years. Or perhaps they were just a little too tired, a little too stiff after hours of lugging heavy equipment around all day in the fields.

There were incidents, however. And one of the most famous, involving a local tough named Scully Wilson, lasted the better part of a day, and involved hundreds of men throwing their fists in the main streets of Petrolia. Chief Jackson was known for being able to work his way into a crowd of fighters and locate the troublemaker, regardless of the pummelling he took in the effort. Observers said Jackson's clothes were torn to shreds before he decked Wilson and dragged him off to the lockup in his patented grip of steel.

On another occasion, Jackson was called in to stop a man from beating his wife and was himself stabbed, yet he still hung onto the attacker until help arrived. In another episode, Jackson was said to have been nearly killed when he walked into the darkness unarmed and was accosted by three men with knives.

Jackson gained the respect of everybody, sterling citizen and ne'er-do-well alike. Legend has it that when he sometimes showed up at a place called the Western Barn, an illegal watering hole, all it would take to send the crowd running were the words: "Here comes Jackson."

A Little Hanging

Not all incidents of lawlessness attracted the police. Once, Petrolia played host to what was described in the day as "a near-hanging."[101] It seems the owner of one of the town's hotels had sold out and deposited $600 in what he reckoned would be a safe spot. However, when he returned to collect the money, it had disappeared. By process of elimination, the man's friends ascertained who the culprit must be, found the man, and led him to the edge of Bear Creek. There, they strung him up to an oak tree.

After "a little hanging," the man was let down to the ground and told to divulge what he had done with the money. Initially he refused, but after the third time he was elevated at the business end of the rope, he relented. He took them to the money, and then the police were called in. The culprit was jailed.

The Sheepskin Hero

The oil lands also attracted their share of heroes. One such person bore the unlikely name of Sheepskin Charlie. He was an odd fellow, most Petrolians would agree. He was an accomplished musician, although for the life of those who enjoyed his music, they never knew just what to call the instrument he played. They described it as looking rather like a coffee pot.[102]

Sheepskin Charlie operated a blacksmith shop overlooking Bear Creek in Petrolia. While the creek stayed calm enough for most of the year, in the spring it could turn into an angry, raging torrent as the snow and ice melted and rushed through the Petrolia Flats. One year when the spring deluge was particularly savage, a teamster drove his wagon into the water. The man quickly realized he had misjudged the depth and tried to turn his team of horses around. The wagon became stuck, and sank deeper into the mud. The horses, in danger of drowning, reared and thrashed in terror. A crowd soon gathered but looked on helplessly.

Suddenly Sheepskin Charlie appeared at the door of his blacksmith shop. With a long knife clenched between his teeth, Charlie waded into the current as far as he could. He then dove into the freezing, churning waters of Bear Creek and cut the trace reins, setting the horses free.

Mischief in the Oil Fields

Children everywhere enjoy highjinks. Ken MacGregor offered recollections of his young days in Oil Springs some years later after he moved to Mount Clemens, Michigan. In one story, MacGregor recounted how he and his brother Bill would take shortcuts through the fields rather than walk around the roads. "We had to jump over, or crawl under, hundreds of jerker lines to reach Oil Springs," he wrote in his recollections filed with the Oil Museum of Canada.[103]

The boys often played in the oil fields, and one day he and Bill were digging a hole near the exhaust pipe of a running steam engine. Fearing they might be scalded by the steam, Ken drove a wooden plug into the exhaust. The boys were amused to discover that once plugged, the engine began to labour, then stop. As Ken put it: "A new Halloween trick had been discovered."

When Halloween arrived, Ken headed over to Pete McArthur's rig and drove a wooden plug into the exhaust pipe. The engine laboured and coughed, then fell silent. Pete McArthur was in a nearby shed when he heard the engine stop. He investigated but could find nothing wrong.

After several attempts to rectify the problem, he called on a neighbour for help, but the two men were baffled.

McArthur then sent for Bob Anderson, a mechanic, more than a mile away. Anderson took one look at the engine — he'd seen it all before. He laughed, pointed to the plug, and asked McArthur: "Don't you know? This is Halloween!"

MacGregor added that a variation on the trick marked many local weddings in the Oil Springs area. Boilers would be filled with steam and then cut loose to blow through hand-made whistles at just the right moment, leaving the parson and other witnesses unable to hear the contracting couple's solemn vows.

A Canine Caper

Newspaper editor Richard Owen Herring was married to a woman who seemed to enjoy imagining she was a lady of means and social standing. Mrs. Herring was known, in the parlance of the day, for "putting on airs," and some of the more earthy of Petrolia's citizenry found her an easy target for their highjinks.

Mrs. Herring was also a dog lover, and she had once sent to New York City for a particularly expensive and rare breed.[104] Some of the town jokesters captured a farmer's stray cur, put it in a crate, and then stuck New York shipping labels all over it. They left the crate on Herring's doorstep.

Mrs. Herring took a while to learn that the unusual looking specimen was not the expensive breed she was waiting for. Once she did, she and the poor farmer were not amused, although reports suggest that husband Richard found the whole thing a great hoot.

Perpetual Paraffin Peace

John McMillan was a man who became very attached to his work. In 1862 while living in Scotland, he sent miners to the Bothwell area to look for oil on land he had purchased from political reformer and journalist George Brown. (Brown had represented the constituency that included Lambton County in the legislature of Canada West from 1851 to 1857.) In 1865 McMillan moved from Scotland to London to look after his oil interests. Soon he sold out and moved to Petrolia, where he managed the Canadian Land and Mineral Company. He became a producer and a refiner and established a branch of that company in Montreal when he moved there in 1873.[105]

Twelve years later, McMillan returned to Petrolia, at which time he became obsessed with his death. One of the products created by refining oil is paraffin wax. McMillan decided he wanted to be preserved in wax and ordered that, when he died, holes were to be bored in his coffin and wax poured in. For one of the strangest interments in Petrolia history, his wishes were fulfilled.

The Big Still

Fire was a constant threat in the oil business, a natural state of affairs considering that all early construction was done in wood, and every single stick of wood eventually became smeared or drenched in oil. Amazingly enough, Oil Springs never suffered a major inferno, but two fires in Petrolia July and August 1867, certainly made that town's citizens sit up and take notice. As noted earlier, the second, larger, fire flattened ten acres, charred the landscape, and put many oil wells and refineries out of commission, and that incident eventually led to the construction of the much safer underground storage tanks and pipelines.

Two years later, town council approved a grant to establish the first "hook and ladder company" (fire department), and three years after that a citizens' revolt forced council to go even further and set up water tanks around the village.[106] Two fire departments were established, one at the east end and one at the west, and a certain rivalry developed between the two as payment was based on which department made it to the scene first. On several occasions, the two would meet head-on in their chase to the fires.

The fire departments didn't put an end to the danger, of course, and in early 1872 a huge fire downtown consumed fourteen buildings, including two hotels. Later that year, fire destroyed a two-thousand-barrel still.

Stills were the central piece of equipment at the refineries. The early ones were constructed of cast iron, but when someone decided to start using boiler plate about 1868, the new material opened the way for larger vessels. Most stills were cylinders that held about 250 barrels of oil. However, the one that for obvious reasons came to be known as The Big Still held ten times that amount. Alas, the Big Still, the pride of the young refining industry, didn't last long. A year after it was built it blew up. It was rebuilt, and the very day it was put back into operation, it blew up again, this time taking the entire Carbon Oil Company with it.[107]

Hard Oiler!

Industrial Neglect

Industrial safety did not always receive high priority. In September 1884 Robert Cluff died what must have been a terrible death. Cluff, an oil-still worker, was on the job early one morning when his clothes caught on fire, and he was soon engulfed. In his attempt to put out the flames, the poor man fell into a ditch of tar and refuse, only adding fuel to the fire. Soon it spread to shipping sheds, which were destroyed along with refinery offices, and engulfed some barrels, some of which contained oil. Firemen arrived in time to save the company books, but not Cluff. The man, no doubt dazed and in excruciating pain, wandered onto nearby railway tracks where he was found by some workmen. His fingernails were nearly torn out in his efforts to remove his burning clothing. He died the next morning at home. He was thirty-three.[108]

The Dreadful Business of Cleaning Stills

Another fire occurred at Imperial in early 1896. This one was referred to by the Petrolia *Advertiser* on April 23 as the largest and most destructive the town had seen in years. About four o'clock one morning, some men were treating the oil in the wax department when gases exploded from what was believed to be spontaneous combustion. The workers escaped with their lives, but one man, Frank Ireland, was badly burned.

The fire could be seen forty kilometres away. The *Advertiser* described it this way: "The thick smoke varying from intense black to a pale grey looked like an enormous cave, in the recesses of which could be seen the glare of the red flame and sometimes ascending like a whirl wind in spiral corkscrew columns, then disappearing in the smoke. As barrels of oil caught fire a series of sharp explosions followed. Several men were knocked off their feet."

It didn't take long after Imperial Oil left Petrolia for Sarnia, in 1898, for the stills to claim their first victim in that city. This time it was a still cleaner, William Tossell, and the incident inspired the *Advertiser* to call for safety improvements.[109]

The job of still cleaner was not pleasant, and for the extra discomfort and danger the men were paid more handsomely than were most refinery workers. When they were in use, the stills became extremely hot, reeking of gases. Each still contained a small "man-hole" at the top and bottom of the vessel, into which the cleaner squeezed to clean it out after each day's use. This usually occurred about two in the morning, after the still had hopefully cooled down a bit and before it was started up for another day's work.

The accident occurred at the end of January, and one can imagine the difference in temperatures between the inside of the still and the frigid out-of-doors, which the *Advertiser* estimated at about 0°F (-18°C). It was speculated that Tossell became dizzy from either the remaining gases or the quick temperature change, for when he exited the still, he fell and struck his head on the ground, breaking his neck.

The *Advertiser* lamented "this dreadful business" of cleaning stills. The heat inside the huge steel cylinders was sometimes so intense it burned the skin on the workers' faces, and the man-holes were barely large enough for workers to squeeze through. "The men prefer to take the risk and physical suffering rather than lose their job," wrote the newspaper. It said exhaustion was not uncommon on the job and, "it is almost surprising that such a disaster has not occurred before."

An Imperial Loss

Petrolia wasn't the only place where refineries tended to burn down or blow up. London had become a major refining centre even earlier than Petrolia, and that city became accustomed to the steady stream of explosions and fires in its petroleum section, which was just across the street from the city limits in the community that came to be known as East London. Between the smells, the fires, and the explosions, the refineries never ingratiated themselves to the London city fathers.

The last straw came in 1883 when lightning struck the Imperial Oil refinery and burned it to the ground. Since railway competition had put an end to the sort of rate structure that had previously favoured London over Petrolia as a refining centre, Imperial went cap in hand to city council seeking assistance to build a pipeline between there and the oil fields. Council had had enough and said there would be no money. Imperial simply moved its refining operation to Jake Englehart's Silver Star refinery in Petrolia, and the company never returned.[110]

Dangers in the Fields

Accidents occurred in the oil fields too. In July 1879 brothers George and Walter Slack were sinking a well on the property of a Mrs. Egan on Petrolia's main street. Assisted by Mrs. Egan's son, William, the men had been at the drilling business since about one in the morning and were down nearly thirty-five metres.[111]

Walter Slack recalled later that it was about five or six a.m. when the water pipe to the boiler that was being used to power the drill broke. They repaired it and continued the work, Walter watching the gauges to ensure a proper pressure was maintained. The men experienced some further equipment problems, and at one time Walter's brother, George, shut down the engine to attend to the repairs.

It was about nine in the morning when the boiler exploded. George "was standing near the drill and I think he had a hammer in his hand, and stepping back he threw it on the floor. This was the last I saw of him alive," Walter said later of his twenty-three-year-old brother.

In the explosion, a pipe flew up and hit Walter's leg, breaking it. The boiler was driven through the derrick, demolishing it, and spun, end over end, about twelve metres. The pointed end was driven into the ground by the force. Boiler plate three quarters of an inch thick (1.8 centimetres) was torn into ribbons like paper, and the pieces scattered like torn clothing. George Slack was driven through the derrick timbers and was later found on the ground between the derrick and the boiler. He was carried to Mrs. Egan's house, where he died about fifteen minutes later. The newspaper called for a boiler inspector to prevent such accidents again.

Eleven years later, a derrick collapsed on top of John Temple of Petrolia, killing him instantly.[112] Temple and Frank Wills were raising a three-pole derrick over a well. The structure was about half up when Wills, who had shinnied up one of the poles, felt the pole giving way. He shouted to Temple to stand clear, but not in time. The structure fell and one of the three poles, twenty to thirty centimetres thick and eighteen metres long, crushed Temple and broke his neck. Wills, too, was struck down by a pole but was saved because a warp in the wood bent upwards, creating a pocket for his body.

Nitro Madness

One of the most dangerous jobs in the oil fields was handling the nitroglycerine that was used to "fracture" the wells and increase production. After R.I. Bradley brought the Roberts Torpedo to Lambton in 1872, there were many accidents involving its production and handling.

For nineteen years Bradley serviced the wells, and until Petrolia council finally passed a bylaw forbidding him from doing so, he used to

Each of Petrolia's nitroglycerine factories eventually blew up, sometimes with the loss of life. In the top photo, a hole in the ground is all that remains after an explosion at a nitro store house in the early 1900s. Below, little was also left of the nearby factory.
Courtesy Lambton County Heritage Museum.

haul crocks of nitro around the town's streets, bumping around in the back of his wagon.[113] Since there was no inhibitor in the nitroglycerine, Bradley would pack the highly volatile material in ice.

For a while he transported the nitro up from Pennsylvania by rail, until the railway company found out and banned his lethal cargo. Then he hauled it in on the back of a mule. But Bradley soon decided it made more sense to manufacture the explosive right in Petrolia, and he opened the first nitro plant on the Blind Line. Bradley Torpedo Works was just a kilometre from Petrolia's main business district.

The most gruesome accident in the history of Petrolia's nitro works occurred in April 1891, an accident that flattened R.I. Bradley's plant and killed three men. The *Advertiser* described it in graphic detail under the headline, "Blown to Atoms."

Bradley's brothers, Albert and Edward, worked with him at the nitro plant. Albert, along with his brother-in-law Duncan McDermid, and James Chambers, were the three men unfortunate enough to be inside the factory when it blew apart, ripping a hole fifteen metres across and nearly two metres deep. The *Advertiser* continued:

> Some 40 or 50 people were employed in gathering together the scattered fragments of what a few short hours earlier were three living healthy human beings. It was a sickening sight to see all those men with two pieces of shingle in their hands, each bearing some infinitesimal piece of human flesh or bone, a piece of broken rib here, a part of a skull covering there. One with a piece of shriveled skin, another with part of a foot, all of them anxiously scanning the ground for further human relics so that as much as possible of the remains of the unfortunate victims might be given a decent burial.[114]

The coroner thought the explosion might have been caused by one of the men striking a crock of nitro by error. There were twenty-nine quarts of nitro in the plant at the time. Bradley rebuilt his factory, and while there were other accidents — one killed a man and left a horse deaf the rest of its life — none was as disastrous as the explosion of 1891.

At one time or another, there was a whole string of nitro plants along the Blind Line and Marthaville Road.[115] But each in succession blew up. Harrison "Tip" Corey operated one of the best-known nitro factories. When he arrived in Petrolia from Shortsville, New York, in 1872, he initially opened the Corey House hotel but that only lasted three years.[116] Later he was a merchant, food packer, horse breeder, oil man, and patron of the arts, leading a series of literary societies and drama clubs and known for entertaining visiting artists and performers. The highlight of many a gala occasion in Petrolia was a poem commemorating the event, authored and read by Tip Corey.

But Corey made his name primarily in nitro, and owned plants in Indiana, Ohio, and Pennsylvania. Like all the men who worked with nitro, Tip Corey was known for having nerves of steel. Inevitably, it

Letterhead from the H. Corey & Son nitroglycerine works operated by Harrison "Tip" Corey and his son Bloss. In marked contrast to his work at the office, Corey was equally well known as a patron of the arts and frequently entertained Petrolians with readings of his self-authored poetry.
Courtesy Lambton County Heritage Museum.

seems, his plant exploded and fire ripped through the jagged remains just three months after the grisly Bradley explosion. Petrolians, no doubt visions of the recent accident still vivid, refused to go near the inferno to put it out.

Everyone, that is, but Corey himself, and a friend, John Scott. Corey climbed onto the roof and doused the flames with pails of water hoisted up to him by Scott, perhaps preventing further explosions. No one was killed in that incident but a few years later, in the early 1900s, the Corey plant exploded again. This time the foreman, who had escaped the first incident, was killed.

Of course it wasn't just the manufacturers of nitro who were playing with their lives. It was tough, too, on the "shooters" — the people who injected the nitro into the wells. The fracturing or "fracing" of wells is practised to this day, although now the substances used are far more stable. Then, as now, fracing broke open cracks in the reservoir rock so that the oil or gas can move more freely, and more of the available material is obtained.

Driller Bill McCutcheon was a young man in the 1870s when he was told to go "shoot" or frac a well near Oil Springs. When he got there, he took a look at the derrick that rose above the well and decided, first thing, to remove some loose planks in its upper reaches, before the explosion he planned turned them into misguided missiles.[117] As McCutcheon was removing the boards he glanced across the field and saw his assistant, a man known today only as Jim, walking toward him with a pail of nitroglycerine in each hand.

"Jim, stay where you are," ordered McCutcheon in a hushed tone, a touch of alarm in his voice. But Jim didn't hear him and kept walking toward the derrick. Once there, Jim set the pails down.

McCutcheon called out again, attempting to keep his nerves under control. "Jim, I'm going to throw down these planks. Take those pails away out of there."

This time Jim heard his boss and called up: "All right, Bill."

McCutcheon turned his attention back to the work of loosening and raising the planks. Without looking too closely, he tossed the first plank over the side of the derrick. As the plank headed groundwards, an expression of horror came over his face. There, right below where the plank was falling, sat the two pails of nitro. The hair on McCutcheon's head stood on end as he watched, paralyzed with fear.

Providence was with Bill and Jim that day. As the board neared the ground, a sudden gust of wind caught the edge and it fell less than fifteen centimetres away from the pails. "I know, Bill," stammered Jim. "I forgot."

Bill McCutcheon could muster a little laugh about that as he told the story years later, at the age of ninety-one. But a Lambton farmer who was fixing an old trough in his farmyard was less lucky. It seems the wood in the trough had once been used as a vat to mix nitroglycerine. As the farmer drove a nail into the trough, it blew up.

Other stories about nitroglycerine circulate around Petrolia to this day. One, which comes in several variations, is about a woman who lived in a downtown apartment. One version has it that a passerby came into Albert Scarsbrook's store to report a strange fluid flowing out of a second-storey window and down the outside wall. The fluid was coming from the upstairs apartment of Kathleen Stokes. An inspection of the apartment showed Stokes was making nitro. Murray Bradley later said he'd heard that rather than flowing from the window, the nitro was seeping through the ceiling.[118] One way or the other, it was good to find out in time.

Finally, there is a photograph at the Oil Museum of Canada that shows a group of men standing inside a hole in the ground, surrounded by debris. The caption states that a nitro plant had stood at the site the day before.

A Very Special Breed

The men who hauled the nitroglycerine around the fields were an eccentric band indeed. Most were thought of as inveterate booze-hounds who spent most of their free time swilling gallons of hooch to

A group of Lambton oil men "shooting" a well about 1908.
Courtesy Oil Museum of Canada.

help calm their nerves. Who could blame them?

Once, after Petrolia passed a bylaw prohibiting the carting of nitro through the town's streets, a man was found with a quantity of the explosive on the back of his buckboard wagon, parked outside a downtown store. The police were called, and the man was confronted.

The man climbed onto the back of the wagon and commenced to perform an impromptu jig on the flatbed. "You afraid this stuff'll blow up, chief?" the man inquired as the wagon's box bounced up and down, its mercurial cargo swaying precariously.[119]

Out of the Reach of Children

Not all those who were injured in those early days were the workers. With all the dangerous equipment and supplies sitting around, it was no wonder that sometimes curious children were seriously hurt.

Ken MacGregor, whom we earlier heard tell the tale of Halloween highjinks, also hearkened back to an incident that occurred in Petrolia in the late 1880s. MacGregor and brother Billy often played with black gunpowder they had no trouble obtaining around their Petrolia home. They would cap a piece of scrap pipe at one end, fill it with the gunpowder, and light it, watching the pipe blow high into the air.

A nine-year-old boy named Sherman Swift watched them, one day, and snuck back after they were gone to see if he could replicate their actions. Sherman collared two friends, and the group drilled a make-believe oil well. As the boys tried to "shoot" the well using a fuse stuck into the gunpowder, the "torpedo" failed to go off. Young Sherman peered into the hole, and the powder flashed, burning his face and blinding him for life.[120]

Hard Oiler!

The story ended relatively happily, however. Sherman Swift attended schools for the blind in Brantford and Lansing, Michigan, and eventually obtained degrees from McGill University. He became a librarian for the Canadian National Institute for the Blind, and edited a Braille newspaper. Sherman Swift was often in demand as a lecturer and after-dinner speaker.

Part Three
A Golden Age

"In the month of November 1867, Messers B.S. Van Tuyl, Geo. Moncrieff, R. Lawyer, Frank Smith, W. Ewing and R. Herring met at the old United States Hotel ... to inaugurate what are now known throughout the entire continent of America, and in many European cities as the famed Petrolia Assembles. Since that time down to the present writing, the brilliancy of these events has never been permitted to wane nor their glory to fade."
— *Advertiser,* Petrolia, 4 November 1892.

Chapter Six
The Oil Barons

The story of Lambton's first quarter-century is a raucous one. It is a story of fortunes gained in a flash and lost just as quickly, of tough-spirited pioneers willing to gamble on a dream. The next twenty-five years unfolded at a more genteel pace. By 1880, a small group of leading families had emerged from the wash of pioneers and had begun to shape a more permanent community in the middle of what had been called "a howling swamp."

Why did a certain few of these pioneers rise to the top in the oil patch? Hard work, inspiration, resourcefulness, and sheer luck, yes. However, those who diversified their interests, who branched out into service industries rather than staying focused only on finding oil, were among the most successful. But while diversification is one of the common threads, the other is oil. The people who most made their mark during that era were the oil barons.

New discoveries at Oil Springs in 1881, continued good production at Petrolia, and steady prices shook Lambton out of the last remnants of the 1870s depression. With the drilling of deeper wells at Oil Springs, a deeper stratum was tapped to give up its reserves of oil. There were no gushers here, nothing to rival the excitement of the 1860s. Instead, in the area of Oil Springs and Petrolia, wells now pumped consistently and productively. The industry had matured.

Conspicuous Wealth

Some of the newly wealthy enjoyed their money more conspicuously than others. The oil refiners, Jake Englehart and John D. Noble, could be seen occasionally dining at Delmonico's in New York City. Several of the wealthier families took winter vacations in California and Florida. John Henry Fairbank's wife, Edna, frequently visited some of North America's and Europe's leading health spas.[121] And, as we saw earlier, the nitro manufacturer Harrison "Tip" Corey was noted for entertaining visiting artists and performers with lavish parties in Petrolia.

Smaller centres such as Oil Springs, Oil City, and Marthaville never quite acquired the trappings of permanence. In Petrolia, however, by about 1880, larger, more sturdy public buildings and homes began to spring up. People complained about the condition of the town's streets and in the mid-'80s, work began on paving Petrolia Street with cedar blocks.[122]

Petrolia's monied existence set it apart from most similar-sized communities. Forms of entertainment expected in larger centres but rarely enjoyed in smaller towns began to appear. While there may have been nothing unusual about the regular arrival of P.T. Barnum or the Guy Brothers Minstrel Show, which appealed to mass audiences, Shakespeare was performed at the Oil Exchange Hall, sometimes featuring top-notch actors of the era. The hall was jammed nearly every weekend for stage productions put on by touring companies. (The Oil Exchange was created by John Henry Fairbank and other producers in late 1884 to set quality controls. The Hall was a place for buyers and sellers of oil to meet. With Fairbank president of the board of management, the Exchange lasted until 1897.)

One performance at the Oil Exchange Hall was the critically acclaimed Harry Miner's *Silver King*, which played for two nights in November 1885. According to the *Advertiser*, the *New York Herald* had hailed it as "the most successful drama of the century ... as good as a sermon."[123] Apparently the production was "embellished by a carload of beautiful scenery."

A horse race track was built in 1882, later used for bicycle racing and fairs. Bicycles were the craze of the decade, featuring penny-farthings, bikes with a front wheel as high as a man's shoulder. All the latest in bicycles could be bought at Noble's store. Lawn tennis, football, and curling became increasingly popular pastimes for players and spectators alike.

In 1885, the Oil Exchange Hall was rented as a roller rink when roller skating swept the land. By the time Sir John A. Macdonald paid an election campaign visit in December 1886 and some two thousand Conservatives crammed the Central roller rink, it was one of three in town.

Upstairs from the brick town hall, the opera house, dubbed the Victoria Playhouse, opened on 4 January 1889. G.S. Pitkin starred in *Dr. Jekyll and Mr. Hyde* that month; in February the London Minstrels put on the play *An Oil Borer's Revenge*. A baptist preacher, Rev. A.E. de St.

Dalmas, stopped by to give a talk on the sin of the theatre for an appreciative audience. Many of the opera house's first entertainments were string quartets, tableaux, and poetry readings.[124] And for the town's leading gentlemen, in the late 1880s, rooms were rented in the Archer Block to house the new Petrolia Club.

There were regular excursions "to commune with nature," a favourite Victorian pastime. One frequent trek involved a train trip to Sarnia, a boat ride down the St. Clair River to Detroit, and a picnic. As well there were various town bands, literary societies, drama clubs, and lectures.

There was no fear in the last two decades of the nineteenth century that petroleum markets might dry up. In fact, the Lambton oil fields could not keep pace with Canada's thirst for oil. By 1890 nearly one-fifth of the oil used in this country had to be brought in from the United States. In 1903, when it was clear that the Lambton oil lands were wearing out, almost two-thirds was imported from that country.[125]

Whatever Lambton Hard Oilers could pump out of the ground could be sold. From $1 a barrel, which crude sold for during much of the 1880s, the price rose to $2 by the 1890s. Oil was certainly king, and Petrolia the undisputed capital of the Canadian oil business. In 1891, a comparison of the manufacturing output of twenty Canadian towns and cities, on a per-capita basis, placed Petrolia at the top.

The Iroquois Hotel

Amid the wealth, a magnificent new hotel was opened in the fall of 1896. The white brick, three-storey Iroquois Hotel boasted fifty rooms. Suites were kept for community leaders like Harrison Corey, Bloss Corey, the hotel's builder J.A. Johnson, and newspaper editor Richard Herring. From the main street, patrons entered the building through doors of Venetian glass. Adjacent to a cavernous main hall nearly one hundred feet long were the dining room, office, card rooms, bar, and reading room.[126]

The opening of the Iroquois was recorded enthusiastically in the *Advertiser*. Described as the finest, best equipped hotel west of Toronto, the Iroquois' cuisine was said to be unexcelled, its rooms elegantly furnished and boasting both electric lights and water. Most of the community's leading citizens attended the hotel's official opening dinner. Conspicuous by his absence from that gala event was the town's leading oil baron, John Henry Fairbank. His wife, Edna, had died seven months earlier[127] and perhaps he felt it inappropriate to attend.

Hard Oiler!

The Merchant Prince of Petrolia

Fairbank was, according to Edward Phelps whose thesis is the most complete chronicle of the man's life, Petrolia's "richest citizen and merchant prince." The Petrolia *Advertiser* told its readers on 16 September 1903 that, "by common consent," Fairbank was "father of the town."

Fairbank and his wife, Edna, had three children who lived beyond infancy. The eldest, Henry, attended the University of Toronto and was in training to become a doctor when he took his own life.[128] John Henry had urged the younger son, Charles, to enter the military and he did so, attending Kingston's Royal Military College before being called home after his brother's death. Daughter May was the youngest of the three.

Edna spent a lot of her time at health resorts and with her parents' family in Niagara Falls.[129] While she often complained of illness, Edna certainly seemed well enough at the many socials she hosted and attended in Petrolia. One of her favourite events was Petrolia's famous Assemblies, dress balls that were held four times a year. From their inception in 1875 — the brainchild that emerged from a meeting of several leading figures, including Benjamin Van Tuyl, George Moncrieff, and Richard Herring — until their demise after the turn of the century, the Assemblies were the poshest social events in the community.

Petrolia's high society met twice annually to attend fancy dress balls known as the Assemblies. Once the Victoria Playhouse was constructed from the town's oil money, the balls were often held there, as this one was in the early 1900s.
Courtesy Lambton County Hertage Museum.

Rose Bal Poudre, Petrolia, Feb. 27, 1908.

The *Advertiser* of 4 November 1892 waxed poetic in its description of these affairs. There, the leading citizenry of Petrolia always enjoyed "the terpsichorean feast with almost unabated enthusiasm."

After the first Assembly in February 1875, Edna Fairbank wrote excitedly to her sons that she "walked through a Quadrille with Mr. Van Tuyl," a reference to her husband's dashing business partner, the American army colonel, Benjamin Van Tuyl.[130]

When the Oil Exchange Hall was built in the 1880s, the Assemblies were held there for a time. Later they took place in the more spectacular Victoria opera house.[131]

No doubt to please his wife, who did not feel their modest white frame home on Petrolia Street was befitting a family of their standing, John Henry Fairbank set to work in 1889 on the Fairbank mansion, Sunnyside. Built next door to their frame home, the magnificent structure took two years to complete and when it was done, was known as one of the finest homes west of Toronto.[132]

The main floor boasted huge dining and living rooms and library. A grand oak staircase led to the second floor's eight bedrooms with baths. The third floor was the ballroom, underlaid with brick, where the Assemblies took place in their latter days. Guy Lombardo and his Royal Canadians performed there. The basement featured a wine cellar along with the two furnaces it took to heat the home. The exterior was built of sandstone and brick, the roof was slate, and two huge iron gates at the street opened to lead visitors up to the home's entrance, two immense oak doors.

Fairbank historian Edward Phelps believes that, at times, Fairbank controlled nearly a quarter of all the business assets of the town. Yet John Henry never "left" the oil field. As the mansion was going up, daughter May wrote to her brother, Charles Oliver, in New York City where he was studying: "I see [visualize] Papa in his old yellow — shall I say overcoat? — black hat, with his shoes muddy, trousers turned up and head slightly bent forward walking around the new house."

In his early days in Petrolia, Fairbank had tried his hand at politics and served three one-year terms as reeve. Then, in 1882, local Liberals talked him into running for national office. In the East Lambton riding where his Conservative opponent was from outside the constituency, John Henry defied the conventional wisdom, traded on his personal popularity, and was elected Liberal MP. He remained in office five years but was defeated in 1887 when the Conservatives found a local man, George Moncrieff, who brought in the prime minister, the aging Sir John A. Macdonald, to make a personal appeal.

As an MP, John Henry never made a name for himself as a national figure; he seemed more comfortable dealing with local issues. He did become a spokesman for the oil industry, however, and just before the election he lost, he wrote to the *Petrolea Topic* (the town's more recently established "Liberal" newspaper) to assure voters he favoured maintaining protective tariffs: "The oil industry labours under disadvantages. If we had the same crude material as the Americans we could be much more independent of this protection. But having these difficulties and being established 24 years, we have grown into it, and like many more things we cannot do without it."

Jake Englehart was a founder of Imperial Oil Company Limited and known for his philanthropic enterprises. At age nineteen he operated his own refinery in London, Ontario, and was well known for his neatly trimmed moustache and beard and immaculate clothes.
Courtesy Oil Museum of Canada.

Jacob "Jake" Englehart

If anyone challenged Fairbank for the title "most influential oil baron," it would have been Jacob Englehart. The wizard of the refiners, Englehart spearheaded the creation of Imperial Oil and became one of the most respected and best loved of Lambton's Hard Oilers.

Born in Cleveland in 1847,[133] Englehart was a young man of nineteen when he took charge of his own firm, J.L. Englehart and Company, in London. He had come to London from New York where, at the age of eleven, he had worked as a clerk in the oil firm of Sonneborn, Dryfoos and Company. In six years he was a partner.

Exactly what Englehart's part in the company was, is not clear now, but the senior partners, Solomon S. Sonneborn, Abraham M. Dryfoos and Leopold Beringer, were known for handling illicit goods — probably whiskey — and were charged with violating national revenue laws. People seeking to escape the American revenue police often slipped across the border to Ontario.

Englehart cut a dapper figure. His pince-nez, held by a broad black ribbon, neatly trimmed vandyke beard and moustache, highly shined shoes, fresh flower in his lapel, and high starched collar made him well known on the streets of London. He lived in the city's finest hotel, the Tecumseh, and often headed out to the oil fields in search of more petroleum for his refinery, looking the part of a city slicker.

He once financed a deal to ship $30,000 worth of kerosene to Germany. When the buyer complained the product was inferior, Englehart dismantled part of his refinery, shipped it to Germany, and redistilled the product to the buyer's satisfaction.

In the late 1870s he moved to Petrolia, where he lived the life of a frugal bachelor in the home of then-mayor Edwin Kerby. On the site of where Petrolia's Big Still had sat before it blew up, Englehart built the Silver Star refinery. He convinced town council to offer him a five-year tax-relief deal, a plan applauded by the *Advertiser*. The building of the Silver Star was "a gigantic gain to this city and neighbourhood in more ways than our public can at present possibly imagine,"[134] the editor wrote in what proved to be a prophetic editorial.

As an employer, Englehart was highly enlightened for his day. He initiated a form of worker's compensation, and industrial safety was strictly enforced. Once, he caught an employee smoking in the refinery. Having warned him before, Englehart fired him. When Jake discovered that the young man's wages were the sole support for his mother, the refinery boss rehired the lad and secretly paid the mother the two weeks' wages her son had been docked.[135]

In 1880, Englehart led in the formation of the Imperial Oil Company Limited (detailed in the next chapter), and two years later he joined Fairbank in the creation of the Crown Savings and Loan.[136] It may have seemed like a strange partnership: Fairbank's interest was to boost crude prices to the highest possible level; Englehart wanted to buy crude at the lowest possible price. But the two men respected one another and saw nothing strange in coming together in a common business enterprise.

Englehart was a perfectionist. When he arrived to visit his Silver Star refinery at Petrolia, everyone was expected to be on his or her best behaviour.[137] They literally rolled out a red carpet for his arrival. Every piece of brass and metal was polished to a high lustre. On one of his visits, Englehart found a man urinating in a corner. "You'd better not let your boss find you doing that," he told the man, "or he'll fire you."[138]

In 1891 Englehart married Charlotte Eleanor Thompson, daughter of a prosperous farmer, and he finally moved out of Kerby's home. He built Glenview, a red brick mansion with a large, circular turret. Next to it, he built a golf course.

In 1905, at the request of Ontario's then-premier Sir James Whitney, Englehart took over the Temiskaming and Northern Ontario Railway, along which the town that bears his name was built.

Charlotte became highly involved in the affairs of the community, among many other things taking over the presidency of the relief fund. Later she would stipulate in her will that upon the death of herself and her husband, their home should be turned over to the town for a hospital. That it was, and the name Charlotte Eleanor Englehart still adorns that institution.

William Henry McGarvey

Not all the Hard Oilers were content to make their mark in Lambton. William McGarvey came to be known as the petroleum king of Austria for his ground-breaking work in eastern Europe. He amassed an immense personal fortune and hobnobbed with royalty.

Born in Huntingdon, Quebec, William's father, Edward, moved the family to Wyoming, where he opened a store in the early 1860s.[139] In the Petrolia boom of 1866, William moved to that town where he opened his own enterprise, the Mammoth Store. Soon he expanded into oil and became an operator, refiner, and oil industry leader. He was elected mayor of Petrolia, served a term as county warden and headed a federal government survey of mineral resources in western Canada.

But unlike many of the oil barons, William H. McGarvey went much farther afield. It was in Europe that McGarvey made his name. (Chapter 9 is devoted to his life and exploits.)

An Italian Count in the City of Oil

Another man crossed the Atlantic in the opposite direction to McGarvey's. Having heard about the Canadian oil find, Count Carlo "Charles" Ribighini left his Italian home and arrived in Petrolia about 1865,[140] hoping to share in the wealth and adventure. Among the works of this highly imaginative man were experiments in the use of oil as locomotive fuel, years before the diesel engine was invented.

When he quickly began to make his fortune, Ribighini approached newspaperman Richard Owen Herring, editor of Oil Springs' *Chronicle*, whom he asked to go to Italy and accompany his wife and daughters back to Canada. Herring accommodated Ribighini, and the family lived in Petrolia for many years.

Ribighini had been a successful merchant in Ancona, Italy, before coming to Canada, where he lived, first in London, then Petrolia. In 1877 Ribighini returned to Europe and worked in Romania's oil fields, helping to introduce Canadian drillers and drilling methods to that country. In July 1878, a daughter, Maria, married Theodore Labatt of the London Labatt family in a lavish New York City wedding. The next year, he travelled back to his native Italy to scout out the prospects for oil drilling, and he sent to Petrolia for drillers. The exploration apparently didn't go very far.

But Ribighini had already developed a name as someone willing to take risks. In late 1873, he was a leader in tests to see whether crude could be used as fuel for locomotives and other engines. With crude prices falling below $1 a barrel, he felt it made more sense to burn oil to produce steam to run the trains, than it did wood, which was going for $2 or more a cord. The *London Free Press* reported on 18 December 1873: "It is fully expected that ere long petroleum will form the staple fuel for the locomotives."

Later that month, the newspaper reported that Ribighini and his engineer, a man named Anderson, were working on a crude-oil burner that would power trains. In one test, an oil-burner-fired engine was attached to seventeen cars, and apparently was successful in pulling them. The benefits went beyond mere cost and availability. Steam could be generated more quickly from oil than from wood or coal. It was estimated that four gallons of crude could run a train for one mile.

Ribighini may have learned of the idea from Charles Brydges, a superintendent of the Grand Trunk Railway. According to A.W. Currie, in his book *Canadian Economic Development*,[141] Brydges suggested oil as a locomotive fuel, but stockholders were cool to the idea. One American account says experiments began in the use of oil as fuel as early as 1860. While the work of these fuel pioneers was groundbreaking, the diesel locomotive, in which an oil-burning engine supplies the power, would have to await the twentieth century to gain acceptance.

Ribighini was in Europe at the time of his death in July 1897, again looking for oil in Italy. He was on his way, by train, from Milan to Amsterdam where he had an appointment as a consulting engineer on the project. He was found dead in the train's sleeping compartment at Cologne, Germany.

Under the Influence of Oil

Others made their names and riches in businesses outside the oil patch but certainly due to its influence. For example, the Scottish-born brothers John and James Kerr founded the J.&J. Kerr Company.[142] Although primarily contractors and builders, they were also in lumber and coal, drilled for oil, and built oil rigs and tanks. During Petrolia's construction boom, they built a fifty-home subdivision, a firehall, school and Masonic Temple. As his residence, John built Nemo Hall, one of Petrolia's many magnificent homes of the era. All the home's fireplaces were built for natural gas, which John Kerr tapped into from his own property. Brother James was a cabinetmaker, was elected town mayor three times, and was secretary of the Oil Exchange.

Then there was Henry Warren Lancey. Born in Maine, Lancey's Petrolia home became a social centre for the community.[143] He built the first residential subdivision west of Bear Creek, and constructed Crescent Park, the site of his own residence and the largest concentration of grand homes in town, Quality Hill. Lancey also built a brick office and retail block across the street from Vaughn's block. But because it was constructed during a depression, it was dubbed Lancey's Folly. Despite the economy, Lancey demonstrated his confidence in the local business market by opening his own grocery store in the building.

When Lancey left the grocery business, the store was taken over by Albert Scarsbrook, who opened Scarsbrook and Palmer grocery. The store catered to the well-heeled. It retailed fine china and crystal, specializing in names like Royal Crown Darby and Waterford. And he sold imported groceries and exotic teas.

A Very Sophisticated Town

In Oil Springs, the boom of the early 1880s was short-lived. But for Petrolia, the Golden Age continued through the 1890s. In some years, more than 900,000 barrels of oil were produced in Lambton,[144] most of it coming from Petrolia. While the rest of Canada stumbled in and out of depression, Petrolia fared well.

Certainly by rural and small-town Ontario standards of the era, Petrolia was becoming a sophisticated community. The newspapers reflected this, delving beyond the normal fare one would expect to find in weeklies of the period. For example, at the outset of Petrolia's Golden Age, an article appeared in the *Topic* of 21 August 1879 that must have seemed like science fantasy at the time. Today we can only look back at it and admire the farsightedness of the editor who selected it.

Under the heading "The Sun's Power," the article was based on a paper published in the periodical, *Scientific American*, by a Professor Langley. It dealt with his calculations of how much power came from the sun to evaporate rainwater. He calculated, for instance, that the power of the heat of a noon-day sun in March, acting on a square foot of the earth's surface after losing some of its energy from the atmosphere, equals 0.131 horsepower. It would be many decades before people began to think about a practical application of that information.

Chapter Seven
This Business of Oil

Lambton's oil story parallels the advent and unfolding of the new scientific age: Oil literally greased the engine of the Industrial Revolution. As a lubricant, it allowed for finer tolerances and bigger, swifter machines. The huge steam-engine locomotives and ships that carried people to the far corners of the world in the latter part of the nineteenth century used copious quantities of petroleum grease.

The demand for lighting oil increased. Cheap oil-and gas-fired lights meant people were able to stay up later, to operate their machines around the clock, to read more and socialize longer.

And then there was the internal combustion engine. Gottlieb Daimler had built a gasoline engine, which, in 1886, Carl Benz fastened to a tricycle, creating the world's first automobile.

Learning by Doing

When the oil pioneers began their work, they had no one else's experience on which to draw. They needed to figure out how to get the crude petroleum out of the ground without aid of text books or other expertise. Charles Nelson Tripp simply chipped off the solidified, asphalt-like secretions from the Lambton gum beds and tossed them into a pot to melt, much the way countless generations of people had done before him. But that experience did James Miller Williams no good when he decided he had to reach below the gum beds, down into the very source itself. Williams was determined to take oil mining out of the realm of prehistory and turn it into a profitable, modern business.

He was the first man in North America — and probably the world — to do so, when he dug his first well by hand. A year later in Titusville,

Pennsylvania, Colonel Edwin L. Drake used the method of the salt drillers to bore a hole to the oil.[145]

The Canadian Rig

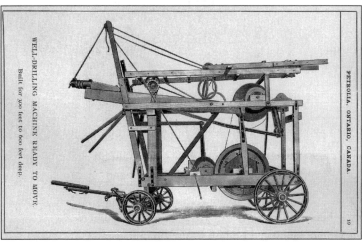

A catalogue from the Oil Well Supply Company of Petrolia, circa 1900, displays a portable well-drilling machine it says is suitable for depths of 300 to 600 feet.
Courtesy Lambton County Heritage Museum.

In Canada, the early wildcatters looked to the drillers of artesian wells for inspiration. After Williams's first hand-dug well, Canadians started experimenting with metal bits suspended from several black ash poles. The bit was raised and lowered, thus pounding or punching its way through the rock..[146]

The science of geology was still young and little was known about the various rock strata in which oil lay. Early oil pioneers found that the pole-tool method worked effectively. Even after the rotary system was developed in the United States, many Canadian crews continued to believe their system was superior. It lowered the bit straighter than the cable-tool or rotary-drilling system, which suspended the drilling bit from a cable. The pole-tool method was shared and adapted in early oil fields all over the world and came to be known as the Canadian rig.

The Canadian rig was really only a minor advancement on the centuries-old Chinese method of drilling for water. There, the cutting tool was attached to a pole that was held vertically, suspended from a cross pole on a post. The end of the cross pole was attached to a springboard, and the driller guided the vertical pole, which held the drilling tool. In ancient China, workers would jump onto the springboard, which would force the drilling tool down, deepening the hole. Instead of using progressively heavier, or more people to jump onto the board and force the tool downwards, Canadians added a treadle. The early drillers literally punched their way through the earth by lifting and dropping a heavy cutting tool or bit.

In 1900, the Petrolia oil baron, John D. Noble, was appointed a delegate to the first Petroleum Congress in Paris, held during that year's Paris Exhibition. It was a singular Canadian honour for the American-born Noble to be asked to read a paper on the oil industry of his adopted country. In it, he described the Canadian drilling method.

Noble explained that the first thirty metres of drilling was through clay. That was achieved by use of a horse-powered auger, which cut through the clay as if it were cheese, he said. Occasionally the auger was pulled out by using a steam engine to power a rope and pulley that went to the top of the three-pole derrick. Then the clay was dumped and the operation repeated. This was continued until the top rock was struck, at which time the horse and auger were dispensed with.

A wooden frame was then inserted into the hole to prevent the clay from caving in. To the bottom of a heavy iron bar, about eleven metres long and nearly ten centimetres in diameter, was attached a steel bit or cutting tool. The bar, in turn, was attached to a line of ash poles, each nine or eleven metres long (reports differ between describing poles thirty feet and thirty-six feet long). Each pole had a screw pin on one end and a screw socket on the other, and stood on end in the derrick until needed.

The driller stood or sat at the top of the well, maneuvering the poles, which were attached by chain and swivel to the working beam. This beam, in turn, was moved up and down by a steam engine. The weight of the apparatus punched or cut through the rock.

By continually turning the poles, the driller ensured a round drill hole. Occasionally the drill bit would become dull. Then the poles would be raised by the steam engine and unscrewed, the bit removed, and a sharpened bit screwed on. The dulled bit would be honed and prepared for its next use.

The debris or cuttings were removed from the hole through a hollow tube that was lowered into the well, with a valve opening upwards at the bottom. The tube's weight, with the poles attached, forced the cuttings through the valve, which was then raised and emptied.

Next, the rock was reinforced with iron casing. Once the oil-bearing rock was reached, a nitroglycerine "torpedo" was exploded in the hole to frac or shatter the rock and let the oil flow more freely into the bored hole.

Since flowing wells were the exception, not the rule, the oil usually had to be pumped to the surface. Early wells were pumped by hand; a man stood all day, lifting and shoving down on a pump handle to fill his barrels or tanks. Later, mechanical pumps that created a vacuum and sucked up the oil were introduced. Steam engines became popular power sources in the 1860s, for both pumping and drilling. The jerker-rod system, introduced by John Henry Fairbank, added the new efficiency of connecting several wells to one power source.

At about the same time John Noble was explaining the Canadian or pole-tool rock-drilling method to his European audience, a group of oil men in Texas was introducing a new system. Based on a drilling concept originally designed by the inventor and artist Leonardo da Vince, about 1500, the rotary drill was first used in the field in 1901.[147] Rather than chip or pound away at rock, this drill chewed it up.

The rotary became known was the American Standard system of drilling, and it enabled wildcatters to go deeper than ever before in their search for petroleum. Both systems are still used today, although the rotary drill is more popular worldwide, including western Canada, while the pole-tool system remains the preferred method in Ontario.[148]

The Oil Well Supply Company

By the turn of the century, the equipment used by the oil producers was usually manufactured at the Oil Well Supply Company Limited, which still operates in Petrolia. The company came about through the amalgamation of two smaller companies.[149]

In 1866, Hector McKenzie, a Scottish artisan who manufactured iron and brass products, set up shop in Petrolia. Four years later, James Joyce (not the writer) arrived from Ireland and began to utilize his skills as a blacksmith and ironworker to make drilling and pumping equipment. The two men combined their efforts in 1890 and, together, the Joyces and McKenzies developed tools and pumping equipment specifically for the local oil business.

In his Paris lecture, John Noble went on to explain that the Oil Well Supply Company was known the world over for its specialized machinery, its expert craftsmen, and its ability to deliver to oil fields in such places as Galicia, Sumatra, and Borneo, and for water-drilling in Australia.

Pumping and Shipping Oil at Petrolia, Ont.

Published by the Bookery.

As the Lambton petroleum industry matured, tank wagons such as this hauled crude oil to central receiving stations where refiners collected it for processing.
Courtesy Lambton County Heritage Museum.

Prior to the amalgamation of the firms, however, Hector McKenzie and his son, William, fell into a disagreement over the company's future. William wanted to gamble on the growing international market, but his father was doubtful. William left and created his own company in Stockport, England, the Oil Well Engineering Company.

Noble explained how, back at the wellhead, oil from several wells was pumped into one tank, sometimes called a "look tank," in which the water and sediment were separated out. According to modern-day oil man Phil Morningstar, and Wanda Pratt, the term comes from the fact that the tank is fitted with a lid that can be opened in order to see how the wells are pumping.[150] The lighter oil separates naturally from the heavier water, by floating to the top.

Tank wagons took the oil — at this point a dark green colour — to receiving stations, or else it was pumped through underground pipelines. From the receiving stations, the oil went to the refiners for processing.

By the late 1860s, it may be recalled, underground tanks dug into the blue clay were used, rather than the earlier above-ground tanks of wood and then iron. The underground tanks were lined with rings of solid pine, to prevent the clay from caving in. The clay was sufficiently impervious to hold the oil tightly, and not let it leach back into the soil.[151]

Refining Oil

At the refinery, the crude went into an iron still, a cylinder three metres in diameter and nine metres long, set up on brickwork, like a boiler.[152] Fire was placed underneath, the oil was boiled to vapor, and the vapor was released from the top through a series of iron pipes that ran through a long box filled with cold water. This condensed the vapor into a pure, clear oil. This "distillate" was then washed in sulphuric acid, which prevented the resulting illuminating oil from smoking when burned.

After the illuminating oil was taken off, the vapor was blown out of the still by the injection of steam, and condensed. The resulting product was sold for making gas or used as liquid fuel. The remaining tar could be used for liquid fuel or paraffin wax, or manufactured into lubricating oils.

The first refineries were often built right in the oil fields, although James Williams had one by 1860 in Hamilton, and the first one in London was built by William Spencer and Herman Waterman in 1863. A refinery at that time consisted of that big iron pot, the fire, and a condenser to recover the liquids that boiled off. Various "fractions" occurred during the boiling process.

Gradually, boiler plate replaced iron, and these boilers or stills became larger. Refineries remained fairly small through the 1860s and '70s, with London alone boasting some dozen at one time. By the 1880s, a refinery consisted of several stills and bleaching tanks. There would often be a barrel works, where the containers for transporting the product were constructed, and a building where the barrels were filled for shipping.

Producers vs. Refiners

The industry's early days saw a constant tug-of-war between the producers and the refiners for superiority, for the ability to set or at least influence prices that would be most beneficial to them. While oil men were notoriously independent-minded business people, several (usually short-lived) arrangements were established over the years to fix prices. The first was probably the organizing, in Oil Springs in 1862, of the Canada Oil Association.[153] It lasted about a year and was unable to do anything more than keep crude at between $1 and $2 a barrel.

In 1867, the producers shut down many wells to reduce supply in an attempt to boost prices, and in 1868 formed the Petroleum Amalgamated Company. Producers leased their properties to this "company" which was really more of a producers' union. Yet many producers refused to join in this effort and its success was limited.

Later in 1868, the major producers created the Crude Oil Association, which was similar to the Canada Oil Association they had created briefly six years earlier in Oil Springs. This time with more clout behind it, oil prices began to rise. Later that year the refiners, perhaps wary of the new-found power the producers were exerting as a united group, formed their own association to regulate prices and promote trade. It didn't last long.

The Fairbank-inspired producers alliance, the Lambton Crude Oil Partnership, followed in 1871, just as prices were about to take off because of a producers' plan in Pennsylvania to withhold oil to boost its value there. Over the next couple of years, the price hit a high of $2 a barrel and then fell to a low of 70 cents.

When the producers formed their own Home Oil Company in 1873 and opened their own refinery, the London refiners shuddered. During the next year the refiners were able to cooperate sufficiently to form the London Oil Refining Company cartel. It survived three years.

When that cartel failed, the producers pounced and formed the Mutual Oil Association, the most successful enterprise to date. Crude sales were controlled, prices rose, and production expanded. In 1878 the refiners reactivated the London Oil Refining Company. When Mutual expired on 1 May 1879, the *Advertiser* the next day called it "black Friday." Crude plummeted to 40 cents, then struggled back to $1.40 through 1880.

Through all this, some of the London refiners evidently remained financially comfortable. In February 1878 refiners Herman and Isaac Waterman were hailed for their public spiritedness in spending $2,000 for an exhibit of Canadian oil at the Paris International Exposition.[154] The principal attraction was a one-ton lion carved from wax derived from Lambton crude. Petroleum products were displayed in cut-glass vials.

That same year, Jake Englehart convinced Petrolia council to grant him five years of tax relief if he built a new refinery there. When they agreed, Englehart packed up shop in London and built the largest refinery ever seen in Canada, the Silver Star.

Englehart's agitator (one of a refiner's mechanisms for treating crude oil) at the Silver Star was described in Belden's Atlas as the world's largest, able to treat 75,000 gallons or 1,800 barrels of crude oil at a time. The oil was barrelled in a shed ninety metres long and nine metres wide. Long pipes extended the length of the building on each side, from which oil was forced by steam into barrels. An automatic feeder shut off the flow when the barrels were full, and they were sealed with boiling glue.

Power for the refinery was generated on site by four large boilers that generated steam for eight engines and pumps. The refinery's waterworks had twelve hydrants operated by an independent engine that pumped water for the refinery. Employees were trained as firefighters. While Englehart's was the largest, there were eight other refineries in Petrolia at the time.

Imperial Oil

The Canadian industry was about to experience a major shift but, as is so often the case, it would take events south of the border to force the change. Enter John D. Rockefeller and the Standard Oil Company.

To this point, the petroleum story in Canada had mainly been one of individual enterprise of both producers and refiners, often working at cross-purposes. Occasionally they would come together, set aside their differences, and work as a group of either producers or refiners. Few had crossed the line from one group to the other, although the Home Oil experiment had demonstrated that producers could also successfully refine.

A number of circumstances conspired to keep the Canadian industry fragmented to this juncture. First, Lambton was pock-marked with more than 1,000 separate wells, most of which, on their own, produced only small quantities of oil. Later experience showed that the Hard Oilers should not have drilled more than one well per acre, but they had no model then on which to base a plan.[155] Second, transportation was fragmented, with three major railways serving the oil lands, and that kept prices competitive. Third, refineries up to that time had been small, and relatively inexpensive operations. And fourth, the industry had been, so far, protected by the national government, since both political parties endorsed protection for oil: the Conservatives through their national policy of blanket industrial protection, the Liberals through a willingness to grant oil an exemption from their general policy of lower tariffs. (Fairbank and former Liberal Prime Minister Alexander Mackenzie of Sarnia were undoubtedly instrumental in achieving this.) The maintaining of duties acted to protect small, inefficient operators.[156]

In total, all these factors acted to disrupt attempts to organize cartels and long-lasting industry cooperatives.

But things were different in the U.S. In the days before the trust-busting laws, John D. Rockefeller had established a huge corporation that cornered the petroleum business. He had acquired his first refinery in 1864, and in just eleven years he controlled the entire American industry.[157] He succeeded in bringing order and efficiency to the American petroleum business, a factor that, together with leaps in American refining technology, threatened to overwhelm Canada's industry.

Finally, Canadian tariffs on the importation of illuminating oil had been eased in the late 1870s, and the increasing popularity of pipelines encouraged a more centralized system of collecting and transporting crude. While sixty percent of Canadian oil products were still being exported to Europe in 1870, within three years the lower-priced and higher-quality American products had taken that market away and were even entering Canada. The Canadian business was ripe for change.

Jake Englehart, it is widely agreed, was the driving force behind the formation of Imperial Oil, the Canadian industry's desperate response to the Standard Oil threat. Some argue that Frederick A. Fitzgerald, Imperial's first president, also deserves strong billing. However it occurred, on 8 September 1880, sixteen oil men, all but Englehart located in London, created the Imperial Oil Company Limited.[158]

The first board included William Spencer, the London refiner who assisted James Williams in taking oil's first tentative steps; Spencer's sons, William and Charles; Herman Waterman who had been Spencer's partner in London's first refinery; refiner John R. Minhinnick and his partner, lawyer John Geary; John Walker, who had worked for John McMillan in the Bothwell fields; Thomas Smallman, who started the first chemical company and, with Walker, built a refinery; barrel makers T.D. Hodgens and his brother Edward; and Englehart, who became vice-president and remained on the company's board until his death in 1921.

Operations were centralized: oil was refined in two plants, in London and Petrolia, while others specialized in some phase of production such as lubricating oil or candles. The London refinery remained until it burned down in 1883. When London council expressed little enthusiasm for its replacement, refining was centralized at Petrolia's Silver Star. Imperial did keep a lubricating oil and wax plant in London, however, until 1895.

Imperial's business boomed. Within a few years it had twenty-three branch offices, from Halifax to Victoria. This was a significant factor in helping to open the Canadian West, and many prairie farmers kept their Imperial oak barrels, turning them into washtubs, rain barrels, and other useful items, rather than returning them for the $1.25 recycling refund.

The Move to Sarnia

By 1895, however, the rush for expansion in the oil industry was so great that Imperial did not have the capitalization to keep up. The demand for kerosene and lubricating oil grew. And the internal combustion engine, although still in its infancy, was increasing in popularity.

American competitors were serving one-third of the Canadian market. Imperial attempted to find new investors in Canada and in Britain but to no avail. Clearly the only source of sufficient capital was Standard Oil, and in 1898 Rockefeller's corporation gained a controlling interest in Imperial in exchange for the capital needed to meet Canada's growing needs.

In Sarnia, the *Observer* predicted that with Standard now controlling virtually the entire Canadian oil business, that city would soon become the petroleum centre. In Petrolia, the *Advertiser* said, not so fast: "The town of Petrolia is all right, and nobody in it should fear that any deluge or other disastrous catastrophe is likely to happen. The industry is not going to be destroyed, but is going to be conducted at full pressure, and Petrolia is and will continue to be right in it."[159] It was a brave and confident-sounding statement, but one that would soon ring hollow.

Twenty-five kilometres from Petrolia, Sarnia had, to this point, been on the periphery of the refining business. Dominion of Canada Oils Refinery Company Limited built a refinery there in 1871, which went through a series of owners.[160] Finally in '97, it came into Imperial's possession. Soon after Standard took control of Imperial, it moved the head office to Sarnia and built a pipeline from the Lambton fields.

Petrolia's loss seemed typical of a trend near the turn into the new century. With the election of the Liberal government of Wilfrid Laurier in 1896, Canada had entered a period of prosperity. And with that prosperity came a reorganization of commercial enterprises that began to favour larger companies over smaller ones, and larger cities over smaller towns.

Petrolia Fights Back

In 1901 a group of businessmen tried to buck that trend. They came together to form the Canadian Oil Refining Company in Petrolia,[161] which survived independently for six years before falling into bankruptcy. An American buyout bid kept it going until the Great Depression, when control of Canadian Oil returned to Canadian ownership.

The company was well-known across the country for its White Rose gasoline, En-ar-co motor oil, and Black Beauty axle grease. It remained in domestic hands until Royal Dutch Shell Group bought it in 1963, but the refinery had left Petrolia eleven years earlier, relocating in a larger facility just outside Sarnia, at the village of Corunna.

For the Canadian petroleum industry, Imperial's move to Sarnia was not a negative factor, merely a response to changing economic circumstances. As a whole, the industry would enjoy tremendous growth during the next century, with great oil finds from the Mackenzie Valley, to Alberta's Turner Valley, and east to the ocean floor off Newfoundland.

However, the transfer to Sarnia also represented the first of two significant blows to Petrolia's economy. The second would come little more than a decade later, when the Lambton wells would begin to dry up. And together, those two events would mark the commencement of the twilight years for this, the cradle of the modern oil industry. This business of oil was about to turn its back on its birthplace.

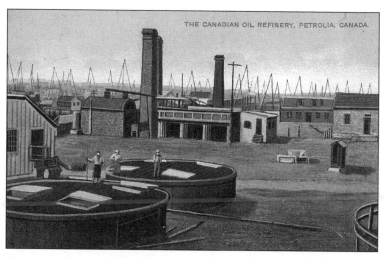

The Canadian Oil Refining Company was created in 1901, a last-gasp effort to maintain a refining presence in Petrolia. But the economic realities of the twentieth century eventually saw the Ontario centre of the petroleum and petrochemical industry moved to Sarnia on the St. Clair River.
Courtesy Lambton County Heritage Museum.

Part Four
To Distant Shores

"A cablegram was received by Mr. D.P. Sisk, on Thursday of last week from his son-in-law, Mr. Charles Wallen, who is in Grosny, Russia, that both he and his brother Ed and their families were safe. Considerable anxiety was felt for their safety by their relatives here, on account of the town having been besieged by a band of Tartars, on December 1, 1917, but who were driven off by the soldiers and inhabitants. As it was, several oil wells were set on fire and several people killed during the raid. The news that they were safe was not only received with thankfulness by their immediate relatives but also by all who knew them."
— *Advertiser-Topic*, Petrolia, 17 January 1918

Chapter Eight
The Travellers

A strange piece of news to be found in a small-town weekly newspaper. Strange, perhaps, for any small town but Petrolia, Ontario. There, hidden among the social notes about people donating to the Victory Bonds fund, people visiting friends and family, and announcements of church meetings, was a hint that this town, in the middle of Lambton County, Ontario, was different. With the growing demand for this black gold, men were searching for petroleum the world over.

But you had to know how to find it, where, and with what equipment. And you had to know what to do when the equipment failed or some previously unexperienced problem presented itself. It was a time when oil workers who had learned their trade well in the Lambton fields were in high demand.

The First Expedition to Java

It all began some time around Christmas 1873, when a group of Petrolians, preceded by an advance guard of the town band, paraded down main street to the railway station. The men of the hour were four in number: Malcolm "Mal" Scott, the oil engineer; Joshua Porter the driller; William Covert, the scaffold man; and a fourth who was probably a driller, Edward Cook.[162] They were headed to meet the Great Western train bound for Toronto. Before boarding they hugged friends, kissed their families, and then waved goodbye from the train's platform.

The train would whisk them away at the heady speed of forty kilometres an hour, through London and eastward to the province's capital, on the shores of Lake Ontario. As the iron beast lurched forward and began its trip, the band broke out into "Will Ye No Come Back

Again."[163] Packed away in the train was the drilling equipment they would take with them, the pole-tool outfit manufactured in Petrolia by George Sanson and Hector McKenzie's young oil supply company.

To Foreign Fields

While the band and ceremony indicated some comprehension of the historic nature of the event, those in attendance could not understand just how special this day really was. Families of the four men understood it would be two years before they would see their loved ones again. But they could not possibly know that these four Hard Oilers were opening up a bold new era in the story of Canadian petroleum, the era of the foreign driller. Over the next nearly seventy years, Lambton oil men would become known around the world as among the best available.

And over that time, the terms "foreign drillers" and "foreign fields" became closely linked in central Lambton to the Hard Oilers. "No one ever said they went 'overseas'," recalled longtime Petrolian Bertha Gleeson in 1998. "It was always the 'foreign drillers' and the 'foreign fields'."

Those first four Hard Oilers were headed for Java in what was then called the Dutch East Indies. They were the first of the Lambton men who would be instrumental in opening fields from Europe and Russia to Southeast Asia, from the Middle East to Latin America and the United States. Their drilling expertise would also be called upon to help find fresh water in Australia and India.

In the day of the steamship, it would take more than two months for the three to reach their destination. They had to cross the Atlantic, continue through the Mediterranean Sea and the Suez Canal (built 1859/1869), cross the Indian Ocean, and dock at Batavia (now Jakarta, Indonesia) on the island of Java. They landed on 5 March 1874, and in a letter written in May and published July 17 in the *Advertiser*, Josh Porter described the scene: "The East India islands present a beautiful appearance — being covered with rich vegetation, from the mountain top to the water edge."

It must have been an awesome experience for these young men who had previously made their living in the oil fields of Lambton County. It must have been equally illuminating for the friends and family back home, who kept abreast of the home-town boys' adventures through the pages of the *Advertiser* and the *Topic*, the two Petrolia newspapers where their letters were often published.

Over the following decades, the residents of Lambton County

became somewhat blasé, no doubt, about the comings and goings of the men who would be known as the "foreign drillers," so frequent were their treks overseas. On the steps of the post office, a child might sit down next to a grizzled oil worker and listen to stories of far-flung parts of the world, not thinking there was anything out of the ordinary about it. The Petrolia newspapers were filled with accounts of arrivals and departures, as if they were nothing different from the social notes about church teas. Headlines such as "Home from Trinidad," "Leave for Peru," "Died in South America," "Drillers in India," and "News from Borneo" became commonplace.

In Petrolia and Oil Springs, streetside conversation turned as frequently to the latest oil strike in Venezuela or the return of some family members from Sumatra, as it did to the price of pork. At the port of New York, the name "Petrolia" became better known than the metropolis of Toronto, as drillers made their way back and forth across the Atlantic.[164] Lambton's oil men could count themselves as among the best travelled, and the most worldly Canadians of their day. It was a way of life so taken for granted, says Dorothy Stevenson, the daughter of a foreign driller, no one ever thought of their town as "different."

Letter from Java

But while the tales of the foreign drillers eventually became routine, we can imagine the excitement with which those first reports were received. In his letter, Joshua Porter described the Javan city of Batavia, population 150,000: "The streets are wide and full of shade trees; hotels are numerous and grand buildings, always back from the streets and surrounded by gorgeous grounds, giving an appearance of rich private residences. The European stores are built in the same style, but the Chinese shops and native markets are a curiosity."

The journey of the four was not yet done. A twenty-four-hour trip by steamship took them to Cheribon, where they remained two days. Then it was onwards by carriage, "passing many plantations, sugar factories, large tracts of rice fields, and peanuts and sweet potatoes."

When they arrived at their destination, the town of Tjibodas, they were in the mountains of West Java, "a beautiful country and healthy climate, rather hot days and quite cool nights."

They lived in comfortable bamboo houses, built on stilts, in which they were waited on by servants who were paid ten cents a day. The food was good and plentiful, although exotic to these Canadians who had just tumbled out of the oil fields of Lambton County where meat and potatoes were the staple of normal meals. In total there were seven Caucasians in the party, including two engineers from the Dutch company that was commencing drilling operations there. They must have been a strange sight to the natives, just as the Southeast Asians were indeed a shock to the Westerners.

Work was delayed as the group awaited the arrival of machinery to begin drilling and refining petroleum. There were further delays as they awaited the company's boiler inspector. "Thus far," reported Porter, "we have had good times, not much work, good health, and our pay every month. After we get one well down here, part of us have to go to Jaerabaga, forty miles away. We expect plenty [of oil]."

Economic Depression

Canadians were selected for these early sojourns in search of crude oil because a London, England based company, chosen to search for workers, could not come up with the Americans for whom they were looking initially. (The connection between Dutch and English oil companies in southeast Asia is explained in a later chapter.) The oil business was booming in the United States during the 1870s, with crude being discovered just about everywhere in Pennsylvania a pick was planted in the dirt. The story was different in the oil fields of southwestern Ontario.

Business was flagging in Lambton: many of the earlier shallow wells were pumped out and new discoveries were few. The third Lambton oil boom was still some years away. However, mushrooming yields in the United States were taking markets away from the Canadian producers. In Sarnia the *Observer* reported on 28 November 1873: "Our Petrolia correspondent informs us that there is an almost complete prostration of business at that place; that labourers are leaving, and that the work of development is making slow progress. The oil refiners limit their operations strictly to the wants of the home market, which means that nearly all of them are shut down, and waiting for a favourable turn in prices."

That was the climate, then, when word came that petroleum exploration was heating up in Java. A general-store owner had begun the region's first oil exploration in 1871 at Tjibodas, at the foot of the volcano Tjarema, south of Cheribon in West Java.[165] Perhaps many people first heard of it from the weekly "Oil Report" that graced the pages of the *Advertiser*. As it turned out, Porter's hopeful prediction did not come true. The yield was poor, and the attempt was abandoned by about 1876.

It would take the coming of the new decade before renewed searches were begun in Sumatra and Java.

But the Canadians came home with glorious stories of their world travels. The pay was better than they could expect in the Lambton fields. And they were housed and transported between home and foreign fields, all at company expense.

A Great Adventure

Was it just the money that drove the foreign drillers? There must have been a certain glamour to the lure of exotic countries, even if it meant saying goodbye to their families for two or three years at a time. For the next six or seven decades, many men made a career of working in foreign fields, faithfully sending money home every month to their families. If there was little adventure left in the fields back home, at least these hardy Hard Oilers could still find it abroad.

Hard Oiler George Bryson penned a letter in 1926 from Singapore that speaks of the lure of the foreign fields. "They say they are glad to be going home. They wink, and tell you that surely they are coming back [to the foreign fields]. I do not know what it is that draws one to the far places of the earth, but there is some pull ... One rather hates to think of leaving."[166]

But certainly the money was good. In 1904 a labourer in Lambton's oil fields could expect about $1.50 a day, but Bill Gillespie signed a contract with M. Samuel & Company of London, England, for $5 (U.S.) a day to work in Borneo.[167] In addition, he received $25 a month for food, unfurnished lodging, including water and light, medical attention, and second-class return passage between Petrolia and Borneo. Gillespie had to furnish his own servant, and pay for his own laundry.

So the money piled up. In the early years, the drillers usually sent their savings back to families through Vaughn and Fairbank, operators of Petrolia's Little Red Bank."[168] Staff there became adept at handling the myriad foreign transactions. Other financial institutions began to move in later, with the Bank of Toronto arriving in 1887.

There is no precise, neat listing of where the foreign drillers went, or when. The picture must be pieced together from family records and memories, letters to the editor and newspaper articles, and from books about oil discoveries in foreign lands. Even the newspaper account of that first departure from Petrolia's train station, and the exact time they left, have been lost. We can only surmise they left around Christmas 1873 —

maybe just after celebrating that holiday with their families — based on the dates mentioned in Porter's letter to the *Advertiser* and the time it took to travel such distances.

After the first expedition to Java, the story of the foreign drillers took a short break, interrupted by a domestic development. In 1874, the Dominion government sent an expedition to western Canada,[169] headed by William Henry McGarvey, a respected Petrolia merchant and politician. They returned without much success.

First Expedition to Europe

Then, in 1879, the Hard Oilers entered the foreign fields in earnest. John Sinclair was hired by Count Carlo Ribighini to round up drillers for work in Ribighini's native Italy.[170] Sinclair later recalled he sent ten men, including his brothers, Neil and Duncan. Most of them returned home within three years but Neil Sinclair stayed to work there with William H. McGarvey and lived in Europe until about 1901.

In 1881, a British engineer from London, England, John Simeon Bergheim, visited Pennsylvania, looking for prospective wildcatters for a location he knew about at Oelheim, Germany, near Hanover.[171] Bergheim was unsuccessful in finding drillers in the United States who were not already engaged. But he was directed instead to southwestern Ontario, to the town of Petrolia. There he met William McGarvey, Hard Oiler, merchant, past mayor, and reeve of Petrolia and Lambton County warden. The two men struck up a friendship.[172]

They collected a handful of local workers and headed off for Germany. Their first attempt at finding oil there failed, but their partnership was cemented. In Germany they heard reports of oil seeps farther east, in Galicia, where attempts had been made to extract crude from the ground, so far with little success. Galicia is a historic region that has changed hands a number of times over the years. Today it is part of the Ukraine and Poland. In the 1880s, it was a province of the Austro-Hungarian Empire. Here, in eastern Europe, the two men tried their luck again, and before they were done, McGarvey and Bergheim would strike it rich — very rich indeed.

Under the direction of McGarvey and his brothers, James and Albert, Canadian Hard Oilers travelled to Galicia and Romania in the 1880s and '90s, and later into Russia. An 1898 record credits William McGarvey with heading a company of up to seven hundred workers; by 1912, two years before war would bring his empire crashing down, McGarvey had a work force of two thousand.[173] Most of the oil-field and refinery managers were Canadians, men known to McGarvey from his days in Petrolia and Oil Springs. (McGarvey's exploits are recounted more fully in the following chapter.)

The Canadian Allure

Canadian Hard Oilers lay pipe through the rain forests of the island of Sumatra to ship the crude to ports. This photo was probably taken in the late 1890s.
Courtesy Oil Museum of Canada.

Canadian Hard Oilers began to develop a reputation as first-rate drillers largely thanks to the exploits of William McGarvey's crews in Europe. Through the 1880s and '90s, Canadians were hired to go to India and Burma, Java, Sumatra and Borneo in search of oil. They looked in Ohio, Tennessee, Texas and California. They travelled to New Zealand and Australia, to Russia, Italy and Spain. In the early years of the twentieth century, they helped to bring in the first wells in Persia and Mesopotamia, now Iran and Iraq.

While the money was good, the work was often dangerous, and

several Hard Oilers perished in those foreign lands. The workers fought yellow fever and malaria in the tropics' intense heat, and laboured under scorching sun among the shifting sands of the Middle East. Huge pieces of equipment sometimes fell on them, and medical help was not always close at hand. Wild beasts roamed around the oil work, and reptiles abounded.

These world travellers returned to tell tales of the accidents and deaths that occurred in sometimes primitive working conditions. The foreign drillers told about how they dodged German submarines in the First World War, and about how they hid from hostile Arabs in the mountains of Persia.

They brought home souvenirs of their travels, which to this day often remain proud family heirlooms in homes all over Lambton County and beyond. Besides the usual bric-a-brac like brass ash trays and desk ornaments, there were Persian rugs, intricate pottery and artwork, furniture, coins and stamps, pieces of clothing, elephants' feet, and leopard skins. And there were photographs of the foreign drillers in distant lands, being drawn in coolies' carts, hunting wild animals, standing next to the Sphinx, riding camels, erecting drilling rigs.

The Canadians were selected for these jobs because they knew their trade. Those first drillers to Java, Italy, and Austria quickly demonstrated what they had learned in the fields of Lambton. In an era before geology was accepted as a valid science, the Lambton men who could drill straight down to the oil pool were highly valued. Their drilling equipment was the typical Canadian system of the time: the drill bit was attached to a series of poles — of hardwood and, later, iron.

Not only could they drill for oil, they were jacks of all trades: pipe fitters, blacksmiths, carpenters, steam engineers and geologists.[174] They fixed broken rods, welded, and did whatever else needed to be done, with little help. One of the first foreign drillers, William Covert, wrote in a letter home from Java in 1874 that he was working four hundred miles from the nearest repair shop.[175] It's not like home where you can send to the shop for a part, Covert wrote. In Java, you simply learned to fix things yourself.

The first Canadians also proved to be very successful at living among people of cultures that were totally foreign to them. As a result, they were usually effective at supervising labourers chosen from the local populations. Perhaps having to shuffle out a living between the cultures of two giants, America and Britain, stood the Canadians in good stead. Certainly Canadians are still known for their skills in the art of political compromise. And perhaps that too has helped to make Canadians such successful peace keepers in various United Nations expeditions. For whatever reason, the foreign drillers seemed to take easily to the societies with which they came into contact. They did not proselytize for democracy as the more boastful Americans might have. They did not threaten and they did not upset the local bureaucracies.

Despite the hardships, it's not difficult to imagine the lure that the life of a foreign driller held for a young man more used to existing on the wages of a field hand or farming his land back home. It was a fast-paced life, full of travel, adventure, partying, and working in exotic places. In their off-hours, the men wore crisp, white-muslin suits, and when they came home on furlough, they were often treated as guests. They were men like Sarnia's Duncan McIntyre, who was born into a home so poor the children had to be split up. His granddaughter, Millicent Woods, recalled in 1998 that McIntyre found the life of a foreign driller "very exciting. He thought he was a very important man."[176] On the back of one photograph of McIntyre in the Far East is written, "General McIntyre."

The "General" even purchased a book on oil exploration published in 1912, probably because it featured a photo of himself and another Canadian driller. Next to the photo taken at Munbu, Upper Burma, of a Canadian steel derrick, McIntyre wrote in pencil: "Joe McGill of Petrolia to right; D. McIntyre at end of boiler; and an American sitting down." The Asian workers were not identified.

Those Left Behind

It was hard on the families who were often left at home in Lambton. When Bill Cole returned from foreign fields, "He would always say to my mother, 'I will not go back again'," recalled his daughter, Dorothy Stevenson.[177] "And Mother would go back to the house and unpack the furniture and settle in. Dad would get a job, and he'd be there a little while. Then he'd come home one day and say, 'I've signed a new contract'. The things would go into storage again, and Mother would move back with her parents, and Dad would be gone again."

It has been said that Petrolia and Oil Springs were Canada's original single-parent communities. So many children grew up hardly ever seeing their fathers; sometimes they forgot who they were. Dorothy Stevenson recalled she was seven and had been suffering from an ear infection when her father came home from an overseas job one time. "He arrived with a little bag, and I ran and hid from him. My mother said, 'Dorothy, you're hiding from your father'. I thought he was a doctor coming about my ear. I didn't know him."

Until the First World War, it was rare for wives and children to accompany the workers on their foreign assignments. Lambton normally remained the home base, with the workers signing on for about three-year stints, returning home for a few months, and then taking on another foreign assignment. The McGarvey expedition to Europe seems the exception to that rule; about 1882 McGarvey brought his wife and three children to Europe, where they took up permanent residences in Vienna and Port Gorlice, Galicia. Several of McGarvey's senior Canadian managers did the same. But for the most part, the drillers continued to look upon their foreign assignments as just that, and quite separate from "home" back in Canada.

With Family in Tow

Later that began to change, and in South America and Southeast Asia, wives and children more frequently joined the men. Margaret Smith recalled how, in 1919, the young man she was seeing at the time, Ray Gregory, came to her with a proposition. "He had a job offer [to drill for oil] in Trinidad. He said he wouldn't go unless I got married and went with him. So I did. Everything was done in a week, the passports, ship tickets. I was only eighteen. I really didn't know what it was all about. I'd worked in Detroit [as a stenographer for an insurance company] but that's as far away from home as I'd ever been."[178]

In the early 1900s, Canadian oil men helped to open up oil fields like this in Trinidad.
Courtesy Lambton County Heritage Museum.

A fifteen-day trip by ship from New York left young Margaret seasick and "wishing I was home. There were men playing cards and gambling on the ship, and I wasn't used to that sort of thing. I thought this ship will sink for sure."

Many others took their families with them, or else married while overseas. James and Arthur Brown were two of five Petrolia brothers who became foreign drillers.[179] James and his wife, Ada, had two sons while living in Sumatra and two more after they were transferred to Sarawak, Borneo, in the 1920s. Arthur married his second wife in Burma, had a family, and never returned to Canada. He died and is buried there.

In 1917 Victor Ross, author of *Petroleum in Canada*, wrote: "No other centre on the American continent has contributed so many expert drillers and oil operators to foreign countries for the production and development of the industry as Petrolia ... [They] have been foremost in locating oil territory, in mechanical inventions, in their methods of production and in the marketing of the product."[180]

The halcyon days of Lambton's foreign drillers were from 1873 until the 1920. There was still sufficient need for workers in the home fields that young men were being drawn into the business until the early 1900s. But as the tap began to be shut off on the crude supplies back home, fewer young men entered the business, and their numbers inevitably dwindled.

Last of the Foreign Drillers

The man known today as the Last of the Foreign Drillers was still living in a seniors' residence in Petrolia in 1998. He spoke shyly and reluctantly about how, at an age when most men were retired, he answered the call to go to the tropical heat of central India in search of water for a parched countryside.

Laurence Oliver was nicknamed "Noisy" in an ironic twist on his unassuming demeanor and his refusal to brag about his worldly experiences. Born in 1901, Oliver has lived his life as a humble, quiet man. When he was thrust into the limelight in the 1960s, you could tell that Noisy wished that all the attention would just go away.

Oliver's early experiences as a driller were typical of many others. In 1922 he began drilling in California for St. Helen's Petroleum Company.[181] In 1932 he joined Shell Oil in Trinidad, and in 1946 began working for the International Water Supply Company, drilling in places like Israel and Guyana for fresh water. The switch from oil to water

Laurence Oliver, last of the foreign drillers, at his home in Petrolia, Ontario, in 1998.
Courtesy Gary May.

shoved Noisy into a spotlight he would just as soon have avoided.

In 1966, after he supposedly retired, Noisy was approached by Dave Matheson, who then was manager of Petrolia's Oil Well Supply Company. In 1998 that company was still producing drilling bits and equipment — one hundred and thirty years after its predecessor was founded. Along with Matheson came a minister for an organization called Action for Food Production (AFPRO), a mission that represented the principal Christian churches in India. The organization's members were looking for someone who could help them find water in drought-stricken Punjab, and they had been directed to Petrolia, home of the foreign drillers.

"The rivers were drying up and were all contaminated and that's where people were getting their water for drinking, and they were all getting sick," Oliver said.

Could Noisy come and help them find fresh water, they wondered. You bet. Noisy just couldn't turn them down.

"The day I got there, I hadn't slept overnight. We got in at four o'clock in the morning. They took me to this confounded meeting. I left, I couldn't even pay attention to what was going on. I went out the next morning to do my job."

In temperatures of 115°F (46°C), Noisy discovered that the drilling equipment was ill-suited to the conditions. Nevertheless, he began what would be a six-month stint that resulted in numerous water wells being brought into production.

Noisy remembered one in particular. "There was a nun who was a nurse at a dispensary right next to a church. Sister Kate," he said, "was from Switzerland. They wanted water right next to her living quarters and this dispensary. I was sort of leery about them drilling that well but that's where they wanted it, up on a hill. I didn't think there was much chance of getting [any water.] We went down deeper there, two hundred and eighty-some-odd feet when we hit it. I was tickled to death."

Noisy recounted how hundreds of spectators used to flock around where he would search for water. "We had to have a rope around the place or they'd be right on top of the [drilling] rig, pretty near."

Of his long career in drilling for oil and water all over the world, Noisy smiles shyly now and recalls simply of his experience in India: "I felt a little satisfied doing something like that."

"But don't make me sound too important," he warned a writer in 1998. "I was just a little guy."

One footnote to the story: while hesitant to speak about it, Noisy often didn't turn in all his expenses for the trip. "I didn't think I was worthy of my keep," he said with a grin. "I was too lazy to turn anything in, I guess."

The "American Gentlemen"

Laurence "Noisy" Oliver was the last of a long and proud line of Lambton foreign drillers who set off in search of adventure. But nothing in later years could compete with the heart-pounding excitement experienced by the earliest foreign drillers. What a thrill that first party under Mal Scott must have experienced as they lived and worked in Java back in 1874. In late September of that year, one of the members of that party, William Covert, wrote to a friend back in Petrolia. The letter, from Tybodas, was published on December 11 in the *Advertiser*.

As they traversed the mountain trails, word spread of their presence. The natives waved and smiled and hailed them as "the American gentlemen." Once they were invited to a party at one of the local chiefs' homes. "I am happy to say nothing stronger than tea [was served]," Covert reported.

> The native band played a number of operas, which appeared to be enjoyed as music, but the sound was all the same to me; my having once belonged to the Petrolia band did not serve me much of late, for I cannot tell any difference between the tunes of the Java band. They presented the chief of the district of Madja with a scarf as a token of respect. Large arm chairs are brought forward to the front for the use of the Europeans, so that they can see the whole of the performance. Then the native ladies go around to the invited guests and present them with the scarf as was presented to the head chief.

133

They came to me with it, asking the honour of my
company in the next dance, and of course it is hard to
refuse any young lady. About three o'clock in the
morning we prepared to leave ...

Like most of the perhaps one thousand Lambton men who became
foreign drillers, Covert was a labourer. Bill Gillespie became a
superintendent. While they both fared well compared to what they would
have earned in Lambton, Covert and Gillespie were working men and
they would never grow rich.

Such was not the case with the Hard Oiler who came to be known as
the petroleum king of Austria, who, within a few years of Covert's work
in Java, began to amass an immense oil empire.

Chapter Nine
The Petroleum King of Austria

Our society worships success and celebrity. William Henry McGarvey was, by anyone's account, both successful and a celebrity. A man of humble storekeeper's-son beginnings, he became, in both politics and business, a leading citizen of Lambton County's oil lands.

But McGarvey outgrew those beginnings. Through a combination of hard work, intelligence, high principles, and good fortune, he built an enormous empire and became known as the petroleum king of Austria.[182] He threw one of the most lavish weddings during Vienna's golden age, was decorated by the Austrian emperor, and was called upon to advise the British Admiralty.

But, at the end of his life, McGarvey had become a tragic figure, watching helplessly as his great company neared the brink of ruin, crushed between two warring armies. He had been turned into a notorious figure by the political whims of Europe's superpowers, cast in the light of suspicion, and watched over by distrusting Austrian authorities. This man, who rose to the heights of European society, then died heartbroken, a suspect in a senseless war.

Arrival in Lambton

The first son of Edward McGarvey was born in Huntingdon, Quebec, in 1843.[183] When William was twelve, Edward took the family to Wyoming, which was about to become a stop on the new Great Western Railway line between London and Sarnia. Soon, James Miller Williams and Charles Tripp would dig their first producing oil well a few kilometres south, and the village of Wyoming would become a central terminus for the new industry. Straining oxen would haul

William Henry McGarvey's quest for oil took him far beyond Lambton County to the Austrian province of Galicia. There, he struck it rich, opening up Austria's petroleum industry, and was decorated by that country's emperor, Franz Joseph, for his work. McGarvey was dubbed the Petroleum King of Austria. **Courtesy Oil Museum of Canada.**

crude oil up the "canal," and supplies and equipment would be loaded for the trip back to the fields.

As a young man, William Henry McGarvey was shrewd and ambitious. He soon ascertained that opportunity beckoned him to the nearby oil lands. In the early 1860s, he left his father and set up his own business, The Mammoth Store, in Petrolia. When Petrolia was incorporated as a village in 1867, McGarvey was selected the first reeve but resigned soon thereafter, apparently too preoccupied with his mercantile and petroleum interests.

On July 10 of that year, he married Helena Jane Weslowski of Mount Clemens, Michigan.[184] It was to be a fortuitous marriage, one that cemented for the ambitious young McGarveys a partnership that took both of them to the peak of social and financial achievement in Europe.

Helena, two years her husband's junior, was a striking woman, tall, auburn hair, hazel eyes. Her father had been born in Poland but was expelled by the Russians for anti-government activities. After the wedding in Michigan, the McGarveys returned to Petrolia where, within a year, they had eighteen producing wells besides the store to operate. Most famous of the wells in which McGarvey held an interest was the Deluge.

When oil was struck at the Deluge, it was said to have spewed skyward and unchecked for several hours. The pump jumped and jerked uselessly under the pressure of the gushing crude, and it took a man named John Scott to tame it.[185] Scott braved the torrent of oil to drag a log, which he used as a lever, over to the jolting pump. He then chained the pump down and finally got the flow under control. An American came along afterwards with some hired help, equipped with long-handled ladles to scoop the oil into barrels.

Three children were born to the McGarveys between 1869 and 1876 — Nellie, also known as Kate, born 1869; Fred, born 1873; and Mamie Helena, also called May, later known as Memmy to her German and Austrian friends, born 1876.

William McGarvey was known around Petrolia as something of a dandy. He enjoyed wearing tailored suits and fine boots, and inspecting his oil wells from the comfortable leather seat of an expensive carriage.

Once, when he arrived at a site in that fashion, some of his workers decided to have a little fun. Decked out in a brand new suit and white vest, and showing off his recently purchased carriage, McGarvey was beckoned by the men to come closer to an oil tank.[186] When he did, one of the workers opened a spigot, showering the immaculately attired businessman. While William's reaction was something short of jumping for joy, the men kept their jobs. One man later said that it appeared his boss was more concerned about the leather cushions in his new buggy than he was the suit.

Looking Farther Afield

In 1874, McGarvey led a group of Petrolians who were commissioned by the Geological Survey to explore the Swan River Valley near Fort Pelly in what is now eastern Saskatchewan.[187] The next year, when Petrolia became a town, McGarvey was asked to take on the mayor's job, and he served as either mayor or reeve from then until the end of 1879. In his last year in office he was chosen county warden.[188] Clearly he was well regarded on his home turf.

As was noted earlier, in April 1879 Count Carlo Ribighini left Lambton and returned to his native Italy to see about searching for oil there. In May, Ribighini sent word back to John Sinclair in Petrolia that he now had the need of a handful of Hard Oilers, and Sinclair hired ten drillers to send over for the tests. They were never very successful.

Neither was McGarvey's first foray into foreign fields, but the partnership he was about to embark upon proved to be the most important of his long business career. Two years after Sinclair left with his crew for Italy, the British engineer, John Simeon Bergheim, arrived in town, having been told in Pennsylvania that Petrolia was where he would have the most luck finding men willing to drill in Europe.[189] McGarvey had recently tried his hand at provincial politics but was rebuffed. Now free of any political attachments, he was able to pursue his beloved oil interests unencumbered. The two men quickly struck up a friendship as well as a partnership, and they embarked for Europe, specifically to Oelheim, Germany, near Hanover.

After about a year, during which the German tests proved disappointing, McGarvey and Bergheim decided to follow stories of oil that lay farther east in what was then the Austro-Hungarian Monarchy.[190] This was the name given the former Hapsburg empire when it was reorganized in 1867. The name stuck until its breakup at the end of the First World War. Besides Austria and Hungary, the empire consisted of several other kingdoms and provinces, of which Galicia was one.

Galicia, north and east of the Carpathian Mountains, extended approximately from the cities of Krakow (now in Poland) in the west, to Ternopol (now in Ukraine) in the east. Its population, about seven million, was a mixture of Poles, Ruthenians, Germans, and Austrians. A monarch, called emperor in Austria and king in Hungary, ruled the empire. In 1881 the monarch was Franz Joseph.

In Galicia, seeps of petroleum had been exploited before, for local and primarily medicinal uses. But early wildcatting efforts had proved discouraging. McGarvey and his engineer friend believed the trouble lay not in the potential of the oil lands, but in the drilling methods. So they brought in some Petrolians who were expert in the pole-tool drilling method, including "Admiral" Nelson Keith and J.P. Connolly.[191] McGarvey relied on Lambton Hard Oilers: William McCutcheon brought in the first big well near Krakow, and Charles Nicholas constructed and operated the first Bergheim & McGarvey refinery at Maryinpol near Gorlice, Galicia.[192]

The McGarvey Reach

Soon, many other Petrolians came to join McGarvey. His brothers, Albert and James, later opened fields south and east of Galicia, in Romania and the Caucasus area, in what was then part of the Czar's Russian empire. Alvin Townsend came, then stayed as a manager for many years. Neil Sinclair, after leaving Ribighini's employ in Italy, went to work for the McGarveys. Several members of the Perkins and MacIntosh families also joined McGarvey. Cyrus and Jacob Perkins each managed Galician fields, and Carl MacIntosh supervised several McGarvey operations.[193]

About 1882, apparently convinced his future lay in Austria, William McGarvey sent for his wife and children. In the coming years, the McGarveys owned a residence in Vienna as well as a castle near Gorlice, Galicia. The latter was close to many of the oil fields and the huge refinery built to handle the crude being pumped out of the ground there. The children all attended the finest schools in Austria and Germany.

With the upheavals, wars, and changes in jurisdictions and place names that have occurred in the region since the 1880s, it is difficult to pinpoint every location where wells and refineries were established. But Mal Scott, one of the crew who first went to Java some eleven years earlier, wrote home from the town of Ustrzyki, Galicia, in 1884.[194] Scott recounted how he had shared quarters with 250 head of Texas steers during his Atlantic crossing earlier that year, and how, after a trip through Netherlands and Germany, he had finally reached the Bergheim and McGarvey company oil lands.

"You breathe the pure mountain air which is most invigorating," he wrote from his location north of the Carpathians. Scott received a personal tour of the oil district from William McGarvey, who then showed the newcomer a flowing well he'd struck a few weeks before. "Mac is in excellent spirits and on a fair road to making a fortune," Scott wrote.[195]

A group of Canadian Hard Oilers poses for a photo, about 1885, at Ropienka, in the Austrian province of Galicia. Seated at the centre is Elgin F. Scott.
Courtesy Oil Museum of Canada.

A few weeks later Scott reported on other area wells, one of which had been put down in the winter of 1882/83 and may have been the original McGarvey strike that led to the creation of Bergheim & McGarvey in 1883. It would be producing more oil, he said, if a decent pump were available. Meanwhile farther east, probably around Borislav, larger strikes were coming in regularly.

"We are all in the best of health and fat as pigs," Scott wrote to a friend.

The business expanded rapidly. On 13 November 1885, the firm of Bergheim & McGarvey advertised in Petrolia for more drillers and rig builders, and sent Albert McGarvey back to recruit. The following year, one of the McGarvey brothers, probably Albert, headed for Romania, the *Advertiser* reported, taking several drillers with them. "They are getting a regular army of Canadian drillers in that country,"[196] the newspaper said.

The Canadians lived well in Galicia, often marrying local women and frequently adopting local customs. Some became multilingual, picking up the German spoken by the Austrians who controlled government, the military and much of the commerce, and a few words of the Polish and Ruthinian spoken by local workers.[197]

A trip home to Canada was not an easy process and those who took it often stayed for long periods. Typical of the better off among them were Albert McGarvey's wife, who, in 1890, returned to Petrolia for a visit and planned to stay a year before going back to Austria.[198]

Often the Canadians lived in fine Galician homes. Managers and superintendents all played tennis, and nearly every field manager had a tennis court. They attended frequent fancy balls, where music was provided by Austrian military bands. At each of these affairs, the band played a march before the first of the waltzes commenced.[199]

Many weddings occurred among the Canadian contingent. The wife of one Canadian driller described what she called a typical Galician celebration: three wagons led the procession to the church. The first carried the musicians, two or three violins, a base, and a gypsy drum. The bride and attendants came in the second wagon, the groom in the third. Parents and guests greeted them at the church door with the singing of a wedding song.

After the ceremony, the bride and groom left in the first wagon and were greeted at the bride's home by her parents. A feast ensued, washed down with beer, wine, and gin. Dancing continued until about midnight, when the bride went to the middle of the room where the other women removed her myrtle wreath and undid her braids, signifying her transition from childhood to womanhood. The bride and groom departed, but the party continued until all the food and drink were gone, a process that could take several days.

A Royal Wedding

Such a wedding was a simple country affair. A much grander celebration was planned for the marriage of William McGarvey's youngest child, Mamie. The McGarveys were enormously wealthy, and only the best would suffice.

In 1895 Mamie married the German count, Ebert Friedrich Alexander Joseph Edward Graf von Zeppelin.[200] Zeppelin was the nephew of Ferdinand Graf von Zeppelin, who a few years later would invent the airship that would rain down terror from the skies over London, England during the First World War. The young Zeppelin was a second lieutenant in the Uhlanen Regiment of German lancers, a rising officer in the German army, and firmly ensconced in Europe's nobility.

It was a time in Europe when titles married money. Few were more titled than Count Ebert von Zeppelin, and few still more monied than Miss Mamie McGarvey. Certainly the two could have met at any number of affairs where the European aristocracy rubbed shoulders with untitled but wealthy families. And once having decided upon marriage, there was no more fitting locale for the grand ceremony than Vienna.

The 1880s and 1890s were a golden age for the Austrian capital. Nearly forty years earlier, Emperor Franz Joseph decided to raze the old wall that had delineated the inner city and replace it with the Ringstrasse (Ring Street.) The boulevard was elaborately landscaped and lined with an eclectic mix of architectural styles. Vienna was the testing grounds for the vast architectural projects of Gottfried Semper, greatest of the Renaissance-revival architects in the Austro-German tradition. His stunning collection of buildings on the Ringstrasse included museums and the Burgtheatre, believed by many to be his finest achievement.

The social schedule for the wealthy and titled was a harried one. McGarvey's wife, Helena, adored the constant carnival atmosphere of the capital.[201] She regaled in the evening musical entertainments, the monthly parties, the elegance of silk and diamonds that was everywhere. While she enjoyed her regular sojourns to the tranquility of her Galician palace on the river, she cherished Vienna.

When it was announced in late 1895 that a daughter of Petrolia would marry into royalty, the Canadian town went mad. Photos of the count and countess adorned the front page of the *Advertiser* on 19 December 1895, along with one of the proud father, William H. McGarvey. The newspaper's headlines screamed:

A COUNTESS!

One of Canada's Fairest Daughters
to Grace the Austrian Court.

Count Von Zeppelin, an Officer of the Emperor's
Guard, woos and wins the Daughter of
William H. MacGarvey.[202]

BRILLIANT EVENT CONSUMMATED IN THE PRESENCE
OF A ROYAL ASSEMBLY.

The newspaper contracted a special "society columnist" to report on the stunning event. The night before the wedding, the bride's parents threw a reception at the Grand Hotel in Vienna, a supper in the dining room that was called one of the finest halls in Europe, followed by dancing to the music of the world-famous Dreschner orchestra.

The next morning, 12 November 1895, a breakfast was held at the Grand Hotel, and at noon, guests assembled at the German Protestant Church. Outside, a cloudless sky somehow befitted the event. Guests had come from as far away as America and included a captain in Russia's Imperial Guard, members of the Austrian and Galician parliaments, members of several of Europe's royal families — and a good representation from the Petrolia drilling crews.

After the ceremony, guests attended another reception and seventy-two telegrams were received from friends from all over the world. "Money was lavishly expended by a generous hand," wrote the *Advertiser's* correspondent. At five in the evening, the count and new countess departed for a honeymoon in Budapest, after which they returned to Vienna to be entertained by a long list of ambassadors and emissaries.

Mamie's family gave the young couple a silver table service, Persian rug, carriages, and horses. The Zeppelins offered a silver tea-and-dessert service and a diamond bracelet. Other gifts included paintings of Carpathian scenes, numerous silver objects, and a fan of white ostrich feathers. The event was described as perhaps the finest of the city's many elaborate wedding ceremonies.

McGarvey also later presented his daughter and the count with a seven-hundred-acre estate and castle, valued at some $70,000, an enormous sum of money for the time, and the equivalent of well over $1 million today.

An interesting footnote: the Zeppelins divorced in 1906.[203] They had no children, and Mamie, known as "Memmy" to her Austrian and German friends, died in Graz, Austria, in 1962.

Nellie married an Austrian judge in Galicia. Like her sister's estranged husband, the count, Nellie's spouse fought the army of the McGarveys' homeland during the First World War. Fred McGarvey finished his studies in Germany in 1896 and went on a scientific expedition with some of his professors to Egypt. He returned to take up work with his father, and in 1901 married John Bergheim's niece, Margaret, in London, England.

Corporate Expansion

The year 1895 had been a busy one for William McGarvey. Besides his youngest daughter's wedding, he and Bergheim reorganized their expanding company under the name of the Galizische Karpathen-Petroleum Aktien Gessellschaft.[204] Bergheim, the engineer, remained in the field, while McGarvey became manager and chairman of the board, spending much of his time in Vienna. But while he may have no longer been directing operations at the wellhead, McGarvey maintained a tight rein on the business to the end.

The company bought land and drilled wells with what came to be known as the Galician drilling rig, built refineries, and bought up smaller firms. One refinery was located near the McGarvey home at Gorlice, at a town then known as Maryinpol. Another refinery, known in its day as the largest in Europe outside of Russia, was constructed in the 1890s on the Adriatic Sea, at the Italian port of Trieste. This led to vast export sales of refined oil products. The company operated a large machine shop, which supplied not just its own needs but those of other companies as well. The drilling division maintained subsidiaries in other countries, including Mexico, Cuba, and Nigeria.[205] McGarvey and Bergheim had become important international players.

McGarvey came to be known as one of the world's greatest petroleum technologists, his name mentioned in the same breath as that of Britain's Sir Boverton Redwood.[206] At the height of McGarvey's influence, Austrian Emperor Franz Joseph held a special ceremony at the Vienna Imperial Palace to honour him for introducing the

This advertisement for William McGarvey's Galician-Carpathian Petroleum Company Limited, formerly Bergheim & McGarvey, appeared in a German-language periodical, Petroleum, in 1910. The advertisement indicates the Galician towns where the firm operates and says it uses the so-called Canadian drilling method or pole-tool drilling. It also refers to a patent held by McGarvey (spelled MacGarvey) on some petroleum equipment.
Courtesy Technisches Museum fuer Industrie und Gewerbe, Vienna, Austria.

Canadian drilling system to Galicia, opening up the Austrian oil fields, and making the country a net exporter of oil and its by-products.[207] Previously, the country had been dependent on imports from Russia and America.

McGarvey was an inventor and an innovator. Advertisements for the company indicate that he held several patents on equipment related to his drilling activities.[208] He was known widely for his scrupulous business principles. "He is a brilliant example of integrity, honour and perseverance," the publication, *Canadian Men and Women of the Time*, quoted a friend as saying in 1898.

There is considerable evidence that he was highly regarded by the people who worked for him, too. In 1892, for William and Helena's twenty-fifth wedding anniversary, a large contingent of friends, associates and employees threw an elaborate surprise party at the McGarveys' Gorlice estate. On the morning of the affair, the couple was awakened at their riverside castle to the strains of music outside.[209] Peering out their bedroom window to see what was happening, the couple was greeted by the sight of a full military band of forty-five players winding its way through the park that surrounded their elegant residence. Behind the band trailed more than sixty Canadian guests, many dressed in the uniforms of the baseball clubs they had formed.

Jacob Perkins, a long-time employee, offered words of congratulations and then invited the couple to join them at a nearby park where even more well-wishers had gathered — the families of the Canadian workers. Two tents had been erected, decked out with flowers and flags, including "the old flag [the Union Jack], the sight of which always gladdens the hearts of Canadians," one observer proclaimed.

A baseball game was followed by dinner for the 150 guests. McGarvey, himself, offered a toast to Canada, and driller George MacIntosh toasted the queen. When Jake Perkins spoke in tribute to William McGarvey, he commented on the oil man's kindness and concern for the welfare of employees, as well as his success in developing the Galician oil fields.

The McGarveys were presented with an album of fourteen paintings of scenes from the region produced by the Krakauer School of Art and signed by the guests.

McGarvey spoke movingly of the large part the employees played in the company's success and said he was pleased that after so many years together he had been able to retain their good will and friendship. Then everyone repaired to the McGarvey estate for music and conversation. Later that evening, another band appeared, to entertain a throng of 150 non-Canadian workers employed at the refineries and wells. A foreman offered his congratulations, McGarvey replied graciously, and a fireworks display was set off in a nearby field.

Undeniably, McGarvey was smooth, politically astute, and quick to grasp new opportunities. When the long arm of John D. Rockefeller threatened to stretch across the Atlantic to embrace McGarvey's company and others, William led the way in establishing cooperatives and cartels with other producers to keep Standard Oil at bay.[210]

But there was a price to pay for fame and fortune. Back in Canada McGarvey's father, Edward, noted with a touch of sadness in a letter to a niece and nephew, in 1897, how his children had spread themselves around the world. "As a family we are pretty well scattered. The most important and serious consideration is how and where shall we meet in the great eternity to spend a never-ending eternity in happiness or more,"[211] he wrote.

Reversal of Fortune

At about the time Edward wrote that letter, Helena McGarvey was visited at her Gorlice castle by daughters, Mamie and Nellie. While they were there, in December 1897, Helena died.[212] There were suggestions that as McGarvey became increasingly successful, he was also increasingly driven by ambition and the need to accumulate even more wealth. Perhaps the periods away from Helena had become longer. At the time of his wife's death, William was in Vienna. There was one report that after Helena died, William remarried, to an English woman he met in Vienna.[213] If this is true, it's uncertain what became of her.

Meanwhile technology was sweeping quickly ahead, and McGarvey's business would prove to be a significant factor. At the turn of the century, the gasoline-fed internal combustion engine was starting to drive the horse from the road, and oil was beginning to power the great machines of war.

In the first decade of the new century, Britain, Germany and the United States all were experimenting with how they could use oil to power their warships. Oil, they knew, would be more efficient than coal, lighter to carry, and it offered the advantage of allowing ships to be refueled at sea, far from ports that might be blockaded during times of hostilities.

Canadian newspapers reported that in the years preceding the First World War, William H. McGarvey, oil technician, was called upon by the British Admiralty to consult on the conversion and installation of oil burners in British ships.[214]

(Bergheim, too, had dealings with the British government. The "petroleum-industrialist" — as German publications called him — had been appointed an advisor to the British Admiralty and was asked to search for oil on British soil. Many decades before the discovery of the North Sea reserves, Bergheim came up dry. He did, however, procure a contract to provide the Royal Navy with fuel oil.)[215]

The quarter-century from 1890 until the war witnessed rapid developments in the technology of large vessels' engines. At the beginning of that period, the reciprocating steam engine, powered by coal, dominated Britain's fleet.[216] A decade later, the steam turbine had taken over in warships and was slowly being utilized in merchant ships. The steam turbine became more economical when oil replaced coal. And in 1908, the diesel engine, which used heavy oil as a fuel, began to be installed in submarines and then in small surface craft.

But problems with diesel power remained to be worked out — for ships requiring a large output of power, such as destroyers, cruisers, battleships and aircraft carriers, steam turbines could not yet be bested.[217] Meanwhile, while they wrestled with that problem, the Admiralty feared Germany was leading the way in the development of the diesel as a main propulsion source for their major fighting ships. Britain was falling behind in the development of oil fuel.

Clouds of War

In the latter part of the nineteenth century, McGarvey would have little reason for concern about relations between his adopted country and the Britain he loved and respected. Both were suspicious of Russia's expansion plans, and between 1887 and 1897, a British, Italian, and Austrian entente countered Russia and France. For a time in the early 1890s, Germany, too, had leant its support to this entente.[218]

The royal families of Europe were closely connected. Queen Victoria's eldest child, Vicky, was married to Prince Friedrich of Prussia, and their eldest child, Friedrich Wilhelm Viktor Albert, in 1888, became Kaiser Wilhelm II ("Kaiser Bill"), Emperor of Germany and King of Prussia.

Nevertheless, by the end of the '90s, three distinct political blocs had formed: the British Empire, the Franco-Russian alliance, and the Triple Alliance of Germany, Austria-Hungary, and Italy. Growing problems at home and in the Balkans forced Austria to turn to Russia for support, a flimsy alliance that began to break down about 1906. By the next year, Britain had made up with France and Russia, and joined in a Triple Entente to encircle Germany.

Between 1911 and the war, the Triple Alliance of Germany, Austria-Hungary, and Italy was countered by the Triple Entente. Feelings were hardening, and Germany and Austria were greatly concerned by Britain's policy of encirclement.

McGarvey would certainly have known of the German book, *Germany and the Next War*, published in 1912. The author, General Friedrich von Bernhardi[219], seemed to be predicting war between Britain and Germany. It was a troubling time for the McGarveys, who had significant interests in Austria, the Balkans, and Russia. Besides William's own company in Galicia, Albert had helped to develop the Romanian industry, and had then moved to Russia, where James was already established in the oil business.

The quickly changing political scene threatened to make any technology gap between Britain and Germany more than just a question of British pride. While McGarvey was certainly glad to help his old friends, the British, in expanding the use of oil to power their warships, in the years leading up to 1914, he must have been confused and increasingly alarmed by the alliances that were evolving across the European continent.

There was trouble on the home front for the McGarveys, too. William's younger brother, James, who managed oil properties at Grosny, Russia, had fallen victim to the kind of violence that was becoming common in that part of the world. In early 1911, word came to William that James had been murdered while at home enjoying a quiet dinner with his wife and a colleague.[220] Armed robbers broke in and intercepted a servant who was running to alert a guard. The servant, a guard, James McGarvey, and his colleague, Talbot Barnard, were all killed with kendzials, short Cossack swords.

Barnard was stabbed trying to carry Mrs. McGarvey to safety. After the raid, she was taken to hospital in nearby Vladikavka and survived, to be taken later to Britain by her daughter. The intruders stabbed the cook and left with about one hundred pounds in cash. Two of the intruders were arrested. A third shot himself. Others escaped.

Violence in the Caucasus was on the increase. Russia was in upheaval, and foreigners were certainly not immune. In the oil fields, unpopular managers were often attacked and killed.[221]

Then, in 1912, McGarvey's business associate and long-time friend, John Bergheim, was killed in a taxi accident in London, England.[222]

At the end of July 1914, war broke out between Austria-Hungary and the Triple Entente. The Russians seized Galicia but later, with German allies at her side, Austria-Hungary began to push them back. The Galician oil fields and refineries stood in the way and became pawns in the battle for supremacy. Over the coming months, the retreating Russians set fire to the wells and blew up the refineries.

For the first time in his life, McGarvey found himself helpless to control his own business prospects. After more than thirty years of success, the tide had turned. He remained a loyal and proud British subject, and friends said later he was heartbroken to find himself living in a nation allied with the country now at war with Britain. An article in *Maclean's* magazine a few years later indicated that McGarvey spent his last days "under surveillance in a magnificent home in Vienna."[223] In November, on his seventy-first birthday, William McGarvey, who so recently had been vigorous and healthy, suffered a stroke and died. An obituary in the *London Free Press* asserted: "He was thoroughly British and worry is supposed to have hastened his end."[224]

If McGarvey was suspect and under surveillance by authorities in

Austria, it may have been as much due to his recent assistance to the British Admiralty as to his nationality. Ironically, it appears he was also somewhat scorned by the press in his native Canada. Despite his huge accomplishments and tremendous wealth, Toronto's *Evening Telegram* devoted just a single paragraph to his death, while in London, three paragraphs appeared in the *Free Press*. It seemed that in the heat of war with Kaiser Bill, McGarvey would gain no further tribute.

Chapter Ten
Escape from Destruction

The First World War made the work of Canada's Hard Oilers crucial. The machines of war demanded huge quantities of petroleum. The oil fields and refineries took on added strategic importance, becoming significant targets for generals seeking to cripple their enemies.

Caught in the middle were the Hard Oilers and their families, thrown into the thick of fighting they did not understand. Their tales of survival and escape add a thrilling yet heartbreaking chapter to the story of those who undertook the quest for oil. Two tales, stories of heroism and determination of two families, illustrate the tenacious and uncompromising actions of these people in their resolution to survive.

At the time war broke out near the end of July 1914, Carlton MacIntosh of Petrolia, Ontario, had been married to Frieda Erika von Espenhan for nine years. The couple had two children, Ralph, age seven, and Molly, age five. Carl had been born in 1879, and at the age of eight had moved to the McGarvey oil fields in Galicia with his parents and grandparents. There he would meet Frieda, six years his junior, the daughter of a successful mining engineer.

By mid-1914 Charles Edward Wallen, of Oil Springs, Ontario, had been field manager of the North Caucasian Oil Company at Grosny, Russia, under general manager Albert McGarvey, for three years. There he had gone with his wife, Florence, and daughter, Elaine. And there was born a son, Charles Jr. Early fighting escaped the region altogether, and even in 1915 it was limited to south and west of the oil lands at Grosny and Baku. That would change with the onslaught of the Russian Revolution in 1917.

Hard Oiler!

Frieda and Carl MacIntosh[225]

As a child, Frieda Erika von Espenhan quickly became acquainted with the Canadian families who had come with McGarvey and company to Galicia to develop the petroleum resources. She was born in Borislav, site of a big refinery, and lived her early years in a series of small villages and towns in the area where oil was the chief source of wealth. A German-speaking Lutheran family in the middle of a predominantly Catholic, Polish, and Ruthinian-speaking province of Austria-Hungary, the aristocratic von Espenhans sent their children away to be educated in good Protestant German schools.

In Galicia, Frieda attended parties with Canadian children and quickly learned their English language. She eagerly swapped little-girl secrets with her young Canadian friends and later danced waltzes with young Canadian men. On Sunday afternoons, families would gather in the park for band concerts. They would frequent theatres and suppers and go for long walks in the beautiful countryside of the Carpathian foothills.

All the oil fields were operated by Canadians, Frieda recalled, and "nearly all these Canadians came from Petrolia." Of the Canadians, she said: "They were a lively bunch and some very funny characters."

One of the liveliest and most clown-like of the Canadian oil men was young Carl MacIntosh, who quickly attracted young Frieda's eye. Recounting how he came to call on her once, she wrote: "One day Carl came in to see us on horseback. The door was open from the dining room into the garden. Carl, always fooling, drove the horse right into the door, so that the horse put his foot right on the step. We all yelled and were frightened that he would come in."

The young Frieda Erika von Espenhan, shown here about 1900, came to know many Canadian children of the foreign drillers in her native Galicia. Frieda married one of the young drillers, Carl MacIntosh of Petrolia, in 1905. That event set Frieda and her family off on an adventure that culminated in their escape from the ravages of war.
Courtesy Lorna Mays, Mississauga, Ontario.

This, the von Espenhans' Polish maid took as a good omen. The young girl would marry the strange, high-spirited Canadian who came into the house on horseback, the maid told Frieda's mother. And in 1905, after having his first proposal turned down, Carl was happy to report to his family and friends that he and Frieda would marry.

Carl's family had a long history in oil, starting in the Lambton fields. His father, George, had taken the family to Austria in 1887, accompanied by George's father and mother, John and Mary MacIntosh. There, the family teamed up with their Lambton cousins to form the Perkins, MacIntosh and Perkins Petroleum Tool and Boring Company Limited. The company, they claimed, was the largest maker in Europe of high-grade drilling outfits. About 1900, Cyrus Perkins opened a branch office in St. Albans, England.

Five years after the company was formed, in 1892, George was the Canadian driller who offered the toast to the queen at the McGarveys' twenty-fifth wedding anniversary. In 1902 Carl spent time drilling for oil in Java.

The first children born to Carl and Frieda, twins, died of dysentery when they were still infants. But by 1909 the couple had two more healthy children, Molly and Ralph. Five years later, when war broke out,

Ralph and Molly, shown here about 1911 in Borislav, Galicia, were the children of Frieda and Carl MacIntosh. Three years later, their idyllic existence in the beautiful foothills of the Carpathian Mountains was destroyed with the coming of the First World War, and for the next nearly four years the family fled from the destructive forces that crushed the Canadian-run oil fields of Galicia and Russia.
Courtesy Lorna Mays, Mississauga, Ontario.

Carl and Frieda were living in the village of Kraznica, near Borislav, at the foot of the Carpathian Mountains.

Frieda's brother was called up by the Austrian army, in anticipation of the fighting with Russia. One day Carl decided to take his brother-in-law some clothing at his barracks. It was a trip Carl didn't give a second thought to making. The politics of war still were foreign to him. Yet, with the coming of war, this Canadian and British subject would now be considered an enemy of his wife's Austria. Amazingly, Carl was never questioned, perhaps because he spoke German fluently. But when he returned home, his Canadian colleagues warned he had been lucky; the days of such freedom of movement for them in that country were gone.

In the shadow of war, the mood in the countryside was changing. A simple stroll became a frightening experience for Frieda, but an adventure for Ralph and Molly. As they walked, they encountered Austrian soldiers heading for the train, a terrible precursor to the troubles ahead. In the coming weeks, terrifying rumours began to circulate, rumours of robberies and the killing of civilians. Since they lived on the main road that crossed the district, Carl and Frieda decided they would be better off in a more out-of-the-way location. They headed for the mountains to get out of the growing war activity.

"To see the running people on their way to Hungary was a terrible sight," Frieda said of the scenes they encountered on their way. "Women, children, cows, dogs, cats, chickens, bedding and other things they could take on a wagon from their homes. One cannot forget the frightened faces."

But their decision to move to the mountains proved to be a bad choice. They left with two trunks of belongings, including some silver and ornaments, planning to come back for the rest later. Part of a group of more than twenty Canadian and British people engaged in the oil business, they soon learned that while civilians could be properly protected in the cities, in the mountains they were at the mercy of nasty characters, and cut off from their usual sources of food.

Young Ralph later recalled: "I can remember our whole family, my Grannie [von Espenhan] holding my hand, going into the forest during the night and staying there until morning. My father [Carl] buried his guns in the forest because if found, he could have got into trouble. Pa never got his guns back."

Once during their three months in the mountains, Carl decided to sneak home to pick up more items. It had not yet sunk in that his citizenship placed him in danger, but a friend warned him just in time. On another occasion, being warned that raiders were coming in search of "the rich oil men," they buried their most precious belongings and retreated deeper into the woods.

The Russians soon overran the Galician oil territory. Thinking now that their British citizenship might be a passport to safety, with Russian occupation, the little group returned to their homes. But it was a sad scene that greeted them. Austrian and Russian soldiers had looted Carl and Frieda's home: pictures were slashed, furniture and china broken, belongings stolen. The couple departed with friends, heading for Borislav, forever vigilant for roving bands of thieves.

The MacIntoshes spent Christmas 1914, with friends, in the town of Borislav, which offered them a tiny respite from the insanity swirling around them. Carl kept his family and friends laughing, their thoughts diverted temporarily from the severity of their situation, blanking out visions of what tomorrow might bring. On Christmas night, Carl and Frieda ventured outside, where the sound of distant cannon brought them back to reality. It had been nice to forget it all for one evening.

After Christmas, Carl obtained a job with a local refinery, where he stayed for four months. There were parties and other fun during those months, a lull before the next storm. Their city had miraculously been left largely untouched.

Some of the foreign contingent began to grow impatient, however, and left to make their way back to Britain, where the men could join the army. Frieda and Carl hoped that perhaps they might stay in Borislav, where Carl could work at the refinery under the Russian occupation. But it was not to be. The Austrians and Germans began to push the Russians back, and soon trains were jammed with the Czar's soldiers fleeing eastward. Carl and Frieda decided they had better join the retreat, fearful of what would happen when the Austrians returned.

As the cannon-fire drew nearer, they packed their things. Carl grabbed the oil company's receipts, planning to return them when he could contact officials in Britain. On the spring morning they left in 1915, they heard the pops and explosions of the oil wells being set afire by the retreating Russians. The air was hot and thick with soot and ash. The sun was nearly invisible through the swirling black smoke, "just a round red ball," recalled little Ralph. The acrid stench of burning oil was nauseating.

They passed through charred villages and towns and watched the Russian soldiers, some holding onto windows and doors of the fleeing trains, some hanging onto the roofs of the railway cars. When the couple arrived in Lemberg (now L'vov), they headed to Frieda's older half-brother's home for shelter. The relatives couldn't even recognize them for the layers of soot that caked their skin.

Carl's parents, George and Margaret MacIntosh, were also living in Lemberg, in a small apartment. It was decided that Carl and Frieda would go to Kiev, far behind the lines of war and, hopefully, out of the fighting.

It was a heart-wrenching departure, saying farewell to their respective parents. Frieda couldn't take her mother who, as an Austrian citizen, would not be welcome in Russia. And George and Margaret MacIntosh decided to stay behind to watch over the affairs of the drilling-tool company. Ralph later recalled of his grandfather, George: "Grandpa Mac stayed in Lemberg and was interned, confined to his own home for the duration of the war."

Waiting for the train, Frieda noted that it was the first time they had been so close to the wounded soldiers who were being examined right there where they were packed onto the railway platform, torn and bleeding. Frieda remarked later how brave the soldiers were, no one crying out in pain as bandages were ripped off and wounds probed.

At Kiev, Frieda was asked by Russian officials whether she was Polish. She said yes, daring not to acknowledge her Austrian heritage. She must have begun to feel like a person without a country, with a husband, who, as a British subject, must avoid the Austrians, and she, his wife, forced to hide her parentage from the Russians. They waited seven months in Kiev, moving from house to house, growing progressively poorer.

Finally it was decided they would go to the Caucasus, where the oil industry was still intact and going strong. Carl found work in Grosny as a manager for Albert McGarvey, William's brother, who was general manager for the North Caucasian Oil Company. That fall, in 1915, some English-speaking families planned to leave the Caucasus for Britain. Some, fearing the prospects of making it through the battle lines, journeyed east through Russia and Japan. Others, including Carl's cousin, George Perkins, and his wife, Annie, travelled via Vladikavkiz, west of Grosny.

Although it was not safe to venture out at night, Frieda felt safer in Grosny, and there was plenty of food for the moment. However, nearly everyone came down with Licheratka, a sort of malaria, and some of them became very ill. The MacIntoshes nearly lost another child, Molly, to dysentery, but after six weeks she finally recovered.

There were terrible dust storms in the Caucasus. Ralph remembered that when the winds whipped the summer dust around, "our parents would cover our heads and tell us to lie on the floor so we could breathe."

Added Frieda: "They came so fast you hardly had time to close the windows and shutters. The sand came in every crack of the house and the house was full of it when the storm blew over … on the road you had to turn the horses away from the wind and lay yourself down on the ground or in the wagon and cover yourself up as much as possible." When it rained, the dust turned to a terrible sticky substance that could suck the boots off their feet.

Tensions were rising in the countryside around Grosny. People still spoke of the murder there of James McGarvey in 1911, and there were frequent raids and robberies. Trips to the market were taken in a buggy, with company — never on foot, and never alone. "One always went to bed with a sort of fear, what will happen during the night," Frieda recalled.

Yet the countryside could also be beautiful. The oil fields and the homes sat on a hill that offered a marvelous view of Kazvek Mountain. Wildflowers grew everywhere.

Carl seemed popular with the workers and 1916 passed without any serious threats to the MacIntoshes' safety. Other managers were less lucky. The workmen had been known to grab an unpopular official and stuff him in a large well-casing or pipe, then toss the casing into a slime hole. The man of course could not escape from the casing, and suffocated.

But Carl had gained the workmen's high regard, soon after arriving, when he sent some wagons on a ninety-minute trek to a river to bring back fresh water. He had been struck, during his first days there, by the large number of coffins that were needed at the oil field, and discovered a huge death toll among the children. No wonder: the local water supply came from the refinery boilers, or rainwater on those rare occasions it rained. A clean water supply improved the health of the local families, and that raised Carl high in their esteem.

The huge Russian fields required several managers to handle the workers. Serving under general manager Albert McGarvey was field manager Charles Wallen of Oil Springs. Wallen and MacIntosh never got along, and just before the Russian revolution, Wallen dismissed MacIntosh over a disagreement, although Carl soon obtained another job nearby.

In early 1917, the Revolution broke out. Military discipline quickly broke down and Russians turned their attention from the Germans and Austrians to fighting one another. The workers took control of work sites, and conditions soon became chaotic. Organization disintegrated, and people began to rob and set fire to shops, offices, and mines. Workers threw out the managers, although Carl, in a supervisory position at his new field, was able to keep his job until the field was finally abandoned in the chaos of the fighting.

The MacIntoshes moved again, this time to a nearby village field where Carl got a job with an English firm, Spies and Company. Fighting between factions was constant. Homes were robbed and people kidnapped for ransom. "Every night we heard the guns, and we used to go into the childrens' room and put them under a window sill in a corner and cover them with pillows and mattresses," said Frieda. "I sat with them, and Carl locked the door and stood with a carving knife and axe and waited until they would come. Then it would mean either their lives or ours. We had no guns or revolvers."

Finally the young couple decided the only move that made sense was a move to Britain. Together with a British family, they prepared to relocate one more time. It would be an adventure that would dwarf all their previous experiences. There were rumors that the Bolsheviks were heading south to do battle with the Caucasus natives, the Chechens and Cossacks. The MacIntoshes slept with knives and axes at their sides as attacks continued, and people were regularly killed in the night. Food became scarce and expensive.

When they left the village for Grosny, it was on a dilapidated wagon powered by two aging horses. Important documents and jewels were sewn into the hems of the women's dresses. Passing two riders on the road, the prospective thieves must have looked at the bedraggled little band and determined them too poor to bother with — dusty, few apparent belongings, and two horses not worth the effort.

Arriving in Grosny, Frieda was at first elated. "What a happy woman I was that night. I wonder if anyone knows how it feels to put one's children to sleep safely, without listening to hear if someone is coming to rob us, and to the shooting. We slept so soundly, we did not hear the shooting that was going on in the town until the next morning." They were going to send for the rest of their belongings, but the field manager called the next day to tell them everything had been stolen.

Frieda and Carl lived in a cramped Grosny office with their British friends for a month. They sold a few things to help finance the coming leg of their escape. With shootings and robberies commonplace, they and their fellow tenants decided that each of the men would take turns acting as night watchman.

Finally, in early 1918, the day of their departure arrived. "We left on the last train to [make it to] its destination," said Frieda. "The next train never arrived. That journey was the worst I ever experienced."

They waited sixteen hours in a crowded railway station for the train. When it finally came, the family became separated in the crush of anxious passengers. Carl had to shove their luggage through a train window and jump onto it as it steamed away. Frieda was terrified he might not make it, and she wondered how she would ever find him again if they became separated. For the next twenty-four hours they travelled on a train so packed that passengers stood in the aisles and sat on baggage. A stop for a change of trains took another fifteen hours at a station crammed with Russian soldiers. Food remained scarce. As they waited, one train that passed by was riddled with bullets.

At Moscow, they got another train to St. Petersburg, by now renamed Petrograd, where they obtained a hotel, and for the first time since leaving Grosny, the MacIntosh family was able to stretch out on a bed. In the week it had taken the family to travel from Grosny to Petrograd, "we never could lie down and slept only in short intervals," said Frieda.

For ten terrifying days, they waited for their passports to be processed. The city was in "a terrible disorder." They couldn't go outside, since anyone could be arrested at any time, for any reason. They hid their valuables in the hotel mattress. Ralph recounted how his catching of the chicken pox may have saved his father from internment: "One night the hotel was searched by the Bolsheviks, looking for spies. They may have thought Pa was one. They came to our rooms, saw a fur coat and hat hanging on the coat rack and wanted to know where the man was." The hotel porter directed them to the next room where, in fact, Carl was concealed. At the last minute, "the porter once again spoke up, saying, 'don't go in there, there's a sick child with chicken pox.' So they left, to the relief of everyone."

Near the end of January, the final leg of their trip finally commenced. Frieda covered her son's pox marks with powder, or they might never have been allowed through Finish customs. They made their way through Scandinavia to the coast of Norway and boarded a camouflaged cattle boat. "The boat lay-to all day and travelled by night via the Shetland Islands," said Ralph, "because of the threat of German submarines."

Once in Scotland, they continued to Cyrus Perkins's home in St. Albans near London. There was a small community of Lambton people there: Petrolian William McKenzie had set up his own oil-well supply company earlier. In wartime, though, the plants were producing cannon barrels. There the MacIntoshes stayed until after the war.

After the war, in 1919, Carl returned to Stryj, near Borislav, where he joined his cousin, George Perkins, back at the drilling-tool works. By now, however, Stryj was no longer part of Austria, but rather Poland. Under Polish law, in order to regain control of the company, the Canadians were required to take on a local partner, and so the Perkins MacIntosh and Zdanowicz Company Limited was formed, with Carl as director.

GALICIAN BORING TOOL WORKS
PERKINS MAC INTOSH & ZDANOWICZ CO. LTD.
STRYJ — POLAND.

C. M. MAC INTOSH
Director.

A business card from the Perkins MacIntosh & Zdanowicz Company Limited drilling firm, re-formed in 1919 after the war. At that time, Polish law required the Canadians to take on a local partner.
Courtesy Lorna Mays, Mississauga, Ontario.

The next year, drawn back to Galicia, Frieda took Molly and joined Carl in Stryj. Ralph remained another year in England to complete his schooling before following.

But it was never the same. The MacIntoshes had lost all their money and property during the war. In 1926, no longer happy or feeling welcome in Frieda's Galician homeland, the family packed up and moved for good to Oliver, British Columbia.

Florence and Charles Wallen[226]

To the Canadian and British families living in the Grosny area oil fields, the Russian Revolution was known euphemistically as "the Smash." When the Smash broke out in 1917, Russian workers took control of most of the sites, throwing managers out or forcing them to remain as puppets of the employees. In the North Caucasian Oil Company field, managed by Charles Wallen, management stayed, working at the beck and call of their antagonists. Wallen's wages were cut to one hundred rubles a week — the same level paid the office boy — and his authority was stripped away.

To a family used to the trappings that came with managing a big Russian oil field, it was a severe blow. They had lived in a luxurious home outside Grosny, where they had been waited on by a small army of servants. The household consisted of an English nurse, an Irish governess for young Elaine and Charles Jr., Cossack guards, a valet, a coachman, a cook, a house boy — and two dogs. In the days before the Smash, the

The North Caucasian Oil Company oil field near Grosny, Russia, managed by Charles Wallen of Oil Springs. Wallen probably took the photograph about 1915, less than three years before he and his family were forced by the Russian Revolution to flee. **Courtesy Mary Wallen, Grand Bend, Ontario.**

Wallens had entertained lavishly and lived like royalty. Dinner parties consisted of caviar, pheasant, wild boar, champagne, and vodka.

Circumstances degenerated further. Later that year, the Chechens gained the upper hand over the region's Bolsheviks. The robbing, kidnapping, murder, and terror increased in ferocity. The family of Charles Wallen, like the MacIntoshes, armed themselves and prepared to fight for their lives and their few remaining possessions. It was a hellish chaos.

The home of Florence and Charles Wallen, standing, right, at Grosny, Russia, about 1917. Standing at the left are Charles's brother, Edwin, and his Russian-born wife, Olga. Seated are Elaine and Charles Jr. **Courtesy Mary Wallen, Grand Bend, Ontario.**

Charles Jr. recalled in later years that when he was two years old, in 1917, his father learned of a plot to kidnap him for ransom. A Chechen had overheard the plot among some workers and had tipped off the senior Wallen. The Chechen, whom the young boy knew as Makmet, had always been friendly to the family, and for the boy's first birthday had given him an ornate kendzial (sword.)

"My father trusted Makmet with my safekeeping, and he took me into his village in the hills for a period of three weeks until the threat of kidnapping had blown over," said Charles.

Soon after the Revolution broke out, roving bands of drunken insurgents ransacked the Wallen home and slashed the furnishings in search of hidden money. Having been tipped off to the danger, Wallen had buried the cash in the garden in glass jars and had tacked bills to the tops of drawers around the house.

On 1 December 1917, the Chechens attacked Wallen's Grosny field. Charles and Florence Wallen could take no more. With the help of some bribe money, and with the oil wells burning about them — a giant wall of black smoke fueled by fourteen thousand barrels of oil per day — they turned their backs on Grosny in early January. Charles Wallen's brother, Edwin, stayed behind to watch over what remained of the oil field, with his Russian-born wife, Olga, and their children.

On the day of their departure, Wallen went into a nearby village in search of supplies for the long journey. Young Charles was almost three years old; his sister Elaine nearly nine years older. While the elder Wallen was gone, the fighting grew more intense as the Bolsheviks attacked Grosny, which was held by Cossacks loyal to the Czar. The sounds of gunfire inched closer. Charles Jr. recalled:

> Our house was being shelled, and Mother, Elaine and I were huddled under the dining room table for protection. The shelling became increasingly heavy and finally mother grabbed Elaine and I and we took off to try and find my father. Running, falling down, getting up and running again, we finally came to a bridge that led out of town. The bridge was under heavy cross-fire from machine guns and Mom threw Elaine and I into a ditch and covered us with her body. A Bolshevik soldier who spoke English rushed over and said, 'for God's sake, madam, follow me,' and took us across the bridge. On the other side of the bridge, we spotted my father and thus started our journey out of Russia.

Like the other Canadians who lived in the region, the Wallens had lost virtually all their belongings to looters, who were often revolutionary soldiers. Most of their money had been deposited in Russian banks and then stolen. But with the money Charles had buried for safekeeping, they had salvaged sufficient funds to help them escape. A paper trail of bribe money paved their way out of the town. But with the intense fighting, friendly Cossacks sent them back, and the Wallens had to keep a low profile near Grosny until April.

Again, although fearful of being detected, the Wallens decided to make a run for it. This time there would be no turning back. With the countryside in ruins, Charles and Florence Wallen led their children into a terrifying unknown, made only somewhat less so by the knowledge that to stay would mean imprisonment or death.

Frieda and Carl MacIntosh had decided three months earlier to move northwest by train, but the Wallens headed northeast, with the help of some hired Cossack guards. Hiding by day and travelling by night, they rode by wagon, walked, and finally sailed along the shore of the Caspian Sea.

"One of my recollections," said Charles Jr., "is of Fanief, a red-headed Cossack, who used to take me in the saddle, cover me with his goat-skin cape, and jog along with me in the saddle."

Fanief had been a guard at the Czar's Imperial Palace, where the Princess Tatiana — who along with the rest of the royal family, would soon be murdered by the revolutionaries — had given each guard a bolt of cloth for a new uniform. Fanief had sufficient cloth left over to have a small uniform made for his son, but now he gave it to young Charles. (The uniform is now on display at the Oil Museum of Canada in Oil Springs, Ont.)

Charles Wallen Jr., in the uniform he wore during his family's escape from Russia in 1918. The material for the uniform was given by Russian Princess Tatiana to a soldier in the Czar's Palace Guard, who later befriended the young Charles during the family's escape.
Courtesy of Mary Wallen, Grand Bend, Ontario.

The senior Charles Wallen led his family to the Volga River, where he obtained passage north. Amid the beginning of spring breakup, they encountered fighting at Kujbysev and Kazan on the Volga. At the first town, their vessel was fired upon and damaged. But slowly they made their way to Vologda, where they met several refugees from the Baku oil fields and the welcome sight of British authorities who were helping foreign nationals escape. Petrograd was the closest port, but British authorities warned it would be impossible to travel there. So the Wallens headed north by rail, a trip that took seven days and brought them to the edge of the Barents Sea.

They had packed themselves into a boxcar along with dozens of other refugees. The only sanitary facility was a hole in the floor of the boxcar, a tin soda-biscuit box placed over it with a hole cut in its bottom. A blanket strung around the contraption was the only privacy.

During the ordeal, young Charles remembered how his father placed his fur coat over him each night. The boy would reach into the pocket and find a single sugar cube his father had secreted there. The discovery would bring a smile to the little boy's face. That simple pleasure, for father and son, helped them through those terrible weeks.

Food was scant during the rail trip, and along the way the only nourishment they could buy was black sunflower bread. A sticky gob when fresh, the dreaded bread dried to rock-hard consistency. Florence Wallen later recounted an incident at Kola, near the end of their trip: a bakery stocked white bread, and the family, sick of the sunflower variety, tried to buy it. The baker, a Bolshevik, refused to sell. To the Bolsheviks, the foreigners were the oppressing Bourgeoisie, not to be shown any consideration.

From the seacoast, the Wallens and their fellow refugees boarded a British troop ship. But danger was not over. The sea around the Orkney Islands was teaming with German subs, and only the fugitives' determined escort kept the enemy at bay. Elaine had developed pneumonia during the ordeal. The sole treatment available was to sleep out of doors where the damp sea air eased her laboured breathing.

In July 1918, six months after fleeing their home, their clothing reduced to rags, their stomachs empty, the Wallens reached the safety of the Scottish coast. They made their way south to London, England, where Charles sought recompense for his losses from the North Caucasian Oil Company, but to no avail. The rest of their own money, which had been deposited in Russian banks, was never recovered.

The Wallens stayed in Britain until after the November armistice and then returned to Oil Springs, arriving Christmas Eve, to live for a while with Florence's parents. Charles Wallen briefly returned to Grosny to check the oil fields, but they were now devastated. He also found Olga, the Russian wife of his brother, Edwin, and was able to help three of her daughters escape. Edwin, by now sympathetic to the Bolsheviks, stayed behind, but later he and Olga went to Britain, where he was living in 1921. Charles would never forgive his brother for siding with his oppressors.

Perhaps the ordeal caused Charles Wallen's premature death. In 1921, in just his forty-seventh year, Wallen died of pneumonia. He had spent half of his life in foreign fields, in Germany, Russia, Barbados, Africa, Mexico, California, and Java.

Hard Oilers in Romania

The oil fields and refineries the Canadians built were tribute to their knowledge and craftsmanship. It would be nearly unthinkable that they would have to destroy what so much skill and effort had created. But if the alternative was to see your work fall into enemy hands, the decision was clear. It was that decision that faced the Hard Oilers in Romania.

One of the most successful Canadian foreign drillers in that country was Charles Drader, says writer Victor Lauriston, who wrote more than seventy years ago that Drader "made a fortune"[227] there. The major refining centre was Ploiesti, north of Bucharest. From there, a network of pipelines linked refineries with the various sources of crude. In 1914 the Romanian government began to lay a trunk line from Ploiesti, across country, to the Black Sea port of Constanta.

Oil has a long history in Romania, but for many years it had been scooped out of seeps and shallow pits in the same primitive fashion utilized all over the world. Then came the Canadian Hard Oilers. In 1886 the *Advertiser* reported that "Mr. McGarvey" (likely William's brother, Albert) was leaving for the Romanian fields, taking several other Petrolians with him.[228] It referred to the "regular army" of Canadians beginning to build up in that country.

Romania did not declare war on Germany and Austria until after the middle of 1916. What followed then was a series of disastrous defeats for the Romanians, with Bucharest being occupied. By the end of the year, most of what was left of the army was driven north into Russia.[229]

With the certainty that the oil fields would soon fall into German hands, the Canadians who had spent thirty or more years building up the oil industry in Romania were now faced with the prospects of having to destroy their work. What was equally certain was that nothing could fall into enemy hands.

Drilling rigs were demolished. Into the wells, they poured concrete and drove in huge beams of steel. The refineries were dynamited or pulled down. The pipelines crushed, pulled apart, blown up.[230]

When the inevitable occupation came, the Germans were at least forced to rebuild, before gaining access to the valuable oil supplies they needed so desperately. And the Canadians who had demolished the industry had made good their escape.

Some Stayed Behind

Not all Canadians left Europe when war broke out. Especially in Austria, many had sunk their roots deeply and found it hard to turn their backs on their life's work, their friends, and their new country.

Among those who stayed were several members of the Perkins family of Lambton. Jacob, who had given the good-natured speech at the twenty-fifth wedding anniversary of Helena and William H. McGarvey, on that brilliant, warm day in July 1892, was one. His brother, Cyrus, was another. Both had managed oil fields in Galicia, and both chose to stay. Both died in the 1920s, their widows and children surviving in Austria and Poland. Records show that, by then, members of the Perkins family lived in places like Vienna, Austria, and in Krosno and Rymanow, Poland.[231]

Those who stayed during the war years often faced hostility from the people with whom they had worked for so long. Many found themselves under suspicion. Some were interned.[232]

Chapter Eleven
The Persian Solution

Canadian Hard Oilers' sweat and toil helped to unlock the great desert secret, the world's largest supply of petroleum, which lay under the sands of the Middle East. Even as resources at home were dwindling, a Lambton driller sank the first Persian well. He and his colleagues helped to ensure that the British navy would ultimately float to victory in the First World War, on what was referred to as a sea of oil.

The Politics of Oil

In the years leading up to the First World War, the world had become increasingly addicted to petroleum. When James Miller Williams was mining Lambton's crude, its primary uses were for lubricating and illuminating oil, liniments and medication. The internal combustion engine then opened up whole new possibilities, with the proliferation of gasoline-guzzling automobiles and the asphalting of new roads they demanded. As well, oil was being used to fuel steamships.

Total world production of crude oil amounted to just one million barrels in 1860 (0.16 million tons), nearly all of it from Lambton and Pennsylvania.[233] In 1880 production had risen to twenty-five million barrels (four million tons). By 1900 it was up to 125 million barrels (twenty million tons), and by 1915 production had reached 368 million barrels (fifty-nine million tons).

By this time, Canada was not a major producer of petroleum. Yet the work of Canadians in the foreign fields remained significant. While Lambton's fields had dominated world production for a brief moment in the 1860s, world demand far outstripped the ability of the tiny Ontario oil patch. And the large Western reserves had not yet been tapped.

167

In the latter days of the nineteenth century, the United States had risen to top spot, with huge new discoveries that stretched across the continent, from Pennsylvania to California. In 1880 Pennsylvania alone produced most of the world's oil. By 1900 Russia produced more than half the world supply but in the next few years huge new discoveries were made in Texas and California, and America regained the lead.[234]

By 1909 American oil accounted for five-eighths of all production, Russia one-quarter. The other eighth came mainly from the Dutch East Indies, Austria (Galicia), Romania, India (Burma), and Japan. Canada hardly measured a flicker on the scale.

As the sun set on Queen Victoria's long reign, in 1900, petroleum was beginning to gain a far greater significance than ever before. And the distribution of that petroleum around the world was a growing political matter.

America, the rising economic and military power, was rich in it. Russia, too, had petroleum to spare. But the other world powers — Britain, France, Germany, Italy, and Japan — were far less comfortable in terms of supply. Certainly there had been attempts to find oil in all five of those countries — often by Canadians — but with little success. There was a growing desperation among those nations as they came to recognize that the era of coal was coming to an end, and the era of petroleum was commencing. No longer could the finding and refining of oil be looked upon as a quaint pastime, to be left to rough-and-tumble wildcatters, Hard Oilers, and roughnecks.

Oil-finding was about to become a sophisticated and highly specialized enterprise. Lambton's drillers and businessmen could certainly not have fathomed what a significant role they would play in the geopolitics of oil.

Private enterprise was beginning to recognize the new realities, too. By 1902 British investors turned to Lambton oil men in search of the resources that could help propel the British economy into the petroleum age. John Henry Fairbank's biographer, Edward Phelps, cites a letter sent to Fairbank by fellow Hard Oiler John D. Noble, who was seeking support for a venture. Apparently Fairbank rejected it, preferring instead, concluded Phelps, to remain small and close to his Lambton roots. Noble's company, Canadian Oil Fields, went bankrupt some years later,[235] as the Lambton resources dwindled.

With supply prospects far from rosy in Canada, Britain began to look farther afield. Burma, then a part of Britain's Indian colony, was thought to be fertile ground, but it was far away and a source that could be easily cut off in time of war. So Britain began to look to the Middle East. Oil seeps and natural gas had been known in the region for centuries. As early as 1872, the Persian government in Tehran had been involved in exploration for oil and other minerals.[236] In 1900 money was obtained to explore in the countries called Mesopotamia and Persia, now Iraq and Iran.

The First Persian Well

The man regarded as the father of Middle East oil was a retired British millionaire, William Knox D'Arcy. But the man who drilled the first well there was a Canadian, Duncan McNaughton.

D'Arcy gained his wealth in the Australian mining business. When he was asked by the British to lead the hunt for oil in the Middle East, D'Arcy selected George B. Reynolds, a veteran of the Sumatran petroleum industry, who once had been employed in the Indian public works department, to head up exploration. In 1902 drilling began at Chiah Surkh, just inside what is now Iraq, near the Iran border. At the same time, survey work also began for a pipeline route south to the Persian Gulf.

That pioneer drilling crew consisted of two Canadian Hard Oilers, Duncan McNaughton and John C. Buchanan, as well as some Polish workers, an American engineer, an Indian doctor, and a labour force of locals.

Lambton Hard Oiler Tom Knapp oversees the unloading of a boiler in Persia during construction of oil fields and refineries about 1910.
Courtesy Oil Museum of Canada.

McNaughton, a Petrolia man, became the first superintendent of the Anglo-Persian Oil Company's Persian drilling staff. Regardless of which of two locations and dates is selected for the "first" Persian oil, McNaughton was there.

McNaughton was working with George Reynolds at Chia Surkh in 1904, when a small and, as it turned out, limited supply was struck. Later, McNaughton helped Reynolds to open up Mamatain and Masjid-i-Sulaiman, in May 1908, the true beginning of the Middle East industry. The working conditions in Persia were horrendous. The sun seared the bleak landscape nearly every day of the year. When shade could be found, the temperature was often 46°C (115°F). Grasshopper swarms clogged the river, and the water stank with their decomposing bodies. The simple act of walking through the camp generated constant squashing and cracking sounds from the booted feet coming into contact with the mass of dead insects that littered the ground. Their bodies were constantly skimmed from the water tanks.

Smallpox was reported at the town where the camp's water and food supply originated. Firewood for the boiler was constantly stolen by the locals. The boiler itself became corroded by the sulphurous water. Letters from home were delayed when the letter carrier and his camel died en route. Finally, a sledgehammer was dropped into a well, gumming up the works.

Not surprisingly, in such unpleasant circumstances, labour problems were frequent. The Poles downed tools so often, the engineer finally sent them packing. The local labourers were balky, until McNaughton and Buchanan took them in hand.

"Our two Canadian drillers are handling them with tact and discretion and have at once been recognized and accepted as masters," the American engineer reported back to head office. Later, more Canadian drillers arrived. Not all of them seemed as adaptable as the first two, however. Apparently one complained he was unable to eat gooseberry jam, and that they had run out of Provost Oats. Another was unhappy with a steady diet of cold boiled eggs and dry bread.

Reynolds was no happier with a crew of Americans who arrived for a brief stay: "The average American driller is quite unfit to be sent to a country like this, as he will not suit himself to new circumstances and conditions."

Despite these human setbacks, the first spot of oil was discovered in January 1904, but the well soon ran dry. More substantial finds were made farther east in Persia in 1908. A year later, the Anglo-Persian Oil Company was formed from the parent firm, Burmah Oil, with the Canadian Donald Smith (Lord Strathcona) its first chairman. The period from 1908 to 1914 saw the drilling of wells, construction of permanent housing, supply of amenities, and the beginning of a settled social life. Pipelines and tanks were built, workshops and warehouses erected, and a hospital constructed. By 1913 a refinery on the Gulf was in operation. Meanwhile in Egypt, oil had been found in 1907.

McNaughton stayed with Anglo-Persian until 1917 when he went to Trinidad, then retired in 1919. He died in 1934 at the age of seventy-four.[237]

Oil Mania

As Canadian Hard Oilers poured into the Middle East, talk in London, England, centred on the need to hasten production and secure supplies. British entrepreneur Marcus Samuel, co-founder of Shell Transport and Trading, wrote to Admiral John Fisher of the British Admiralty, the self-styled "oil maniac." Samuel urged quick action to replace coal-fired ships with oil burners.[238] Fisher, in turn, began to pressure his friend, Winston Churchill, who, in 1912, had become the cabinet minister responsible for the Royal Navy, to take the necessary action. Churchill trusted the oil maniac's expertise and did his best to press the case for petroleum.

"Find us oil in sufficient quantities and at a reasonable price in peace, and without interruption in war," Churchill wrote Fisher in May 1912. "Make us feel that we can count on it and swim on it; guarantee its supplies and reserves and you will have added another to those silent victories of peace of which I spoke last night."[239]

Under Churchill, the British Admiralty took on an increasingly dominant role in directing the search for petroleum. In 1914 and just before war broke out, Britain took a controlling interest in Anglo-Persian, its two directors holding veto power over corporate decisions.[240]

The war that came to be known as the Great War, was the first fought in such large part because of petroleum. Germany, also thirsty for crude, directed its Middle East intelligence operations toward inciting local uprisings against Britain, which enjoyed considerable influence in the area.[241] The seas around the Middle East were unsafe, convoys were decimated and supply lines interrupted. In November 1914, Britain landed a force in the Persian Gulf region, its objective the defence of the country's political interests and oil supplies. Those supplies, in turn, became the primary Turkish objective.

But Britain successfully defended its crucial supply, and British oil production grew during the war, ensuring ample supply for its fleet. From 1914 to 1919, production from the Middle East oil fields grew from 1.7

million barrels to nearly seven million barrels. The Canadian Hard Oilers were on the front lines and proved themselves a significant factor in ensuring that happened.

Fred Edward

One of those men was Fred Edward of Petrolia. Son of A.C. Edward, Fred followed his father into the foreign fields. Having first worked in Lambton's oil fields at the age of fourteen, Fred earned his steam-engineer's certificate by the time he was seventeen and struck off for Mexico.[242] Like many of the Canadians who worked in that country, Edward routinely carried a pistol for protection. Once, he became involved in an altercation with a local worker who drew a knife on Edward. The Canadian pulled out his pistol and shot the man through the arm.

After three years in Mexico, Fred Edward returned home with $2,000 in his pocket and a case of malaria. Three months later he was off to Egypt, where he drilled on a barren island off the Sinai Peninsula.

In 1913, as the war clouds thickened, he left for Persia. In the foothills of western Persia northwest of Ahvaz, Edward's crew drilled. All the camp's supplies came overland by camel, train, and mule-drawn wagons. The labourers were Turks, Arabs, Persians, and Indians. Edward had an ability to pick up languages quickly, and he gained a working knowledge of several, which helped him communicate with the workers.

The drillers faced constant problems: as they drilled, the sand kept collapsing into the hole (it was quite a different material than the familiar heavy Lambton clays); pipe-casing was required all the way down the shaft, and, occasionally, the rotation of the percussion drill would unscrew the bottom length. Then the entire six- to nine-hundred metres of casing had to be withdrawn, a length at a time.

In the merciless heat, the men worked amid constant threat to their safety. With the Middle East oil lands taking on increasing strategic value, the British sent in rifles and ammunition at the beginning of the war. It was not uncommon for the drillers to be working in the fields with a steady background of gunfire. For further protection, an oil line was set around the perimeter of the field so that, if the workers were attacked, oil could be released and set on fire. Inside the wall of fire, the men were presumably safe from the intruders.

Edward recalled one well that came in with such a roar it could be heard for thirty kilometres. Oil blasted upwards to a height of sixty metres. The steel rig was torn apart, and drilling tools spewed across the field by

Canadian driller Bob McCrie took this photo in 1923 at #2 well, Mesopotamia. The picture shows the drillers "shooting the well" with the use of nitroglycerine.
Courtesy Oil Museum of Canada.

the pressure of the rushing crude. The well caught fire and flames shot into the sky. The men had to use water from the boilers to douse the fire.

About two years after his arrival, Edward contracted rheumatic fever. He needed medical assistance, but he was more than one hundred and fifty kilometres from the nearest doctor, and surrounded by hostiles. The resourceful Canuck obtained a camel and slipped through the enemy lines dressed as a Persian.

When he arrived at the Gulf, where medical help could be obtained, Edward later claimed to have met T.E. Lawrence, who was overseeing the evacuation of British subjects on a gunboat. If Edward could get out of the oil fields, the man (known better as Lawrence of Arabia) said, then he could certainly get into them. A swap was agreed to — Edward's camel for Lawrence's help in obtaining passage on the boat. The last thing Edward recalled as he watched from the boat's deck, was Lawrence heading into the desert astride camel.

Returning to England where, upon arrival, he weighed just ninety-seven pounds, Edward went home to Petrolia to recuperate. In five months he had signed up to drill for water in Australia, but by 1918 he was back in the Middle East where he stayed until 1922.

Hard Oiler!

Ernie Kells

Ernie Kells commenced working on Lambton's oil rigs when he was seventeen. He worked in New Brunswick and Quebec, but little oil was ever found there, and in 1922, at age twenty, he headed to Mesopotamia and Persia.[243] Initially he worked for the Anglo-Persian Oil Company at Ali Gharbi, and later moved on to Dehluran, Ahwaz, and Quaraguli in Persia.

"Lots of times you'd work seven days a week. You mostly just worked and slept, and read a lot," he said years later.

"I was young. I had good health. You'd get malaria fever occasionally but you'd get over that. We had different kinds of diseases, smallpox; every few years you'd get an outbreak of cholera and that would kill a pile of the native people; there was a bit of bubonic plague, but not much. That came from the mites and fleas off the rats. Cholera was the worst."

In the 1920s, "we got $312 a month. You worked about ten hours a day and six days a week." After he'd had his fill of the Middle East, Kells returned to Petrolia in 1932, married a teacher, and bought his own oil field.

The Canadians supervised large workforces of local labourers in the construction of the oil fields, refineries and pipelines through the Persian desert. Here a Hard Oiler poses with his native workers during construction of a pipeline from Dehluran, Persia, to the Persian Gulf, about 1923.
Courtesy Oil Museum of Canada.

James Brown

In 1903 at the age of eleven, James Brown began to work as a rod boy in the Lambton fields, carrying rods away when they were pulled out from the well-casings.[244] This was Jim's apprenticeship as a driller, and in 1915 at the age of twenty-three, he left Petrolia to drill for oil in Persia. In the course of the fourteen years he spent overseas, Brown sent home to relatives a large collection of Persian rugs, and Arabian-style swords, knives, and battle axes, some of which remain treasured family mementos.

At first, Brown wasn't sure if he ought to be drilling for oil while the First World War was on. Maybe he ought to join the armed forces instead, he wondered. But the authorities quickly assured him that his contributions would be just as valuable helping to maintain the supply of oil to the British war machine. At the time, the Persian oil fields were called the lifeline of the Royal Navy.

(On 7 July 1915, Sarnia's *Observer* reported that many of the Lambton drillers in foreign fields had earlier been forced to return home on account of the war, but that they were, at that time, leaving again to resume their work. Burma, Egypt, Persia, and Venezuela were among their reported destinations.)

Once, when Brown was working on a Persian pipeline, German soldiers and their Arab allies attacked the camp, driving the Canadians into the surrounding mountains. Brown's grandson, Murray Brown of Petrolia, recalled Jim's stories in later life.[245]

"Their attackers killed some of the workers, so they took off into the mountains and hid," said Murray Brown. "The company at first wrote them off as dead because everyone else had left, and people on other rigs had been killed. They lived up in the mountains on raw birds and raw mutton because they didn't want to build any fires that would be spotted."

More than one hundred kilometres from their base, the small group survived for four months before they were spotted and returned to the camp.

At another time, a drilling rig fell on top of Brown, crushing his leg. With no doctor available to set it properly, he developed a limp that he carried with him the rest of his life.

A Fateful Trip

The ordinary details of everyday life sometimes brought the Hard Oilers into contact with history's unfolding tapestry. In 1912 in London,

England, James McRie, aged 35, was just back from drilling in Egypt when word came that his wife was ill in Sarnia. McRie told his friend, Gus Slack, another Lambton boy.[246]

Slack had an idea. He had a ticket home but really, he wanted to stay in London for a while longer, to do some sightseeing and to visit his friend, fellow Canadian William McKenzie, at the Oil Well Engineering Company. Take the ticket, insisted Slack. I'll go home on a later ship.

The grateful McRie thanked his friend, shook his hand and took the ticket. Passage was on a brand-new ship and McRie was sure to be home in no time flat.

The last glimpse of McRie that Slack ever caught was walking up the gang plank of the *Titanic*. Like fifteen hundred others, McRie perished on the ship's maiden voyage. Slack later returned home on the *Lusitania*, three years before it was sunk by a German submarine.

Gus Slack was not the only Hard Oiler who had a close brush with the *Titanic*. Returning from Egypt, Fred Edward had a ticket on the ill-fated liner too, but was delayed in London traffic and missed its departure.[247] He joined Slack aboard the later *Lusitania* voyage. It's easy to imagine their talk on the long trip home.

Chapter Twelve
Expedition to Sumatra

For the most part, the foreign drillers were average men looking for a decent living. More money could be had in the foreign fields than in the oil fields of Lambton. And along the way, these Hard Oilers could enjoy more adventure than they could ever expect to experience at home.

Some made a career of working overseas. They would sign a contract for two or three years, come back home occasionally, and then return to their overseas job. They might leave their families in Lambton, or they might take them along.

Edward Winnett was not one of the drillers who made the foreign fields his life's work. He tried it once, made a good deal of money, but returned home to his wife and children. The foreign fields had proved a lonely existence for Winnett, a deeply religious man with strong family ties. Alone in the wilds of Sumatra, he missed his family terribly and never felt compelled to try it again.

Edward Winnett was born on 8 January 1849, in Killaloe, County Clare, Ireland.[248] The second oldest of seven children born to a Protestant family, he was six when his parents, Henry and Ellen, left their village at the south end of Lough Derg, near Limerick, and headed south to the port of Cork on the first leg of a voyage that would take them to the new world.

Leaving behind the grinding poverty of the Ireland of the mid-nineteenth century, the Winnett family arrived in Canada in 1855. They located in London in what was then Canada West. Edward was about fifteen when he went to work as a messenger at the Tecumseh, London's premier hotel. The Tecumseh had been built in the mid-1850s during a time of strong economic growth and boastful civic pride. The plumbing alone had cost $5,000.

But no sooner had its doors been opened to the public, than London and the rest of Canada West tumbled into a deep depression, and the

Tecumseh fell on hard times. In 1856 London's population reached 16,000 and was still growing. Four years later, the population had sunk to just 11,000.[249]

That began to change, though, in the years after the discovery of oil in Lambton County in 1858. London was a railway centre. The Great Western line split at London, one branch wending its way southwest to Windsor and Detroit , the other heading due west to Sarnia. It was the Sarnia route that carried fortune-seekers and their equipment into the oil lands of Lambton County, and was used to cart the crude oil out of the bush and east to the larger population centres.

Working at the Tecumseh imparted considerable status on the second child of the Winnett family. In 1860 the hotel had hosted a breathtaking royal ball upon the arrival in the city of Albert, Prince of Wales.[250] When his mother, Queen Victoria, died, Albert would become King Edward VII. It was the first visit of British royalty in the city's history. Four years later, young Edward Winnett donned the uniform of a hotel messenger and went to work at what was then the largest Canadian hotel west of Toronto.

Later, Edward worked in his father's boiler shop, and in 1873 he married Annie Jane Winnett, a first cousin, who had been born in Dublin in 1853. Between 1874 and 1896, Edward and Annie Jane Winnett had eleven children. In 1883 Edward and Annie had moved to Oil Springs. Two years later when Edward's father opened a boiler shop in the village, Edward agreed to manage it.

Fourteen years after moving to Oil Springs, Edward decided to take a contract to work in the oil fields of Sumatra. Six of the Winnetts's eleven children lived beyond childhood and were alive when he left in 1897. No doubt part of the reason for the decision to take the contract to work in foreign fields was the cost of raising a family.

Then, too, the eldest of the children were now of an age where they could help their mother in Edward's absence. By 1897 Frederick Walter was twenty-three. His brother, Albert Henry, was twenty-one, and Edward Richard, was nineteen. It seemed a good time for Edward to give the foreign fields a try.

Today, Sumatra, South Borneo, and Java all are part of the nation of Indonesia. In the 1890s they were Dutch colonies, part of what was referred to as the Dutch East Indies. While small quantities of oil had been found in Java in the 1870s, it was not until 1889 that the first big strike was made in Sumatra.[251] In the Netherlands, the Royal Dutch Company was quickly established to exploit those resources. In Britain the London merchants, the Samuel Brothers, were not far behind, arriving in the Dutch East Indies initially to distribute the oil and acquire land. (The Samuel Brothers company was quickly gaining a reputation for its oil expertise and had been involved in recruiting Canadians for oil exploration in other places too.) In 1892 Samuel Brothers built its first oil tanker, and five years later established the Shell Transport and Trading Company.[252]

In 1902 the Samuels's Shell Transport and Trading Company merged with the Royal Dutch company to form the Asiatic Petroleum Company to transport and market eastern oil. Shell and Royal Dutch later completed their integration under the name Royal Dutch Shell.[253]

Lambton drillers were in high demand in the latter days of the nineteenth century, as the oil industry expanded quickly in Southeast Asia. On 29 April 1897 the *Advertiser* reported that a group from Oil Springs and Petrolia was leaving for Borneo. This group, under the supervision of Lambton Hard Oiler Alva Townsend, opened the lucrative fields at Sanga Sanga.

In October of that year, another group of Hard Oilers headed for the Sumatra fields. John W. Crosbie was in charge of the Sumatra group, accompanied by John Hall, George Luxton, John E. Crosbie, and Edward Winnett. A newspaper story said the group would help Crosbie erect and operate a large refinery.[254]

On 7 October 1897, hundreds of friends and family met at the Petrolia train station to say farewell to the parting group. "It was a sad parting to leave my home and dear wife and children," Winnett told his diary. "I never shall forget that parting."

Among the crowd of well-wishers were Edward's elder brother, Fred, and his wife, Jennie, who would figure prominently in Edward's thoughts over the course of the nearly eighteen months he would spend away from home. Fred would take over the Oil Springs boiler works in Edward's absence.

But if Edward missed his family, it was also the adventure of a lifetime. After London and Toronto, the group went on to Montreal where they stayed at the Richelieu Hotel, went sightseeing by carriage, walked up Mount Royal, and finally made their way to the harbour, where they boarded the four-hundred-and-seventy-foot-long steamer, *Labrador*, for the voyage to England. On board, Edward attended a Methodist service at which the minister preached a sermon he felt appropriate for the occasion — Jesus walking on water.

Passing through the Gulf of St. Lawrence and nearing Newfoundland, they encountered icebergs before heading out in to the Atlantic. Once into the ocean, Winnett wrote: "The sea is boiling mountain-high, coming over the hurricane deck." Almost alone among the two hundred passengers, Edward said he was not feeling too badly the effects of the heaving sea and wolfed down a healthy breakfast while most others were ill. Sixty were in sick bay, and Edward recounted one man standing on the hurricane deck when a wave knocked him down and "bowled" him along the deck six metres.

There was a burial at sea after a man died, apparently of natural causes. Then they spied the coast of Ireland, which Edward had not seen since his departure from Cork forty-two years earlier, and on to Liverpool, where they disembarked and took the train to London.

The British capital left Edward Winnett awe-struck. He marveled at a city of six million: "The streets are one living mass of people. Also the streets [are] blocked at times that it is impossible for one to move." A metropolis of that size must have made a fantastic impact on a man who had never lived in any place larger than London, Ontario, then no more than a good-sized town.

He visited the Crystal Palace, St. Paul's Cathedral, and Hyde Park, then on to White Chapel, where not long before, Jack the Ripper had conducted his gruesome work. "I saw some of the dirtiest women I ever saw," Winnett remarked. Then in an uncharacteristically uncharitable comment he added: "I thought it a pity that Jack the Ripper did not put some more of them out of existence."

Before returning home, Winnett was to witness many scenes of dirt, of hunger, of poverty, and people living in societies terribly foreign to what he was used to in Canada. His experiences broadened his mind and made him much less critical of those who lived differently.

The Canadians left London for Southampton to catch the steamer, *Prince Hendriek,* which took them to India. They set sail November 10 with six hundred other passengers. The *Hendriek,* said Winnett, was a floating palace. Equipped with electricity and a brass band, the ship measured one hundred and fifty metres in length and eighteen metres abeam.

He noted the Bay of Biscay was termed the sailors' grave, where "no less than six steamers have been lost within the last two years. Thank God He has favoured us with a beautiful passage."

Along the coast of Spain, past Gibraltar, and into the Mediterranean the voyage continued. Winnett watched porpoises, which, he thought, looked like large pigs jumping out of the water. Then on to Italy and Genoa where the harbour was covered with small boats. When they left, Winnett remarked on the Italian warship that saluted a visiting British warship. On board the *Hendriek,* Winnett said, "the band plays 'God Save the Queen'."

In Port Said, Egypt, Winnett was upset by the immodest clothing of the native workers who loaded coal into the *Hendriek* for the next leg of the voyage. He noted the "dirty cloth" tied around their loins and another they tied around their heads. "You can see hundreds of them ... they carry the coal on their heads in baskets. You can imagine how many there was when they loaded four hundred and eighty tons of coal into our vessel in an hour."

Ashore, he saw "sights never to be forgotten. There seems to be no civilization there. You can see them, women and children, one mass of rags. Nothing but canvas bags to cover their nakedness." Winnett and his colleagues were beginning to experience culture shock. He clung to the friendly, familiar things, wielding them as a shield against the foreignness he experienced for the first time in his life. He countered a description of women in veils with the band striking up "'No Place Like Home,' which made me feel lonesome as we passed along out into the [Red] Sea."

The sun grew hot, and someone strung up canvas on deck to protect the northerners from the beating rays. By November 25, seven weeks from home, Winnett saw passengers dressed in white muslin suits to protect themselves against the tropical heat. Later in Asia, Winnett would, himself, don a white suit, the unofficial uniform of the Canadian foreign drillers.

They crossed the Indian Ocean and docked in Colombo, Ceylon. Here they had access to fresh fruit and took a rickshaw ride. Winnett commented on the poverty and hunger. "I think if you put half a dozen in a row, you could see the sun through their arms and legs," he wrote. He shuddered at the meat hanging in the hot sun, covered in flies and maggots.

Through the Strait of Malacca, which separates the island of Sumatra from the Malay Peninsula, they arrived in Singapore. By the time they disembarked, they had spent a month on board the *Hendriek*. Departing the ship for the final time, the passengers picked up the hymn the band played, and started singing the words to "God Be With You Till We Meet Again."

If London was the foreign drillers' gateway to the oil lands, Singapore was the crossroads. "Drillers, geologists and engineers are constantly coming and going," wrote driller George Bryson in 1926. "Here they come to take boat for home from Burma, Borneo, Sumatra, Java, and India."[255]

To Winnett, Singapore offered "the most beautiful sights I have seen in my travels." The drillers were housed in the Hotel Del Europe, which occupied fifty acres of trees and gardens. While he did not record the cost, which his employer picked up, another driller of the same era stayed at the Criterion Hotel for $19 a night. A view from Winnett's hotel, across the street, opened onto the harbour.

But the journey was not yet finished, and after a brief stay in Singapore, Winnett and his colleagues boarded another boat for the five-hundred-kilometre voyage south to the mouth of the Musi River on Sumatra Island.

Sumatra is a mountainous island. The peaks run its length, north to south, creating a series of short, fast-flowing rivers on the west side and wider, navigable rivers on the east. There on the east side, ocean steamers of the era could navigate ninety to one hundred kilometres upstream from the ocean, while small steamers, mostly stern wheelers, could ply the waters of a river, like the Musi, for a distance of two hundred and fifty kilometres.

The mountains of Sumatra include many volcanic craters, and earthquakes are common. The most famous of the volcanoes of Winnett's era was Krakatoa, off the southern tip of Sumatra, which erupted just fourteen years before Winnett and company arrived, causing a tidal wave that swept inland and took fifty thousand lives. The natives later told drillers the ocean was black with ash for eight days after the explosion. (The eruption scattered debris as far as Madagascar, a distance of nearly 5,000 kilometres.)

Winnett's ship steamed up the Musi River to Palembang, about eighty kilometres from the ocean. The group was housed in a hotel with rooms that stuck out over the river. In the morning they saw hundreds of small boats on the river, loaded with fresh fruit. When some of the younger locals caught a glimpse of the white foreigners, they "ran for their lives," Winnett laughed. "They seem to be afraid of a white man."

He watched, bemused, as a wedding passed. It consisted of small decorated boats, a band on board, "which puts me in mind of the 12th of July [Orange parade] at home."

Winnett learned that one of the Wallens from Oil Springs was in hospital in Palembang and went to visit him. This could have been any of the three Wallen brothers — Charles, who later made the escape from Russia, Edwin, or Fred — who all worked in Sumatra.

Finally on December 15, Winnett caught a boat from Palembang to the location of the refinery and his future home, about eight kilometres from town. He settled in at his new bungalow with his roommate, John E. Crosbie of Sarnia.

The homes were nine metres by eight metres, contained four large rooms, a hall, a kitchen, and a large verandah on the front and back. Located within two metres of the river, they were "surrounded with the most beautiful fruit trees, such as coconut and banana and pineapples and other fruit I don't know the names of." Ships passed day and night. A steamer brought the mail daily. The men were required to buy their own furniture so they headed out to do so and to obtain provisions.

In Southeast Asia, the Canadians lived in thatched roof bungalows like this one in Borneo, often right at the water's edge. The slow-moving rivers offered the best transportation routes through the dense rain forests of what is now Indonesia.
Courtesy Oil Museum of Canada.

Winnett took a stroll along the route a new pipeline would follow. "Here were hundreds of [local] men up to their middles in mud and water, chopping down trees, also trying to make a walk along through this Savannah," he wrote. The area was flooded at high tide, and natives went from house to house by boat, selling fresh fruit.

When he returned, he found some native workers erecting a bathroom and water closet, built out over the river. Apparently plumbing was pretty basic.

Over the coming months, Winnett was sent frequently to Palembang to pick up supplies for construction of the refinery. Because of his experience at his father's boiler shop, and his knowledge of the oil industry, Winnett oversaw a wide variety of construction work: a railroad, oil tanks, and a two-hundred-kilometre pipeline that connected the oil fields to the coast.

On one of his typical daily rounds, Winnett wrote: "The refinery is like a beehive today. Hundreds of Chinese and Malays, some loading a vessel with pipe [for the oil pipeline], some unloading boiler plate from small boats, more getting timber out of the river that came in a raft for the tanks. Some building a storehouse."

During his first winter at the site, he wrote that about 300 men worked on the refinery and another one hundred and eighty-eight on the pipeline. He worked with John W. Crosbie on supervising the pipeline work. Besides overseeing the work, he took inventory and frequently went on trips to Palembang to purchase supplies. On one buying trip, he was sent to Singapore to purchase some machinery and was handed $125 for a week's expenses and boat fare for the thousand-kilometre round trip.

During one trip to Palembang, Winnett passed a funeral procession.

> I met a boat and twelve Chinese men rowing for all they were worth. On this boat was a coffin and corpse. As they passed they were all shouting and laughing as if going to the races. I watched, then also [went] to the place where they landed to see the rest of the performance. When they landed down the river about two miles [from] here, they all collected around the coffin and got ropes and placed them under the coffin. They got two bamboo poles and placed them through the ropes, then got the poles on their shoulders and shouted, the whole lot of them, laughing and shouting at the top of their voices.

This was too much for Winnett's Christian sensibilities. He described the scene as "one of the most unhuman affairs I ever saw."

On another occasion, Winnett described what happened after a Chinese worker robbed a vessel of its provisions, and the policeman who had been sent to arrest the suspect was attacked and killed, his heart cut from his chest and cooked. "All this, they confessed to, and gave their reason for it. It was [that] they were hungry, so they paid the penalty of death by being hung here in Palembang a few days ago."

It was not to be the only hanging Winnett described. When a young girl was murdered for the gold bracelets she wore on her ankles, a man and woman were convicted and executed in the same way.

Wildlife was bountiful and curious to the Canadians. Winnett described sitting on his waterside verandah and watching a large crocodile swim up the river. His attempts to shoot the animal failed, the musket balls bouncing harmlessly off its thick hide. A few days later a crocodile emerged from the river in search of some chickens. "I made for my gun … I had a good look at it as I was within twenty-five feet of him when I fired. I aimed straight for his eyes where I have no doubt but I hit him, for his actions in the water were terrific. They say there is no such thing as killing these monsters with one shot. This is the only way I can account for me not getting him," Winnett concluded.

Other times he observed three-metre-long cobras and other snakes.

Winnett and George Luxton walked through the rain forest for a visit one day. The pair started for home at about six in the evening. "It got dark shortly after we left, so it can hardly be imagined what a dangerous and lonely trip it was through the jungles where there is all kinds of wild beasts," he wrote. "The night was so dark, I could not see my hand before my eyes. However, we arrived home about nine o'clock, mud to the eyes, and awful tired." Winnett's diary made no further references to night-time sojourns through the jungle, so it appears he and Luxton learned not to repeat their mistake.

The Sumatra soil was fertile; it produced some of the world's finest coffee. Winnett was always struck by the bounty of the island's farmland, and he described the acres of coffee, pineapples, bananas, and rice. "I often think God made this part of the world for poor people, as everything grows wild, fit for provisions."

What followed was perhaps an indication that Winnett's Protestant sensibilities were moderating somewhat, as he became increasingly exposed to these radically different cultures. His first encounter with the Egyptians dressed only in loin cloths left him scandalized, but by now he only commented about the heat in the Sumatran jungle, and that the natives "never need cloth or clothing of any kind."

Yet after one of his walks through the countryside, the tone of the Canadian's writing demonstrated he was not totally comfortable with everything about life here: "We had to walk two miles through the jungles with my umbrella and satchel over my shoulder and my stockings outside my pants to keep the blood suckers from getting at my legs. In this jungle, there is elephants and tigers, also wild boars. I had to have my revolver where I could get it without much trouble. The only thing I saw was a … wild boar. Those are very fierce creatures. They will face a man like a dog."

During a visit to the nearby home of fellow Lambton driller Robert Rawlings, Winnett described how he learned to sing hymns in the Malay language. In fact, among Rawlings's own belongings, now in the possession of the Oil Museum of Canada in Oil Springs, is a book of Malay hymns. Produced by the American Mission Press in Singapore, it consists of translations into Malay of English-language hymns such as "Holy Holy Holy" and "Onward Christian Soldiers." The hymnery offers the first line in English so the Anglophones can quickly identify the song. Occasionally, Rawlings scribbled several lines of English in the margins.

Several times in his diary, Winnett referred to visiting his friend, Wallen, at the Palembang hospital. Now, on 13 March 1898, Winnett himself came down with what was diagnosed as yellow fever: his leg swollen, his arm from the elbow to the wrist swollen, his temperature 105 ° F.

Since there was no doctor at the camp, he had to rely on Rawlings for assistance. Finally, a doctor at Palembang was contacted, and the diagnosis was made. Winnett was ordered to bed, unable to work and in great pain. Eventually, when his condition did not improve, he was moved to the Palembang hospital, where he stayed for the next four months. On July 24, John Crosbie and George Luxton came to take him back to camp.

There are no entries in his diary during those months of illness, probably indicating the diary was left behind at his camp. But soon after returning to duty, Winnett was writing again. On 28 July 1898, Winnett wrote: "I can say what no one else can. I was the first to do a piece of boiler work on the island of Sumatra."

Supervising the boiler works would now take up the bulk of his time. Occasionally he looked on where the oil storage tanks were being erected. The tanks would hold 20,000 barrels of oil when completed. The workers, about five hundred in total, were mostly Malay and Chinese.

Away from the coastline and at a higher elevation, the climate is cooler than at sea level. In August, Winnett said "the weather is lovely every day. When I woke this morning, I was cold, although I had a good warm blanket over me. The weather is all that could be desired." The wet season arrived in October and although it lasted four months, the daily rain did not continue that long at a time, he said. The situation was different, however, on August 19 when Winnett and Crosbie were on their way to Palembang for provisions.

> There was a tremendous storm of wind and rain, so on our return trip we had to cross the river which is one mile wide. The river was worked up like a sea. When we got well out, the waves washed clean over our boat which half filled... We also had with us about fifty dollars worth of provisions which made quite a load. We had to make for a vessel that was anchored in the river for shelter, as our boat was just about to go under. We also had to hire another boat to take the provisions ... the waves were washing over the side of our boat. But thank God He spared us for a while longer. I was awful frightened for my knee was awful sore and was doubtful if I could swim with it.

By the end of August, cities around the Dutch East Indies were readying themselves for the coronation of a new Dutch monarch. Winnett described the scene in Palembang during a visit on September: 1

> The street is arched for fully half a mile from one side to the other, and decorated with flags and banners and Chinese lanterns ... They have all kinds of wild beasts — elephants, tigers, monkeys, gorillas, snakes, baboons and all kinds of reptiles that inhabit the island. We went to see the boat race on the river. Boats were forty feet in length, each boat was manned with forty-two coolies. Forty of those had paddles ... one to steer and another standing up in the centre of the boat with a white handkerchief in his hand, waving it so as to make the coolies all keep time. I never saw such a race. The boat actually raised out of the water and the waves flow fully ten feet high.

Usually, Winnett got along well with the workers. On one occasion he told how some of them killed a boar and gave him ten pounds of the meat. "It was as lovely a piece of meat as I ever ate."

However, there were occasional labour problems. On the morning of 12 September 1898, the workers struck for more money. It was a frightening scene Winnett described: "There was five hundred and sixty men ... they were all collected around my bungalow. They were a dangerous looking lot, nearly every one of them had a cleaver or what they call a prong with them, and others with large knives in their belts."

Their tactics seem to have worked. "We had to give them a raise of pay," concluded Winnett. "Soon we had them all satisfied and back to work."

Then on November 4, while out walking not far from his home, Winnett encountered six workers. "As it happened, I had my walking stick with me, so I turned around and leathered them with it right and left. In one second there was not one of them to be seen. So I went into the bungalow and there could hear them gabbling near all night, but had my gun close to me all night. They are a dangerous lot."

Winnett made no further references to danger from the workers.

While the work was hard, the evenings and days off were often lonely for the Lambton drillers in far-off Sumatra. Winnett made frequent references to "my dear wife and children" and how he missed them. Christmas day, 1897, "was a very lonesome Christmas for me," he told his diary. He wrote a letter to his wife, Annie, one to his brother and sister-in-law, Fred and Jennie, and then went out to oversee construction on the various projects then under way.

His wedding anniversary was October 1. His wedding day had been "the happiest day of my life ... It makes me feel so sad to think of being parted from her [Annie] and my dear children." Six days later came another sad day, the anniversary of his leaving home. Then another blow, when his roommate, Crosbie, announced he was taking a better paying job with another drilling company. The pair had become good friends in Sumatra. At a farewell dinner, Crosbie presented Winnett with a sword and shield. "It makes me feel so lonesome to think of him going away and leaving me all alone among strangers and 14,000 miles from home."

While Crosbie was leaving for better money, Winnett too was making a good wage. He sent home ninety dollars a month to his family.

Work heated up as the end of the year neared. On November 13, a steamer from the Netherlands arrived, loaded with 2,500 tons of freight, including thirteen stills, each 9 metres high and 2.5 metres in diameter, made from steel plate 2 centimetres thick; enough boiler plate for five tanks of 20 metres diameter and 11 metres high, and eight boilers of 9 metres by 2.5 metres; six tanks, 6 metres in diameter and 1.5 metres high; iron for thirteen condensers; an iron building 45 metres by 18 metres; corrugated galvanized iron for the roof; steam pumps; fire brick; and cement. When it was laid out on the ground, the boiler plate covered fifty acres, Winnett estimated.

In Sumatra, Canadians supervise local labourers who erect an oil derrick and power house for a drilling rig. **Courtesy Oil Museum of Canada.**

The unloading was a dangerous job, and accidents were frequent. Just as work began, a sailor and a worker fell into the river. A man broke his arm when it was caught between a plate and the vessel's hull; more people fell into the river; a worker had an eye poked out when a piece of freight broke loose; a worker received a serious injury when his foot was cut on some equipment; a worker was crippled in a fall onto the dock; another fell into the river. And not all those unloading the ship were men, apparently, since Winnett noted that a woman slipped on the steps and fell.

It was the last significant piece of work Winnett would oversee in Sumatra. While the money was good, the loneliness and homesickness proved too much. On December 12, just a year after arriving in Sumatra, Winnett prepared for the trip home.

He left four days later, taking the steamer along with Robert Rawlings, George Luxton, and Jonathan Hall, for Singapore. The trip was a rough one, and Winnett, known for a sometimes wry sense of humour, indicated that "three of our party are feeding the fish." Winnett, who suffered few ill effects from rough seas on the way over, was still healthy.

There was a close call with the steamer, *Galitania*, but finally they reached Singapore. Two days after Christmas, still in Singapore awaiting passage home, Winnett and Rawlings attended a Methodist service. During the service, "Mr. Rawlings stood up in church and told how he had been for the last year in the jungles of Sumatra where there was no place to hear the word of God preached. He also said it put in him mind of the old saying you never miss the water until the well runs dry."

Singapore was known as the oil drillers' eastern crossroads for good reason. Winnett was sitting in a park on December 28. He looked up and stared ahead in disbelief. There, coming toward him, was a familiar face from his days in Lambton, a Mr. Yeager. Winnett didn't indicate which Yeager it was, but two brothers, M.L. and Robert, both served in the Sumatra fields. Yeager, who at first did not recognize Winnett, was on his way, with Fred Lawson, into Sumatra. That evening the two men joined Lawson, Rawlings, and Luxton for an old-style Lambton Hard Oilers' reunion. "We had quite a time," was the simple manner in which Winnett described the gathering. "We spent the evening talking of old times and home and friends."

The following day they said goodbye. Yeager knew Winnett's third son, Edward, who was by then twenty years old. "I was so glad to have Mr. Yeager tell me Ed was such a good boy, and also that his girl was the best girl in Petrolia as he knew her and family. He even said she was one of his Sunday school scholars."

When Winnett returned to his hotel room after dinner, he searched out a photograph of Ed and "his girl," and gave it to Yeager. "He said he would not be alone while he had it in the jungles," Winnett wrote.

After stretching his legs in Singapore, Rawlings was now returning to Sumatra for another tour of duty and had to catch the steamer back. The two bade farewell. A few days later, on 5 January 1899, Winnett boarded a steamer for Hong Kong. When another passenger, this time a Chinese man, died on this voyage, Winnett was scandalized by the cavalier actions of the Japanese sailors who buried him at sea.

> They had quite an amusing time, cracking all kinds of jokes about the poor fellow. They pitched him up in their arms and gave him a pitch overboard into the sea like a log, and then all had a laugh and sport to see him go. It was one of the most unhuman pieces of work I ever saw. There is not much sympathy for a Chinese or anybody else in this part of the world when the wind is out of him.

This was monsoon season, and the seas were heavy for the voyage to Hong Kong. When trouble brewed among the three hundred Chinese passengers, the Japanese sailors calmed them down with threats to spray them with the scalding water from the ship's boilers. It was on this trip that Winnett turned fifty, and three days later, on January 11, they arrived in Hong Kong. The next day he bought passage on a Canadian Pacific ship, the *Empress of China*. He paid for the trip right through to London, Ontario, and handed over thirty-two British pounds, about $160 (Canadian).

After a stop at Shanghai, they continued to Kobe and passed Mount Fuji. When he caught a glimpse of snow at Yokohama, it was "the first snow I saw since I left home." It was a mere 7,000 kilometres across the Pacific to Vancouver, and as Winnett looked east under a sunny sky, he dreamed of his return home.

In early spring Winnett was home again, and while his diary had stopped by that time, we can imagine the joyous homecoming. He was a pious man whose family was terribly important to him. Winnett would not leave them again, despite the lure of the money of the foreign fields. The cost was too great.

Edward Winnett was always, in the words of a niece, Marion Winnett

Berdan, "a jolly sort." After his return from Asia, Winnett and his family moved to Sarnia, and then crossed the St. Clair River to Port Huron, Michigan. He lived in Port Huron and vicinity for another eighteen years, until his death in 1917. Annie died seventeen years later and was survived by five of her children. The last, Daisy May, died in 1964.

Chapter Thirteen
They Sought Adventure

William O. Gillespie

Among the more travelled of the foreign drillers was William Gillespie, born 15 February 1878. He spent twenty-four years oversea, in Cuba, Borneo, Sumatra, and Burma in Asia; Egypt and the Sudan in Africa; and in Australia.[256]

His passport described him as five foot, ten and a half inches tall, a broad high forehead and long face, hazel eyes, dark hair, with a ruddy complexion, and a dark moustache.

It was just after the Spanish-American war when Gillespie first ventured into foreign fields, drilling for water in Cuba. It was water, too, he was searching for when he went to work with the International Boring Company in Queensland, Australia. Later still, he spent six months in Central Africa to report on drilling water for the Cape-to-Cairo Railroad.

Gillespie entered the oil business in Egypt on the Red Sea. Later he spent three years on the northeast coast of Sumatra, and several more years in Brunei and Sarawak, on the island of Borneo.

While in Sarawak Gillespie wrote home:

> Don't think that romance and adventure are dead out here. Piracy still goes on to a certain extent. Last year the Chinese pirates captured a fair sized steamer under command of Europeans between Singapore and Hong Kong; they boarded the steamer at Singapore as passengers at Miri [Sumatra] in July 1923. The Chinese broke out, not exactly in rebellion. No one knows exactly what they intended to do. When it was all over, twelve were dead on the spot. Several died in the

hospital afterwards. Two Europeans, government men, were hurt. One Sarawak ranger jumped, it is claimed, ten or twelve feet at the word 'charge!' but he took the head off a [Chinese] at one strike — took it absolutely clean off.

In Australia, Gillespie later recalled, he once struck a supply of water that literally boiled not far beneath the surface. "A sheep fell in about a hundred yards from the bore after I struck it and they just pulled it out in pieces."

In Australia, the men lived on "dried food and bad water," he said. Men became ill, not fit to work. Gillespie himself fell ill there in 1909 and returned home to Petrolia, where he rested for five months. By December of that year, he was back at it, this time in Egypt, where he stayed until 1913 before heading to Upper Burma for three years.

Bill Gillespie was typical of the driller-of-all-trades. In Egypt, he shod all the company's mules when not busy running his drilling rig. During one eight-month period in Sarawak, he worked on several bridges, cut down seventeen dangerous trees, and built a timber dam, a horse stable, a feed house, and homes for the rig crews. All of this he did in his "spare time," he wrote his employer, "such as Sundays and after leaving the rig." Being an engineer, he turned discarded casing protectors into horseshoes for the work animals.

Part of his job in Egypt was to teach local workers how to drill using the Canadian pole-tool method. His contract was for a one-year term, with an option to extend it for up to two six-month periods, and to work twelve hours a day. In exchange he would be paid thirty British pounds a month plus board and lodging and would get free passage and half-salary during the time he was in transit to and from Canada.

Gillespie was also an enthusiastic book collector and reader, his daughter, Kathleen Gillespie, recalled. He loved to learn about the geography and culture of the areas he visited, and among his many purchases were books on head-hunters and other tribes who lived in the areas of Southeast Asia where he worked.

The Prince and the Sultan

These simple country boys from Canada sometimes found themselves rubbing elbows with princes and sultans, sometimes dining with the wealthy and powerful. Several of the drillers who went to Persia reported meeting the Shah of Iran. And Bill Gillespie wrote home in 1922 about encountering the Prince of Wales and the Sultan of Brunei in Borneo with the officers of HMS *Renown.*

> The Sultan arrived shortly after the way was closed to the public, dressed in gold silk and robes of state, with his ministers, advisers and guard of honour, and took his seat just in front of where the Prince would land. Shortly after twelve o'clock the Prince arrived, and landed to the salute of twenty-one guns. The Sultan handed him ashore. After a few minutes with the Sultan, the Resident presented us all, and he shook hands with everyone. He then entered the Royal Chair, with the Sultan, and was carried to the audience hall ... The Prince, dressed in shorts, army shirt open at the neck, looked quite one of the boys, hard as nails and fit for anything, and I believe a long shandy made him feel about right. About one thirty, the Sarawak Oil Fields Limited motor ship *Miri* arrived with the officers of the *Renown* and *Cairo* who were allowed leave. We were served a splendid curry tiffin in the courthouse while the Prince with the Resident and his wife went out to the falls, about fifteen minutes' walk from the courthouse, for tiffin. About four o'clock the Prince and his party left. He went around on his own, shook hands with us all, and remarked that he had had a splendid time.

From drilling to blacksmithing, from wiping grease from brows to eating a curry tiffin in the British empire's Far East reaches, the Hard Oilers did it all.

Borneo's Canada Hill

It was a Petrolian, Charles Macalpine, who opened the Borneo field at the north-coast city of Miri, known as Sarawak's oil city. Near the coast is a high, long ridge, known as Canada Hill.[257] Here, the first oil well was put down in 1910, which continued producing until 1972. A plaque is located at the site indicating the first Malaysian oil well drilled by the cable-tool method. Total production from the well is estimated at 660,000 barrels.

The work was hard and the off-hours often lonely in the foreign fields. But the Hard Oilers enjoyed good wages and adventure. In Borneo about 1910, a group of Canadians is decked out in their white muslin suits, the unofficial "uniform" of the off-duty foreign drillers. Front (l to r): James Brown, Gus Slack, Fred Webb, James McCrie, John Brown, Charlie Macalpine. Back (l to r): Ben Osborne, Wallace Saunders, James Rawson, Tom Hamilton, Harry Milligan, Fred Zimmer, W. Eady, Jay Zimmer.
Courtesy Oil Museum of Canada.

Frederick Saunders

Saunders was born in Petrolia, in 1881, and at the age of sixteen he joined Imperial Oil in that town.[258] With a subsidiary of Imperial, he was appointed superintendent for a refinery on Curacao in what was then the Dutch West Indies.

From 1913 to 1919, he was with the Anglo-Egyptian Oil Company at the Suez, where he also built Shell Oil's first Suez refinery. Later he managed Shell refineries in Mexico and the West Indies, before retiring from foreign fields in 1927. Saunders once explained that, during his time in South America, refineries were built on islands instead of the mainland because governments were not always considered stable. By locating their equipment on the islands, the operators felt safer from local trouble.

In 1922 Saunders left Tampico, Mexico, where he had been

superintendent of the Corona Refinery. A letter of thanks for his work
was sent by his manager:

> Dear Mr. Saunders:
> Before your leaving Chijol I wish to express my heartiest
> thanks for the splendid work you have been doing as
> Superintendent of the Corona Refinery ... During the
> time of construction as well as during the time of actual
> operation we have always been in very friendly and very
> close cooperation, and during this period I have always
> admired your clear insight in refinery operation as well
> as in all other details, which necessarily belong to the
> running of a refinery and to construction work.
> Gradually the refinery production was increased up to
> an intake of 55,000 barrels daily, and it certainly is proof
> of your conscientious work and your good
> superintendency that during this period not a single
> accident has happened.
> — M. Milo, manager

Saunders died in Windsor in 1964.

Bill Cole

From the time of the First World War until 1930, Cole worked in oil
fields in Mexico, Venezuela, Persia, and Sumatra.[259] In Venezuela he
contracted malaria which afflicted him until his death in 1961.

Once, while he was superintendent of a Venezuela field for Royal
Dutch Shell, a group of local workers laid down their tools and marched
on the home of the field manager, demanding higher wages. They carried
a scaffold, as though they were ready to hang the manager if they didn't
get what they wanted. For the adults it must have been a frightening
time. But for little Dorothy Cole, age eight, it was fun, "like Halloween,"
she later recounted, "because they had masks on their faces." After that,
though, Dorothy's father always kept a car at the ready, its tank filled with
gasoline, just in case.

It was also the one and only time Cole's wife and daughter joined him
on his foreign trips. After other assignments, Cole would return home
and assure his wife, Lottie, that he wasn't going back. After a while he'd
change his mind.

"He had his own calling card," said daughter Dorothy Stephenson.

> I was amused at that, this little country boy with his own calling card. He was always beautifully dressed in the white suits for the tropics. One of the pictures we had was him sitting in a chair, his feet up, and next to him is a leopard [skin], and beside him is his man-servant, with a top hat on. And he's there with a bottle of beer in his hand. Now, what more could a king have than he had at that moment? And I'm sure that for my mother, he was a great man of mystery when he came home.

A Well-Travelled Water Boy

William Frederick Tichborne was a boy of fourteen when he convinced his mother he should leave school and join the foreign drillers heading off to Germany.[260] Once he'd overcome that hurdle, he coaxed the drilling superintendent to take him on as a water boy. By 1880 Tichborne was heading to Hanover with the William McGarvey expedition.

On board ship, young William was the youngest and smallest worker, and was teased mercilessly by the men. The ship's captain took pity on him and invited William to take his meals at the captain's table. In Germany, the boy was befriended by the landlord of the boarding house where the workers stayed, and ate his meals with the family.

William dreamed of saving his earnings and presenting them to his mother, who was home, confined to a wheelchair. All the way home he carried his savings in a money belt, but he had to stop over in Oil Springs on the final leg of his journey. Fearful that some men who were drinking heavily might steal his hard-earned funds, William Tichborne hunted up the local bank manager and deposited the money.

"He was always disappointed that he couldn't drop all that cash into his mother's lap as he'd planned," said Tichborne's grand-daughter, Jean Mearce.

Later, Tichborne gained his credentials as a hydraulic engineer and went to Australia to drill artesian wells. There, he met his wife-to-be, Grizel Hamilton. They lived in field-tents near Charleville, Queensland, and two children were born. The family moved back to Canada where Tichborne bought a farm, but Grizel remained homesick for Australia the rest of her life.

First Well in Colombia

Fred Webb is credited with drilling the first oil well in Colombia.[261] In 1906 he signed a three-year contract with the Royal Dutch Shell to drill in the East Indies. He spent time in Borneo, Sumatra, and the Celebes Islands (east of Borneo). Later, with Imperial Oil's subsidiary, International Petroleum, he went to Ecuador and spent two years there before retiring in Petrolia.

Just Like Home

Mrs. Fred Webb wrote in a letter sent to Petrolia from Miri, in Sarawak, Borneo, in 1922: "There are so many from Petrolia here and some of us that were in the same class at school, so that it does not seem that we are really in a foreign country."[262]

In later years, families of the foreign drillers often accompanied the Hard Oilers, and substantial colonies of Canadians sprang up in the foreign fields. On New Year's Eve, 1924, the drillers, many of them Canadians, threw a costume party at Miri, in Sarawak, Borneo.
Courtesy Oil Museum of Canada.

Hard Oiler!

Just a Little Guy

In his earlier days, Laurence Oliver tried threshing grain on the prairies, but much preferred the life of a driller. "I lived better in the drilling fields than I ever did back on the farm," he said. "On the farm we never had any electricity or running water. We walked half a mile across the fields to a spring for a bucket of water."[263]

In 1922 he went to California where he joined the St. Helen's Petroleum Company. For the next forty-six years he worked around the world, on five continents. After California he went to Venezuela and Trinidad. He returned to Canada in 1940 and spent the next twelve years drilling blast holes for Northern Ontario mining companies. In 1952 he went to work for a water-drilling company, and he spent the next fourteen years, until his "first" retirement, in Israel and Venezuela.

In 1967 he was coaxed out of retirement to find water in India, and after successes there, went to Venezuela, Guyana, Niger, and Dahomey (now Benin) until finally calling it quits in 1973.

"Don't make me sound too important," Oliver told a visitor in 1998. "I was just a little guy."[264]

Inventor of Horizontal Drilling

Leo Ranney, engineer, inventor and philosopher, created methods of horizontal drilling that are still a key characteristic of modern oil-drilling techniques.[265] His idea was to sink a horizontal shaft directly underneath the oil pool, then drill thousands of small vertical oil "wells" upwards from it, into the oil pool, and "drain" the oil. This led to greater recovery rates. Ranney later recalled that when his first vertical drill pierced the overhead rock and the oil gushed downward into the horizontal shaft, "I just stood there and let it pour over me."

Ranney had a brilliant and always-active mind. During the 1930s he designed and built giant water-collector systems for London (England), Lisbon, and Paris. In the Second World War, Ranney's water-well systems helped many American gunpowder plants function. At his death, he held three thousand patents on everything from drilling machinery to bathtub toys. He once proposed creating an earthquake in Japan as a way of creating havoc and winning the war.

He was the step-grandfather of Charles Oliver Fairbank, current owner of the world's longest continuously-operating oil company, in Oil Springs, Ontario.

A Town of Strangers

The drillers' children who stayed behind sometimes felt their fathers were like strangers to them. Arnold Thompson once recounted: "When I was six, my father left for foreign fields, and from then on my father was a stranger. This was a fact of family life, with a number of families in Petrolia.[266]

"My wife, Lila, was the same way," Thompson continued. "Her father was away in a foreign field when she was born. Our mothers brought us up. When my father came home, he was just another man. I didn't know him. I didn't know what to talk to him about. He didn't know what to talk to me about because we had nothing in common."

His parents had little in common, too, Thompson said, with his father being away for three years at a time. And with the money they were earning, there were enticements to gamble.

"He loved drilling, which was a gamble. And he loved a deck of cards, which was [also] a gamble. There were people in this town [Petrolia], and I knew them, who waited for such men as my father, with a bottle of booze and a deck of cards. So it wasn't long before a small fortune was dissipated and they returned to get a new drilling contract."

One place in town was renowned for gambling, Thompson said. "Upstairs was the gambling den. Nobby Morrison was a great gambler, and he lived alone, and his house could be used for gambling any time he wanted to play. The petroleum industry in its infancy was a big gamble. [Petrolia] was a gambling town."

A Whiskey Dispute

In 1923, a Canadian driller from the village of Fullerton (Clifford West), wrote that "A man to live in [Borneo] and combat malaria must be a heavy whiskey-drinker, which appeals to many, as the company furnishes all the whiskey free of charge."[267]

A dispute quickly arose. A nameless driller wrote the *Advertiser-Topic*: "He is the only one I have heard of whom the company furnished free liquor to. We are all drafting a letter to the general manager for the return of money spent in the past for liquor. My own item will amount to quite a sum if I get it."

Hard Oiler!

A Family Affair

Whole families would enter the oil business in Lambton County — fathers, sons, brothers, uncles. The Fairbank family is the best example, with the current Charles Oliver Fairbank the fourth generation to operate the family oil business since it was established in 1861. But there were other examples where several brothers, or up to three generations went to foreign fields. And some stayed.

John MacIntosh left Petrolia in the mid-1880s to work for William H. McGarvey in Austria.[268] Three of the four children born to him and his wife, Mary, also went to the foreign fields. One of those sons, George Clayfield MacIntosh, married Amelia Mitchell of Petrolia and they had three children. The youngest, John, was born in Austria in 1889. George's second son, Carlton, married Frieda Erika von Espenhan of Austria, and they, in turn, had two children who were born in Austria. Carlton was the third generation of MacIntoshes to work in the Austrian oil fields.

When John and Mary MacIntosh's daughter, Margaret, married a driller named Perkins, in Austria, another generation of foreign drillers commenced. The Perkins family stayed during the First World War, and several were still living in Austria and Poland in the 1920s.

The Browns of Petrolia

Another famous family of foreign drillers was that of Joseph and Elizabeth (Foster) Brown, who married in Lambton County in 1874. The Browns had twelve children, and five of the boys became foreign drillers.

One of them, James Brown, was part of the earlier story of oil in the Middle East. Later, Jim and his wife, Ada, went to Sumatra and Borneo. They had two children in Sumatra and two, later, in Borneo. One of those sons, Bob, whowas born in Sarawak, Borneo, in 1928, said: "I can remember the grass huts we lived in. There were a lot better places than that to live." He recalls, however, that they had servants and "my mother liked that."[269]

The social life among the colony of foreign drillers was good. There were regular tea parties and masquerades. School classes were set up for the children, often with Canadian teachers, and they conducted Christmas concerts just like they would have back in Canada.

Not everything was like home, though. In the Asian jungles, the Canadians had to be prepared to deal with army ants and pythons. The ants would devour anything in their path, and the pythons took a liking

James and Ada Brown of Petrolia at their home in Sumatra, about 1922. Sons James, in the chair, and Edward, in a servant's lap, were born in Sumatra.
Courtesy Murray Brown, Petrolia.

to the family's pigs. On one occasion, Brown's drilling crew was forced to kill a three-metre-long bush snake that took a liking to their drilling rig.

When the family moved back to Lambton in 1932, the boys' helpful Uncle Harry announced to them that snow came in many colours. They were disappointed when they learned that it only came in white.

Jim Brown's brothers, Gilbert, William (Jack), Arthur, and Henry (Harry), all spent time in the foreign fields. Gilbert went to the Middle East before going to Maracaibo, Venezuela. Jack drilled in India, leaving a wife and daughter in Petrolia and then marrying and raising another family in India. Arthur worked in Burma, then part of Britain's Indian colony, and helped the British army blow up wells when the Japanese invaded in the Second World War. He lived in Burma until he died.

The Crosbies

Another of the great Hard Oiler families were the Crosbies. Gilbert Crosbie was born in 1858 near Sarnia and at the age of twenty-two went to Petrolia to work in oil.[270] Soon he was working for the Southern Pacific Railroad Company and was sent to Texas and New Mexico to drill for oil and water. Then it was off to Germany and Galicia, where he hooked up with the Bergheim & McGarvey company, managing one of their fields for nine years, followed by a trip back to Germany to operate a field for a group of Berlin bankers. In 1902 he went to work for the North Caucasian Oil Company near Grosny, but soon found himself sent to West Africa.

After little success in finding oil there, he was next sent to Sachalin Island, a prison colony off the east coast of Siberia. Security was strict. Under the protection of ten soldiers, Crosbie and his fellow drillers were escorted on the Trans-Siberian railway to Vladivostok, and then by steam ship to the island, where he was received by the chief of police. After six months prospecting, the party returned to Port Arthur on the mainland, and there, in late 1903, the British consul warned of the impending war between Russia and Japan.

The party left for the twenty-two-day rail trip back to Moscow, then they returned via Britain to Canada, where he died at Oil Springs in 1905. His wife, Martha Wallen Crosbie, travelled with him nearly everywhere, and they had seven children while living abroad.

A Very Wealthy Crosbie

When John E. Crosbie of Sarnia died in Tulsa, Oklahoma in 1938, he died a multi-millionaire.[271] This Crosbie had been the roommate of Edward Winnett in Sumatra, in 1897 and 1898, and he later drilled for oil in India. Then he moved to the United States, and about 1905 began to buy up oil leases. He possessed, in the words of C.B. Glasscock, chronicler of Oklahoma's oil history, the most valuable characteristics of a promoter and banker. In the days before federal income tax, Crosbie once earned $800,000 a day.

He bought a controlling interest in the Central National Bank and Trust Company of Tulsa and became its president. Over the course of eighteen years, he increased the bank's capital holdings ten-fold, and its deposits by more than twenty-five times, before selling out.

Crosbie's passion was said to be trotting horses, but only as an owner and spectator — he never bet. Despite his immense wealth, Crosbie lived an austere life and was said to be "contemptuous of display."

To Our Foreign Subscribers...

Notice in Petrolia's *Advertiser-Topic* on 27 October 1921: "The Post Office Department having increased postage from one to two cents a copy to foreign countries, the United States excepted, the subscription price of the *Advertiser-Topic* to Borneo, India, South American, Australia and other foreign countries is now $3 per year."

The Man Who Cheated Death

In a Burmese jungle, Duncan McIntyre was crushed under a two-ton oil pump and lived to tell the tale, cared back to health by the unwavering dedication of a Scottish nurse.[272]

McIntyre came from a very poor family. Born in Scotland in 1870, his family moved to Michigan, where the children were split up because their parents couldn't afford to keep them. While still a boy, he moved to Lambton County and entered the oil business.

For twenty-six of his forty-six-year career, Duncan McIntyre worked in foreign fields. His wife and children stayed at home. Duncan became a stranger to them, a guest in his home during his infrequent visits.

McIntyre left for Persia in 1905. Over the years to come, he went to Burma and Borneo. Every few years he would make the trip back home — on furlough, as he put it — decked out in his white Panama hat and white suit.

McIntyre would bring home with him souvenirs of his adventures. A leopard skin was carted to and from so many show-and-tells at school by so many McIntyre children that it eventually wore out and only the head remains today. An elephant's foot and tooth were in equally great demand, but they have withstood the childhood ravages more successfully.

Among his belongings, McIntyre saved a book, *Oil Finding*, by E.H. Cunningham Craig. Published in 1912 by Edward Arnold of London, England, it was one of several volumes that company produced on applied science.

An introduction by the oil expert, Sir Boverton Redwood, called the book, "a laudable and successful attempt to deal with a subject which has hitherto received far too little attention." Considerable money has been wasted, Redwood continued, due to the unscientific manner in which oil exploration was being conducted. Geology was just beginning to gain greater respect from the petroleum industry. McIntyre, himself, was featured in one of the book's photographs taken in Burma.

In Yenangyoung, Burma, on 8 September 1914, McIntyre experienced an accident that would have finished a lesser man. Only the quick work of a Scottish nurse, who for years later remained in contact with the family, and McIntyre's iron will, saved his life.

The leopard that Duncan McIntyre of Sarnia said caused the accident that resulted in his suffering twenty-one broken bones in the Burma rain forests was later shot by the others in McIntyre's party. They presented McIntyre with the animal's skull and pelt in honour of his miraculous recovery under primitive medical conditions, in the care of a Scottish nurse. **Courtesy Gary May.**

McIntyre was a field superintendent. In typical fashion, on this day, a two-ton pump was being towed on a wagon pulled by an elephant. Although oxen and horses were often used to pull heavy equipment in many foreign fields, the availability of elephants in Burma made them welcome alternative beasts of burden.

When McIntyre checked the wagon, his keen eye discovered something amiss. The huge pump was not level on its platform — it was shifting. McIntyre ordered a halt. With a crowbar in hand, he tried to straighten the pump.

There are two versions of what happened next. McIntyre's grandchildren, John McIntyre and Millicent Woods, say the story their grandfather told them is that a leopard frightened the elephant. The news report of the day does not mention the leopard, but says only that McIntyre's own work with the crowbar destabilized the pump. In either case, the equipment toppled over, knocking him down, and rolling on top of him.

The horrified crew members quickly jumped into action but even as they worked to free McIntyre, they must have feared the worst. Far from proper medical facilities, McIntyre was carefully placed on a makeshift stretcher. It took a day for a crew of native workers to carry him through the jungle to the camp hospital. He was conscious all the way.

When they arrived at the field hospital, a Scottish nurse, Margaret E. Clark, counted twenty-one bone fractures, including his left knee, both collar-bones, left jaw-bone, right shoulder-blade and right arm — in two places. When the news was sent to his family in Sarnia, they were warned there was a very good chance McIntyre would not survive. But tragedy sometimes takes an unexpected turn. Annie McIntyre, alone at home with five children and warned her husband might not survive, could take no more. She walked into the nearby St. Clair River and drowned herself.

In Burma, nurse Margaret Clark worked valiantly to save the injured man. After several months of recuperation and still not knowing of his wife's death, McIntyre walked out of the field hospital with the aid of a cane, and boarded a ship for home. Only in April 1915, when he was met at the train station in London by his eldest son, George, did McIntyre learn that Annie had taken her own life.

After three months at home, McIntyre was back on the road again. A three-year-contract with the Burma Oil Company would take him back to that British colony, where he stayed until retirement in 1930.

Wartime Observations

Rumours of sabotage and close calls at sea filled the pages of local newspapers as Lambton drillers moved to and from the foreign fields during the First World War. On 15 March 1915, the *Oil City Derrick* recounted the wartime tensions observed by driller Tom Ivison, who was home in Petrolia from his work in Borneo.

In December 1914, said Ivison, Royal Dutch Shell feared sabotage in its Borneo fields and refineries, so all the known Germans in the Dutch colony were rounded up and interned. (The same thing happened in the British colony of Singapore, where German citizens had their businesses confiscated.)

The trip from Borneo to Java, normally six days, was extended to eleven days, due to the wartime conditions, Ivison said. At one port in Sumatra, he counted sixteen German merchant ships and another twenty Austrian ships, laden with goods, tied up in the harbour to avoid capture by the British. He heard of two German spies and a wireless operator being captured by the British and shot. Another German jumped out of a third-storey window to avoid capture, and was killed.

While travelling through the Suez Canal, Ivison watched thousands of New Zealand troops waiting to do battle with the Turks. Ports were guarded with gunboats and torpedo boats. Lights were doused throughout the canal, and the ship's pilot's bridge was built up with sandbags to stop stray bullets. Passengers were ordered below deck and portholes darkened with cushions, curtains, and blankets.

Ivison saw gunboats at every station along the canal and, on the Egyptian side, trenches were heavily fortified. He witnessed a skirmish where Turks and Germans tried to cross the canal but were thwarted by the British.

The Bay of Biscay was filled with German submarines, and the passengers watched as a Norwegian craft was sunk, he said. Those on Ivison's boat were told to put on life preservers in case of attack. Ivison's two-hundred-and-eighty-five-pound bulk required the fashioning of a special preserver, but it was never needed.

The same edition of the *Derrick* reported that two Lambton drillers had returned a few days earlier from Borneo, and in mid-ocean their ship had been challenged by a German armoured merchantman. The ship fled and the Germans abandoned the pursuit.

But Where was Santa?

Christmas 1922 in Borneo was described by an anonymous writer to the *Advertiser-Topic*: "Christmas Day itself was much as it is at home but without the cold and snow. Church in the afternoon, dancing early in the evening at the Rest House, and then everyone off to the various dinner parties, music, song and story, until the wee small hours of the morning."[273]

The Canadian contingent in Southeast Asia made Christmas as much like home as possible without the snow. The young participants in a 1929 Christmas concert at Miri, in Sarawak, Borneo, show off their costumes.
Courtesy Murray Brown, Petrolia.

A Young Woman's Adventure

Margaret Scott was the daughter of a Lambton oil inspector. She was just nineteen, a clerk in a Detroit insurance company office, when Ray Gregory asked her to marry him and accompany him to Trinidad where he had a job offer to drill for oil.[274]

Margaret was doubtful her parents would ever agree, but she thought her young man might have a better chance with her father than with her mother. So she advised Ray to wait until her mother was out, and broach the subject with John Scott.

Ray Gregory had come from an oil family. His father, George, had drilled in Borneo, Burma, Persia, and Sumatra, leaving his wife at home to raise three boys and a girl. With the local petroleum business dying, it was natural that Ray looked to the foreign fields for employment.

To Margaret's surprise, John Scott said it was all right with him if the young couple got married. Now she felt she had to say yes. Before long, they were married and living in Trinidad, in a house built on stilts that were dipped in creosote to keep insects out. Food had to be kept in tin cans surrounded by water and creosote.

"The cockroaches were so big, we used to call them Trinidad canaries," she said. "I'd go into hysterics when I saw one."

The $375 a month Ray Gregory earned was a lot of money then, Margaret Scott Gregory said. Along with that ,they received free accommodation, utilities and transportation. There was a clubhouse next door, where Margaret loved to play the piano.

"White ladies [from the camp] didn't go shopping," she said. "You sent your servants. I said, 'how do I know what they've got in the store?' I said, 'I'm just going to go because I don't know what I want'."

One day, she recalled, Ray returned home. "He said, 'get in the car, I've found something.' There was a pond or little lake, and the fish were just jumping. We thought the fish were going to be easy to catch with our hands, but they weren't."

Margaret Gregory's first child, Marion, was born in Trinidad in 1922. Soon after, they moved to Venezuela where Ray got a job with Royal Dutch Shell. The homes were of poured cement and sat on the ground rather than the stilts of Trinidad, with the servants' quarters in a separate building at the back.

Hard Oiler!

Pass the Medical Bag

Not only were the Canadians jacks-of-all-trades, sometimes they were called on for medical assistance, too. In 1898 R.W. Laird wrote home from Sumatra.

> "I have fifty-seven men to look after. Five of them are policemen. In the morning they all sit down in rows around me and I count them to see they are all up. Then I give each one his work for the day. I will be able to write 'doctor' after my name when I get home, for I have to play at that here. There were three had fever, so I gave two quinine and the other one castor oil, and it cured them."[275]

Apparently, while there was a doctor not far away, the men were afraid to go to him because they might lose a day's pay. "There was not very much the matter with them, or I guess they would be beyond my skill," Laird wrote.

A Poet's Touch

Although many of the foreign drillers received a minimum of schooling, some were quite poetic in their descriptions of what they encountered. James Alexander Rowe was on his way to Java in 1899 when he penned these words about the Mediterranean Sea: "It is very striking. As far as the eye can reach, the water is the colour of sky and one feels the very job of being alive."[276]

In the Suez Canal, despite the British warships engaging in target practice, Rowe had time to note: "The first thing to attract our attention is the myriad of flamingos in the marshes near the canal. They assemble on the water systematically and do not look unlike a regiment of tiny white soldiers."

Canned Butter, Again

An anonymous writer from among the Canadian contingent in Sumatra wrote home about the food in 1899.[277] Nearly everything came in cans, he lamented, including corned beef, salmon, kippered herring, soup, condensed milk, and butter ("not very nice"). However, they enjoyed a daily feed of fresh chicken, cooked in every way imaginable. It was the only meat they had, although there were potatoes, bread, tea, and coffee. And every day they had pudding or fruit cake. The writer marveled at the cook, who prepared their food over an open fire.

The One that Got Away

The same writer told of how a snake got after the chickens. The men got a rifle because the reptile was so large they feared a revolver would not be sufficient. It escaped their first effort to kill it, but it returned.

They wounded the snake but again they did not kill it. This time it took after them, "causing us to make tracks toward the house with the snake following closely. The men with the guns made a stand and fired at his head, but only succeeded in tearing another hole in his side, and he came at us again and got into the coolie boys' room where he was shot to death." [278]

The beast measured in at 3.5 metres (eleven feet) long and 10 centimetres (four inches) in diametre. The Chinese staff had a feast of it, undoubtedly grateful for the change from chicken. The Canadians, apparently, did not share their enthusiasm.

About the Arabian Pirates ...

Jokes and pranks were commonplace in the oil business. From the squirting of William H. McGarvey's new suit and leather-seated carriage, to the Halloween prank of plugging the exhaust of a pump engine, Hard Oilers would be Hard Oilers.

The jokesters were loose in the foreign fields, too. Chatham journalist and writer Victor Lauriston told the tale of two young drillers on their first voyage through the Suez Canal. The boat moved south through the canal, and as night fell, it rounded Cape Ammel in southern Arabia. All day, the veteran drillers speculated, for the young men's benefit, on the chance of attack from "Arab pirates." [279]

At darkness, the vessel crept across a smooth sea. Suddenly, over the side of the ship emerged several men armed with axes, pikes, and cutlasses. With blood-curdling yells, they rushed the passengers, the veterans among them running for cover. But the two younger men stood their ground, one of them grabbing a heavy iron bar and belting an invader behind the ear. The assailants unexpectedly turned and ran, vanishing over the side.

Strangely, the only victim was one of the ship's sailors, who nursed a sore head where he had obtained a bump, he said, "trying to drive off the pirates." After, the two young men could not recall any of the sailors helping out during the brief skirmish.

This story was recounted in a letter sent home and published in one of the Petrolia newspapers. Someone sent a copy to the Anglo-Persian Oil Company where officials were left scratching their heads. They had heard nothing of such an incident from official sources, and knew nothing of the so-called Arab pirates. The officials called on the man whose name had been attached to the letter, but when he stood before them, he just stared at them blankly. The man insisted he had never written such a letter.

The "pirate" attack was written off as a little initiation rite for the two young foreign drillers.

... But Sometimes they were Real

From a letter from Miri, in Sarawak, Borneo, published in the *Advertiser-Topic* 13 March 1926:

> There have been three steamers attacked by pirates while under British officers and a good many lives have been lost in the last four years, besides numerous native craft [being lost]. Holdups in true western style and murders are common affairs. Have had a little touch myself [with pirates] on my last vacation — but who would not live out here. There is about as much notice taken of [the pirates] as there is of a driller returning to Petrolia after being away for from three to twenty years, and travelling 14,000 miles to be in time for an Old Boys' Reunion.
> — signed, Just a Driller

Part Five
The Legacy of Oil

"This is where it started. This is the kickoff to the twentieth century, our whole modern age."
— Charles Fairbank, 19 December 1997, author's interview.

.

Chapter Fourteen
Farewell to the Barons

When Imperial Oil, by this time under Standard Oil's control, closed its Petrolia headquarters and moved to Sarnia in 1898, it took one-third of the town's economy and part of its soul with it. The founding of the Canadian Oil Refining Company in Petrolia a few years later helped somewhat to revitalize the town's economy, but did little to repair the soul. Then, as the first decade of the new century unfolded, the old oil fields grew tired, and their production slackened. By 1910, wells were being regularly shut down, and another third of Petrolia's economy went with them.[280]

While refining was on the rise in Sarnia, oil production was in definite decline in Lambton County. A few wells continued to disgorge crude, but more and more of what the pumps brought to the surface was the accursed brackish water. As time went by, the water choked off more and more wells.

With his large holdings, however, John Henry Fairbank continued to enjoy a profit from oil, although his income from them certainly declined. Most of his other enterprises fared well, although an attempt to diversify the town's economy further by opening a wagon-works business was one of his few failures.[281] Wagons were in considerably less demand by this time, because automobiles were fuelled by one of Fairbank's other products.

Edna Fairbank, who had become much respected and admired by Petrolians for her numerous charitable endeavours, died in 1896.[282] In 1912 Fairbank's own health began to fail, and in February 1914 he died.[283] On the day of his funeral, businesses closed in tribute as hundreds turned out to pay their respects, flags were dropped to half staff, and the town band played the Death March.

A newspaper obituary noted that to some he might have appeared cold and reserved, but those who knew John Henry understood that was

WINTER SCENE ON THE FLATS, PETROLIA, ONT., 20 YEARS AGO.

Behind this peaceful winter scene, trouble brewed for Petrolia in the early 1900s. Oil wells ceased producing, Imperial Oil's refinery was moved to Sarnia, and the golden age of petroleum was drawing to a close. But the trappings of success remained. On the hill, the third building from the left is Sunnyside, the Fairbank mansion, which remains to this day a symbol of the town's Victorian-era oil heritage. **Courtesy Lambton County Heritage Museum.**

only his business face. Fairbank had showed a steady hand at the helm of a family enterprise that had required a clear head and quick actions in times of trouble, it said. He survived the experience with few scars and a "princely pile" of worldly goods to his name.

In Vienna, word of Fairbank's death came to a still-healthy William Henry McGarvey. Healthy perhaps, but the Canadian-born Petroleum King of Austria was growing increasingly distraught over the dark war clouds that threatened his family and his business concerns. McGarvey, himself, became increasingly despondent and ill later in the year, and on his seventy-first birthday in November 1914, he died.[284]

For McGarvey, however, there would be no spectacular funeral, no great outpouring of public sentiment back in Petrolia. Divided from his Lambton home by thousands of kilometres and the cruel fate of politics, there were just short notices of his many amazing accomplishments in the Canadian newspapers.

Yet McGarvey's death, like that of Fairbank, hit some very hard. One such man was another of the oil barons, Jacob Englehart. Many of the pioneers, most of whom he had known, had died within a few short years, and he had also lost his wife, Charlotte, in 1908. He remained on the board of directors of Imperial even past retirement age. Then, after a short illness in 1921, and after more than fifty-five years in Canadian oil, Englehart died.[285]

At his funeral were the cream of Lambton society as well as the political and business movers and shakers of the province. A special train was chartered to carry the body and mourners from Toronto to Petrolia, for the service and burial. At the funeral, an address was delivered by the Anglican bishop of Huron. To Englehart, said the bishop, success in business was never an end in itself, but rather a means to an end. He was interested chiefly in humanitarian endeavours, and was known as a great public servant above his calling of businessman.

The three men — Fairbank, McGarvey and Englehart — created a sort of triumvirate of Hard Oilers. There were certainly many other important and well-known people who contributed to the building of the Canadian oil business. Charles Nelson Tripp and James Miller Williams, for instance, were crucial in its early stages. But these three were somehow special, standing out from their colleagues and competitors for their longevity and far-reaching influence.

Fairbank had demonstrated an initial success in oil production and had then diversified his enterprises to encompass most significant aspects of life in Lambton County. He was the beloved leader of a community who frequently and quietly leant a hand to those in trouble. He had immersed himself in the mercantile, social, and cultural life of central Lambton, never swaying from his unbridled confidence in the community. Declining all opportunities to expand his influence and wealth beyond that community, he was truly one of the great small-town entrepreneurs of nineteenth-century Canada.

McGarvey looked not just beyond Lambton but beyond Canada to cement his reputation as a great oil man. His acumen for finding and developing oil made him very wealthy. Yet he never lost touch with the people who depended on him for their livelihoods. The huge party that his employees — Canadian and European alike — threw for him and his wife, Helena, on their twenty-fifth wedding anniversary demonstrated the respect and love they held for him.

Englehart was the refining genius. But not only did he know refining, he knew human nature, and he was an organizing wizard. Before he masterminded the formation of Imperial Oil, each previous attempt to bring the refiners together had failed. He was the one who finally convinced the disparate refining factions that their future was in cooperation, and then he worked as Imperial's vice-president to keep them together. And he, too, as the outpouring of community sentiment at his funeral demonstrated, never forgot the people who helped him achieve success.

None of the three avoided misfortune. McGarvey lived just long enough to watch his empire begin to crumble under the weight of war. Englehart must certainly have felt bitterness in watching his old nemesis, John D. Rockefeller, consume his beloved Imperial. And even Fairbank, who had chosen to remain closer to home than his fellow Hard Oilers, suffered a huge financial loss from the wagon-works enterprise. Each also lived to see the death of his wife, women who in each case had contributed significantly not only to their husbands' business successes, but to their families' reputations as generous, public-spirited, and leaders in their communities.

In total, each was a builder in his own way and in his own particular sphere of influence. Each had adopted the oil patch rather than being born into it. Each had been born in extremely humble means, and each had parlayed a very small amount into a great personal fortune. Each had created opportunities for great numbers of others to earn a living and benefit from the products they manufactured. And each remained, to the end, respected for their dignified and honourable approach to the business world and their deeply held belief that they owed much to the people who had helped them obtain their success.

In a hall of fame of Hard Oilers, these three men would stand ahead of all others because, in their quest for oil, they did more to build a new industry whose global reach spans beyond that of all others today.

During their lifetimes, these Hard Oilers had watched tremendous change take place, and had been responsible for much of it. In 1861 Fairbank had arrived in Oil Springs when the village was a wild, grease-smeared collection of bumptious saloons, rustic frame buildings, and oil-spattered fortune-seekers. He had laboured over primitive cauldrons of bubbling bitumen and been intelligent enough to fear for his own safety amid the open flames and volatile kerosenes and gases.

From those humble beginning, he introduced the jerker-rod system that combined many wells to a single power-source and he was the first to try floating barrels of crude down the Sydenham River to ships in Lake St. Clair. Fairbank became a leader among the oil producers and in bettering their business prospects through cooperation of their efforts, he contributed to the overall wealth and well-being of his community.

Edna Fairbank, initially reticent to move to the Lambton frontier that reeked of oil, eventually embraced her new home wholeheartedly. She became known as a diligent worker for the welfare of the poor, and she contributed to the social, religious, and cultural wealth of the community.

McGarvey branched out from his Mammoth Store in the 1860s, determined to learn the oil business, and he soon mastered the Canadian or pole-tool drilling system. Then he was astute enough to understand, when he went to Galicia, that the problems oil hunters experienced there were not rooted in the ground, but in their methods of drilling. He applied what he had learned in the Lambton fields, built refineries, and helped Austria-Hungary become self-sufficient, even a net exporter of oil.

Helena McGarvey, while content to let her husband enjoy the limelight, was active in the social and cultural affairs of the time. She presented herself as a perfect partner to her husband, helping in his early political activities, and then, later, to solidify his position as a well-rounded businessman.

When Englehart opened his first Canadian business in London, Ontario, he donned his dandy duds and went out, himself, to the Lambton fields and knocked on doors in search of crude to run his refinery. Later, he oversaw huge technical improvements in those refineries, that which not only enhanced the quality of the finished product, but turned the refineries from the highly unstable facilities that initially and frequently blew up, into places where safety was valued. He was one of the first to understand the importance of assuring a happy, productive workforce that did not need to fear constantly for their well-being amid the explosive materials with which they worked.

Charlotte Eleanor Englehart was truly adored by the town of Petrolia for her never-ending works of kindness and generosity. Even before she won the heart of Petrolia's most eligible bachelor, she determined to immerse herself in church and civic affairs. Known affectionately as Minnie to her legions of friends, she was president of the local relief fund. Noted for a generous nature, on her wedding day she presented each of her bridesmaids with a diamond ring. And she decided to invite the town's residents, once a year, to pick flowers from her extensive Glenview gardens, to place as memorials on the graves of loved ones.

In the approximately six decades between the time James Miller Williams began manufacturing oil products, to the deaths of Fairbank, McGarvey, and Englehart, the business of oil had undergone a monumental revolution. Before the time of the Hard Oilers, petroleum was scooped up in ladles or sopped up in woolen blankets from where it seeped to the surface or pooled in shallow pits. It was poured into little medicine bottles for internal use, slapped on the outside of wooden vessels and barrels to prevent leakage, or dabbed on cuts and wounds to fight infection and entice healing.

Initially, the Hard Oilers chipped it out of the "gum beds" with picks and shovels, boiled it down, and formed it into blocks to asphalt roads in Paris. Then they scooped it up in barrels or pumped it up by hand from wells that were at first hand-dug, then "punched" through the rock with crude percussion drills that pounded their way downwards.

Then horses were used, and then steam engines, in the drilling and pumping of the oil. Instead of refining the crude in makeshift stills that sat in the fields, plants were built, and the crude was hauled there for refining. New products were imagined and developed; new uses were created for crude, as fuel for cars and ships.

New drilling instruments were invented, new tools for repairing damaged equipment and wells. After the turn of the century, geology began to enjoy increasing respect as a method of better judging where oil would be found. Oil began to be moved from source to refinery in pipelines, and it was shipped in railway tanker-cars, and ships were built specially to transport it on the high seas.

New methods and practices were learned from the mistakes made in Lambton's oil fields. For instance, the pioneer Hard Oilers believed that by drilling more wells, they would increase total production. They believed there was a nearly endless supply of crude oil waiting to be tapped, and the more wells that were dug, the more oil could be pumped. Out of that Lambton experience, oil men learned that all they accomplished was to let the natural gas escape, which could have helped push the oil to the surface. The Lambton fields were a testing ground for the oil industry; lessons learned the hard way there became lessons applied in fields all over the globe.[286]

A stack of oil barrels at a Petrolia refinery.
Courtesy Oil Museum of Canada.

All this occurred in the lifetimes of these three key Hard Oilers. When they began, the business of oil was still very much in the purview of the hard-bitten individual who learned by doing, who got his hands greasy every day, and who risked his life to find oil and bring it to market. As twilight fell on their careers and their lives, it was becoming a business of large corporations and of professionally trained people who drew up maps and charts to tell them where crude would likely be found.

Their passing, within a brief seven years of one another, just after the Ontario oil fields had largely played themselves out, represented the closing of an era. But their existence and experiences contributed significantly to the development of an industry that remains so crucial to our modern world's way of life.

Chapter Fifteen
Looking Ahead

As you stand in the hollow, out back of Charles Oliver Fairbank's home in Oil Springs, you find yourself in the very spot where Hugh Nixon Shaw's big gusher of 1862 came in. Right here, at the edge of the village of Oil Springs, is where Shaw, nearly penniless and laughed at as the "insane Yankee," determined that he would punch down into the rock just one more day.

And right here, in what is now Charles Fairbank's backyard, is where a great roar began deep in the bowels of the earth. It thundered and shook the ground, as a pillar of crude oil shot skywards to escape its rock vault, and poured over the landscape on that January day. Four years after James Miller Williams struck free-flowing oil, this was Ontario's first gusher. The oil filled this hollow, flowed down Black Creek and the Sydenham River, and then emptied into Lake St. Clair.

Right here. On this spot.

By the time that happened, Charles Fairbank's great-grandfather, John Henry Fairbank, had been in the oil business for several months. And through John Henry's son Charles, to his son Charles, and now finally to Charles Oliver III, the family torch has been passed. It is too soon to know whether the world's oldest continuously operating oil company will pass to a fifth generation of Fairbank children. It will be up to his children to make that decision, on their own, Fairbank says.

In the 1960s, Charles Fairbank III was a science teacher who had gone away to work near Toronto, and his father wanted to sell out because he thought it was a dying business. When young Charlie returned to Lambton at the age of thirty-two, he just got hooked. "You have to taste the oil before you get infected," he says.

Today he has 318 wells, each producing an average of one-fifth of a barrel of oil a day.[287] That amounts to about sixty-three barrels a day, or over 22,000 barrels a year. Oil isn't Charles Fairbank's only business — he has sixty acres of soybeans and about a hundred sheep, and still runs the Van Tuyl & Fairbank hardware in Petrolia, started by his great-grandfather in 1865. But oil is Fairbank's passion.

There is a sparkle in his eye, a reverence in his voice, as Fairbank talks about what it all means. "The biggest industry that we have in the world right now is the petroleum industry. It's made the kind of lives that we live now, possible. This is where it started. This was the kickoff to the twentieth century, our whole modern age. It started right here."

He pauses, casts a paternal gaze over the fields of which he considers himself less the owner than the current guardian. Quietly, respectfully, he continues: "That's the importance of this place. It's absolutely magnificent that something that started it all, would still be going on today."

Fairbank is the largest of about thirty producers in the historic fields of Ontario. Even with the Oil Well Supply Company and Baines Machine Shop, with oil-well repairman Ken Girard, the oil haulers, and the other workers employed in the business, it is a small industry. Yet those who love the business and the heritage it represents are a determined lot, and they have worked hard to maintain its visibility, at least locally.

It is a rich heritage. You see it represented in the two museums that maintain a friendly rivalry — the Oil Museum of Canada in Oil Springs and the Petrolia Discovery site, a working oil field.

You see it on the street signs: Gum Bed Line in Oil Springs; Discovery Line and Eureka Street in Petrolia; The Plank Road, which connects Petrolia and Sarnia; the Oil Heritage Road, a former provincial highway, which connects Petrolia and Oil Springs to the nearby throughway, Highway 402.

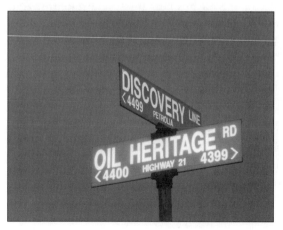

Remembering Lambton's petroleum past: the corner of Discovery Line and Oil Heritage Road in Petrolia.
Courtesy Gary May.

You see it in the names of Oozloffsky, Ignatiefna, and Valentina Streets, named by a former Petrolia mayor and developer, A.C. Edward, in honour of people he had met as a foreign driller.[288]

You see it in the buildings that remain to tell you something of Petrolia's glorious and rich past: Victoria Hall, which was rebuilt after fire destroyed it a few years ago; Charlotte Eleanor Englehart Hospital, the former home of Charlotte and Jake Englehart; the Little Red Bank, which survives as a lawyers' office; the Van Tuyl & Fairbank hardware store; Baines Machine Shop; the Oil Well Supply Company; Crescent Park; Nemo Hall; and perhaps the most magnificent home ever built by the oil barons, Sunnyside, known locally as the old Fairbank mansion.

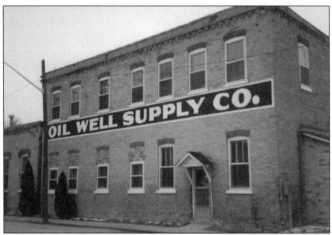

More than 100 years after its predecessor was founded, the Oil Well Supply Company still does business in Petrolia, and still occasionally sends drilling and oil well supplies to distant corners of the globe.
Courtesy Gary May.

You see it in the murals depicting the story of oil, which are painted on buildings, and oil tanks, and the sides of barns.

You see it in the pump-jacks that dot the landscape, and the names of Marthaville and Oil City.

And you see it in the twinkling lights and cracking towers, and in the tanks of Chemical Valley along the St. Clair River.

For the Petrolia weekly newspaper, there was a legacy too. In the days when foreign drillers travelled the globe, the *Advertiser-Topic* went too, both in the reporting of news of Hard Oilers' adventures, and in the circulating of the publication to distant lands. Slowly, as the old drillers came home and few left to replace them, the newspaper's overseas circulation dwindled until 1962 when its last Borneo subscriber died.[289] The woman whom the Hard Oiler had married there could not read English.

There are less sterling examples of the heritage of oil, too. Along with the romantic past of exploration and riches have come the troubles associated with cleaning up the messes, such as the chemical "blob" that sat at the bottom of the St. Clair River some years ago.

Inevitably, it seems, one of the consequences arising from our dependence on products made from oil is the degradation of the environment. Soon after humans began to capture and refine petroleum, the waste started to foul the surrounding wilderness. From the recollections of an early Oil Springs resident of the black sludge in the waters of Black Creek, to stories of crude from early gushers flooding the landscape, and millions of litres of the black stuff flowing down the waterways into Lake St. Clair, oil made a mess of the environment.

In modern times, the consequences have grown more grave. On the morning of 3 December 1984, in Bhopal, India, a pesticide plant leaked a highly toxic cloud of methyl isocyanate into the atmosphere. Of the 800,000 people living in Bhopal at the time, 2,000 died immediately, 300,000 were injured, and as many as 8,000 have died since. Five years after the accident, studies showed that survivors suffered from one or more ailments that included: partial or complete blindness, gastrointestinal disorders, impaired immune systems, stress disorders, and menstrual problems. A rise in spontaneous abortions, stillbirths, and offspring with genetic defects was also noted. Lamentably, that is also part of the heritage of oil.

In reaction to what is now infamous as one of the world's worst industrial disasters, the United Nations Environment Program (UNEP) created the Awareness and Preparedness for Emergencies at Local Level (APELL) program. APELL was designed to improve public awareness of possible hazards within communities, encourage plans to respond to emergencies, and promote accident prevention. Among the founders and early participants in APPEL's work were officials from Sarnia's Chemical Valley. So, in the birthplace of the modern oil industry, we also saw the establishment of solutions for dealing with the problems it created, says Allen Wells, Lambton's administrator of community awareness response for APELL.

Certainly there is room to remember the quest for oil in a more grand fashion, too. For all the effort and dedication put into preservation of the story by the volunteers and staff at the Oil Museum of Canada and at Petrolia's Discovery site, it is simply not enough. All one need do is travel to the other side of Lake Erie, to Titusville, Pennsylvania, to see what an infusion of cash and a simple plan can accomplish. Its excellent museum and interpretive centre is a far more fitting way to preserve the history than the shoe-string operations in Lambton that are left to the limited finances of the county historical society, local government, and a small band of tireless and determined history buffs.

In total, Ontario's wells have produced an estimated seventy-one million barrels of crude since James Miller Williams and Charles Nelson Tripp dug their first well in 1858.[290] Of that amount, 9.7 million barrels came out of the Oil Springs field and another 17.8 million from the Petrolia field. Those 27.5 million barrels, nearly forty per cent of all Ontario's crude, came from those two historic fields.

Canadians should be proud and take heed of the part their ancestors played in the founding and development of this crucial industry. And the petroleum companies, too, should take a far greater interest in letting more people know where it all began. For in this day of squeezed public finances, we cannot expect governments to open their wallets and hand over thousands to those two tiny museums.

What is needed is a joint government-and corporate-led campaign to create a first-rate interpretive centre that encompasses both the oil museum and the working oil field. Resources are needed to catalogue and file the myriad boxes of letters, diaries, clippings, photographs, scrapbooks, notes, documents, and other materials that exist, but which will some day deteriorate to the point of uselessness unless action is taken soon. What more fitting memorial could there be to the lives of John Henry Fairbank, James Miller Williams, Charles Nelson Tripp, Hugh Nixon Shaw, Jacob Englehart, William Henry McGarvey and the dozens of other Hard Oilers than a centre for the study and understanding of their pioneering work?

An expanded Hall of Fame at the museum could tell the stories of these petroleum pioneers. Dioramas could depict the significant events: the first well, the Shaw gusher, and the departure of the first foreign drillers. A library — perhaps at the old Fairbank mansion — could preserve the priceless documents that are now in boxes. Summer-student guides dressed in period costume could show visitors through the only working oil field in Canada that's open to the public. Maybe add a replica of the old Imperial Oil refinery of the 1890s. And a re-creation of the wild and woolly main street of Oil Springs that was once traversed by omnibuses day and night.

The jack-pumps that keep hundreds of wells operating in the historic fields are part of the oil heritage too. These Devonian-age oil fields now produce about 75,000 barrels a year. To put that into perspective,

Ontario's total annual oil production is about 1.7 million barrels — most comes from new wells drilled in deeper Ordovician-age rock formations — and even that accounts for the equivalent of just one day's production in Alberta.

Geologist Terry Carter of the Ontario Ministry of Natural Resources estimates that the seventy-one million barrels of oil and 1.1 trillion cubic feet of natural gas taken thus far from Ontario wells represents about half of all the oil and gas that is recoverable. It's impressive, Carter says, to have a business still operating on such a healthy footing, 140 years after it began.

Ontario oil production peaked in 1995 when 1.8 million barrels were pumped, and revenues peaked the following year at $47 million, Carter says. He credits improved seismic technology, which more accurately identifies new sources and reduces the risk in what still remains a very risky venture.

But the buoyancy and healthy glow is entirely within the deep-well business. No one expects the old wells, some of which have been pumping for more than one hundred years, to suddenly begin to produce great quantities again.

The economics of the old oil in Lambton are based in large part on whether it makes financial sense to get rid of the pesky water that accompanies it. As a barrel of oil is pumped from the ground, a barrel of water flows in to take its place. As more and more oil is removed from the reservoir, more water flows in. Eventually, the amount of water is so great that it becomes prohibitively expensive to pump oil. When the price the producers obtain for their crude is too low, the trouble and cost of dealing with the water makes the wells unprofitable, and they are shut down.

Environmental costs of the old wells are significant. Until recent years, the producers just separated the oil from the water and let the water run back onto the land. But that's not environmentally acceptable today. The water is salty and filled with suspended clay. Now the water has to be pumped into a settling tank, where the suspended particles separate. The water then is pumped back down into the earth to a depth of about one hundred and twenty metres, cleaner than it was when it was pumped to the surface.

For Charles Fairbank, the need to dispose of all the water, the large number of wells, which individually produce very little oil, and the maintenance, electricity, and hauling costs means the expense of producing one barrel of oil from the historic fields is about $20 a barrel. Since producers are paid on the basis of "sweetness" (sulphur content) and the lightness of the oil, the producers in the historic field receive a bit less per barrel than do their counterparts whose crude comes from the modern, deeper wells and which is lighter and lower in sulphur. The historic well operators' enterprises are very sensitive to the price they receive for their crude.

In the 1970s when the Persian Gulf crisis boosted prices, new producers were enticed back to the historic fields, andthey opened long-closed wells by infusing them with water to get the oil flowing again. Another price boost would likely do the same thing, says London, Ontario, oil- and- gas consultant Bob Cochrane. "There will always be oil," Cochrane says. But the price at which it's available will go up because all the big fields have been found."

Having said that, Cochrane worries that even substantially higher prices may not be enough and that, over time, the producers will dwindle in number. "The work is really hard. It's a miserable, horrible job being out there in the cold of winter and the heat of summer. It's a different kind of mentality than with the modern industry. I don't know how appealing it is to young people."

Because the fact is, the mystery is gone. The adventure has been all used up. The fortunes have been made. The howling swamp has been tamed. The thrill of discovery is no more. The only job remaining is to make sure Canadians do not forget the Hard Oilers and their quest for oil.

Appendices

APPENDIX I
A Chronology in the Quest for Oil

1827 — Lambton County is part of the lands the Chippewa Indians cede for settlement.

1838 — Samuel Eveland settles in what will later be Petrolia.

1842 — The Geological Survey of Canada is established.

1846 — Nova Scotian Abraham Gesner demonstrates that kerosene can be made from asphalt.

1850 — James Young obtains patents on a process to obtain illuminating oil, lubricating oil and paraffin wax from coals and oil shales, from which the name "coal oil" issues.

1851 — Henry and Charles Tripp arrive in the Oil Springs area, planning to mine gum beds.

1852 — Henry and Charles Tripp apply for a manufacturing charter. They buy up lands and start manufacturing asphalt as an experiment.

1854 — A charter is granted to the Tripp brothers under the International Mining and Manufacturing Company name. In the United States, Abraham Gesner founds the North American Kerosene Gas and Light Company on Long Island, to produce lighting oil.

1855 — The Tripp brothers' asphalt exhibit gets honourable mention at the Universal Exhibition in Paris.

1856 — Charles Tripp sells the first of his holdings and soon must unload the rest to pay debts. One property is bought by a group that includes James Miller Williams of Hamilton, who chooses to dig for oil rather than boil the asphalt. Railway construction helps to open up southwestern Ontario.

1857 — Williams and Tripp dig a well in Bothwell, but they fail to find oil.

1858 — In August, Williams strikes oil at his hand-dug Oil Springs well, sets up a refinery and begins to market the product; thus the first integrated commercial oil operation in the world commences. Decimal currency replaces sterling in Canada. The Great Western Railway extends a branch past the oil lands to Sarnia.

1859 — Williams sinks deeper wells. One is thirty metres into the bedrock, making it the first rock oil well, and the world's attention turns to Oil Springs. In August in Titusville, Pennsylvania, Colonel Edwin Drake strikes oil and that country's oil industry is born. Whereas Williams dug his first well, Drake drilled his, leading to the American claim that they can boast the first "drilled" commercial oil well.

1860 — Canada's first flowing surface well is found at Oil Springs. By the end of the year Williams has taken out between 200,000 and 400,000 gallons. More wildcatters arrive, including surveyor John Henry Fairbank who soon turns his attention to oil. Williams advertises illuminating oil for 70 cents a gallon, machine oil for 60 cents, and starts selling crude in bulk. Drillers begin to look for oil near Petrolia.

1861 — Hugh Nixon Shaw is one of the early wildcatters and begins drilling deeper than anyone ever has before. The Oil Springs *Chronicle* is founded.

1862 — On 16 January, Shaw hits the region's first gusher. More wells follow, land prices spiral, untapped oil flows across the landscape and into the creeks and rivers. Oil sells for $1 at the well. By the end of the year 1,000 wells produce 12,000 barrels a day, teamsters haul 500 loads a day to Wyoming, ten refineries are in the fields. Williams wins awards in London, England, for being the first to produce crude and refined oils.

1863 — In January, heavy production sharply reduces prices. Salt water begins choking off the oil flow. The Oil Springs *Chronicle* calls for deep tests but less spectacular wells are found and production remains high.

1864 — This second oil reserve dwindles while kerosene demand increases, and the price of crude climbs to $4 a barrel. Jacob L. Englehart opens the Baltic Works in London, converted later to the London Refining Co. In the United States, John D. Rockefeller acquires his first refinery.

1865 — By the end of the year crude is $11 a barrel. A Chicago firm builds a 108-room hotel in Oil Springs and the village population nears 4,000. Drillers have started wells in Bothwell and more in Petrolia.

1866 — The Civil War has ended and Fenians threaten Canada, frightening American workers out of Oil Springs. Oil is struck in Petrolia, Pennsylvania wells begin full production again, and attention switches from Oil Springs. Oil Springs's population drops to 300, the field is nearly empty. The Great Western Railroad builds a branch line to Petrolia.

1867 — Overproduction at Petrolia and Pennsylvania keeps prices low. A huge fire at a Petrolia well in August spreads across oil fields and burns for days.

1870 — Sixty percent of Canadian oil production is exported. In the United States, John D. Rockefeller forms Standard Oil and captures most of the market, while the Canadian industry remains fragmented.

1871 — Sarnia's first refinery is built.

1872 — A disastrous fire in March consumes much of downtown Petrolia. Crude prices are falling in Canada.

1873 — Depression in Canada and U.S. competition cut Canadian exports.

Near the end of the year, the first foreign drillers leave for Java.

1874 — Petrolians are sent to western Canada to explore for oil, but results are disappointing.

1879 — Count Carlo Ribighini hires Lambton drillers to look for oil in Italy.

1880 — In September, Imperial Oil is founded at London by a group of London refiners, and Petrolia's Jake Englehart.

1881 — John S. Bergheim and William H. McGarvey begin searching for oil in Germany. While they fail, an important new partnership is formed.

1883 — When fire destroys Imperial's London refinery, the company moves its headquarters to Petrolia. Bergheim and McGarvey begin making oil strikes in the Austrian province of Galicia. Another short-lived oil boom hits Oil Springs.

1886 — Gottlieb Daimler makes the first gasoline engine, which Carl Benz fastens to a tricycle mounting, and the first automobile is born.

1888 — The Victoria Playhouse is built in Petrolia, starting a building boom that sees new oil barons' mansions and other substantial buildings constructed.

1891 — The use of crude oil and oil by-products has spiralled and Petrolia is declared the biggest manufacturing town per capita in Canada.

1898 — Imperial sells a majority interest to Rockefeller's Standard Oil in exchange for expansion capital. The company leaves Petrolia, moving its headquarters and its primary refinery to Sarnia.

1901 — The Canadian Oil Refining Company is formed, and a refinery is built in Petrolia, temporarily resurrecting the town's economic prospects.

1906 — Lambton oil production is in serious decline. Producers begin to close down many wells.

1908 — Canada's first gasoline service station is opened in Vancouver.

1910 — Most old oil wells have been closed as production falls and salt water chokes off the flow of crude.

1914 — John Henry Fairbank and William McGarvey die.

1921 — Jake Englehart, last remaining founding director of Imperial Oil, dies.

1952 — Canadian Oil Refining moves to Corunna near Sarnia. Petrolia's last refinery is gone.

APPENDIX II

Typical Foreign Drillers Contract:
A contract between W.O. Gillespie, of Petrolia, Ontario, and the Bataafsche Petroleum Maatschappij, of The Hague

Agree as follows:

1. The party of the first part enters into the service of the company for (three years) commencing with the date of arrival of the steamer in the first port of the Dutch Indian Archipelago or in Singapore and binds himself to do any work, which he may be ordered to do by one of the Managers, the Head

Administrator, or the Administrators, to the best of his knowledge and ability.

2. The party of the second part reserves itself the right to employ the party of the first part not only in her own service, but if so desired, also in that of one of the allied companies, viz:

a) De Koninklyke Nederlandsche Maatschappy tot Exploitatie van Petroleum-bronnen in Nederlandsche-Indie, having its registered office at The Hague.

b) De Nederlandsche-Indische Industrie — en Handel Maatschappy, having its registered office at The Hague.

c) De Dordtsche Petroleum-Maatschappy, having its registered office at The Hague.

3. The party of the second part shall pay to the party of the first part his traveling expenses as passenger (second class) by steamer to his destination. His initial salary amounts to (Fls.500) [five hundred guilders] per month. This salary comes in force as soon as the party of the first part will have reached the first port of the Dutch Indian Archipelago or Singapore. Half salary (Fls. 250) [two hundred fifty guilders] per month to be allowed while travelling to destination and returning provided the contract is completed.

4. Further the party of the first part shall during the term of his service with the said Company in the Dutch East Indies, be entitled to free medical attendance and free dwelling.

5. The party of the second part binds itself to pay to the party of the first part, after the latter has spent three consecutive years in the service of the Company his traveling expenses as above, provided he returns within six months after having left the service of the Company and has not entered into the service of any other company or person in the Dutch East Indies after his leaving the employ of the party of the second part.

6. The party of the second part reserves its right to dissolve the agreement at any time and to discharge the party of the first part –

(a) On account of misdemeanor or inability of the party of the first part.

(b) Without stating any reason why.

7. In the case as mentioned sub 6a the salary ceases from the date of his discharge and the party of the first part has no claim for return fare.

8. In case 6b and also in the case of illness, contracted in the service of the Company and not caused by own fault (to be established by the physician appointed by the Company) the Company shall pay to the party of the first part three months' salary and return fare second class.

9. Should the party of the first part leave the service of the Company within three years after his having entered same, except by reason of illness as set forth above he not only loses all claim for return fare and payment of salary from the day he leaves the service of the Company, but he shall also owe the Company an amount of (Fls. 700) [seven hundred guilders] equal to the passage fee to the Dutch East Indies.

10. This agreement has been entered into, under the provision that the party of

the second part may consider it null and void, if the party of the first part does not arrive in the first port of the Dutch Indian Archipelago or Singapore within three months, unless his not arriving in time is due to delay of the steamer by which he has left.

This contract executed in quintuplicate at Pittsburgh, Pa.

N.B. In all instances where this agreement speaks of "party of the second part" it must be taken to mean the four companies together.

Witness our hands and seals this Fifth day of December, 1916
Horace Cornish — W.O. Gillespie
Oil Well Supply Co.
By N.W. Anderson Agent for the Koninklyke Nederlandsche Maatsschappy tot Exploitatie van Petroleum in Nederlandsche Indie the Bataafsche Petroleum Co., the Nedrl. Indische Industrie & Handel My. & the Dordtsche Petroleum Co.

Author's Sources and Notes

Interviews (In their own words):
Family histories, diaries, and recollections were particularly important in compiling anecdotal information that made the story all the more personal and compelling. Besides Edward Winnett's diary donated to the Oil Museum by his niece, Marion Berdan of Petrolia, Mrs. Berdan also provided a family history to fill in details of her uncle's life.

Several others offered material compiled either by themselves or family members. Maureen Bradley and her mother, Mildred Bradley, both of London, shared family stories, articles, newspaper clippings, and a video-taped interview of Maureen's uncle, the late Murray Bradley, long-time operator of the Oil Well Supply Company. Murray Bradley's interview included the story of the Roberts Torpedo and its adoption in Lambton, and many of the incidents in which nitroglycerine played a part. Those records were also crucial to the understanding of the history of Oil Well Supply.

Murray Brown of Petrolia offered his family history as compiled from a variety of sources, including his own memories of stories passed down through the generations. As owner and operator of the Bluewater Energy Quest firm, Brown also explained the modern-day work of exploration and the obtaining of drilling rights from landowners.

Jane Day in Bury St. Edmunds, England, and her cousin, Lorna Mays of Mississauga, Ontario, provided the diary of Frieda Erika von Espenhan MacIntosh, which chronicled the MacIntosh family's incredible escape from Austria and Russia, which was augmented by excerpts from the recollections of Frieda's son, Ralph MacIntosh.

Charles Oliver Fairbank III, current owner of Fairbank Oil and great grandson of the founder, shared details of his illustrious family's long association with petroleum and with the everyday life of Lambton County. Fairbank also provided a guided tour of his historic, but still-producing, oil field.

Kathleen Gillespie of Petrolia shared stories told to her by her father, William O. Gillespie, as well as accounts written by her father and souvenirs he brought back from the foreign fields.

Pete McGarvey of Orillia provided details of his family's long history in oil, both in Canada and Europe.

John McIntyre and his sister, Millicent Woods, both of Sarnia, loaned material owned or compiled by their grandfather, Duncan McIntyre, from his days as a Hard Oiler in Southeast Asia and Persia.

Jean Mearce of Corunna shared stories of the experiences of her foreign driller grandfather, William Frederick Tichborne, who as a teenager first went off to the foreign fields with William McGarvey's ground-breaking expedition to Germany, in 1881.

Laurence Oliver, the last of the foreign drillers, chatted about the biggest adventure of his life, the time he was called out of retirement to help several drought-parched Indian villages find water.

Margaret Smith shared her own experiences with her late husband, foreign driller Ray Gregory, and other recollections of Lambton's oil past.

Dorothy Stevenson is the daughter of a foreign driller, the late Bill Cole, and wife of Lambton oil man Charles Stevenson, and recounted stories and memories.

Bertha Gleeson, long-time Petrolia resident and widow of the late journalist Lew Gleeson, provided anecdotes and observations of life and the people of Petrolia.

Fay Bertrand of Vancouver provided the story of her ancestor, Andrew Lucas, who travelled into central Lambton in the 1830s in search of oil he intended to use for medicinal purposes.

Details and anecdotes from Petrolia's oil past were provided by Charles Whipp, former owner/publisher of Petrolia's *Advertiser-Topic*, and Marlynn Jolliffe, former manager of Petrolia Discovery, a working oil field now open to the public.

Geologist and consultant Bob Cochrane of Cairnlins Petroleum Services in Komoka, Ontario, explained the basics of oil and gas formation and how it is exploited, as well as providing maps and details of how much oil has been taken from the historic fields in the past 140 years.

Doug Gilbert, executive director of the Ontario Petroleum Institute in London, Ontario, provided a description of the current industry in the province.

Terry Carter, geologist with the Oil, Gas, and Salt Resources Library of the Ontario natural resources ministry in London, described the modern face of the oil and gas business in Ontario.

An explanation of the United Nations sponsored Awareness & Preparedness for Emergencies at Local Level (APELL) program came from Allen Wells, Sarnia-based administrator of Community Awareness Response.

Museums:

The Oil Museum of Canada: Early recollections and descriptions of Oil Springs came from letters and other non-published accounts filed with the Oil Museum of Canada in Oil Springs. Included were those compiled by the Women's Institute of Canada. The W.I., founded at Stoney Creek in 1897, provides researchers of Canadian history with a wealth of material in a series of locally compiled publications called the Tweedsmuir Books, named after Baronness Tweedsmuir, wife of the former governor-general, John Buchan, the Baron Tweedsmuir.

Museum displays highlight the people and events connected to oil in Lambton and the story of the foreign drillers. Among the displays is the very coat worn by a little boy, Charles Wallen, during his family's escape when the Canadian-managed oil fields and refineries at Grosny, Russia, were torched during the Russian Revolution. That coat was made from material given to a palace guard by one of the daughters of Czar Nicholas. Another display is an honour role of known foreign drillers, a pillar containing some five hundred or so name plates.

Beyond its public displays, the museum also contains diaries, letters, pictures, memorabilia, early newspaper and periodical articles and other donated materials essential to the piecing together of this remarkable story. They include the hand-written diary telling of foreign driller Edward Winnett's work in Sumatra; pamphlets; family histories; letters from former University of Western Ontario head librarian J.J. Talman; and the history of oil prices and attempts to form cartels.

Petrolia Discovery: This working oil field and interpretive centre in Petrolia contains producing oil wells, a drilling rig, and hundreds of displays and artifacts that help to explain oil's early years and the people who made it happen. Petrolia Discovery has, on file, tape recordings of interviews conducted in the 1980s and 1990s of family members recounting their experiences and recollections of stories from the early oil days. Those interviews are with Margaret Gregory Smith, Ernie Kells, Robert Brown, Laurence Oliver, Dorothy Stevenson, and Arnold Thompson.

Also among its papers on file are biographical sketches of some of the early Hard Oilers, compiled from family members in the Oil Springs and Petrolia area.

Drake Well Museum: In Titusville, Pennsylvania, stands a fitting memorial to the birth of the American petroleum industry, the Drake Well Museum. Edwin Drake drilled the first commercial well in North America. That's the operative word: "drilled." Williams and Tripp dug their well a year before. Nevertheless, the Americans claim their well represented the birth of the modern oil industry, rather than the one at Oil Springs. The dispute notwithstanding, the Drake museum is a highly informative and entertaining interpretive centre, which only emphasizes what could and should be done in Canada to chronicle the story here. The museum in Titusville tells the story of the oil boom town in a docu-drama produced by the Petroleum Institute of America, starring Vincent Price, and in displays, dioramas, and working models.

The **Technisches Museum fuer Industrie und Gewerbe:** Located in Vienna, Austria, the museum's staff tracked down early records of the Galician-Carpathian Oil Company Limited of William H. McGarvey and John Bergheim.

Historians:

Colonel R.B. Harkness: Many of the early events that took place around the founding of the oil industry in southwestern Ontario have been culled from the memories of old-timers and saved for posterity through the exhaustive work of the late Colonel R.B. Harkness. Harkness served as Ontario's oil and gas commissioner for many years, but in addition, he had a passion for history and was determined that Ontario some day claim its rightful place for early contributions to that business. Besides his letters, many of which are filed with the Lambton Room of the Lambton County Library at Wyoming, Ontario, and the Oil Museum of Canada in Oil Springs, Harkness wrote articles for newspapers and periodicals, including *Canadian Oil and Gas Industries,* which published his "Ontario's Part in the Petroleum Industry" in its February/March 1951 edition.

Harkness insisted that Charles Nelson Tripp and James Miller Williams be remembered for their part in the story. He tracked down newspaper articles and land transaction records, copies of which remain in his files.

One day, while I was visiting the office of Terry Carter, geologist with the Ontario natural resources ministry's Oil, Gas, and Salt Resources Library in London, Carter asked whether I knew who Harkness was. I said I did, and he handed me an old ledger book he had found in some dusty cupboard. It was a series of oil and gas production records, some dating back to the late eighteen hundreds, detailing specific wells across the province. They had been kept, and many of the later ones compiled by, R. B. Harkness.

Victor Lauriston: Another man to whom we owe a debt of gratitude for preserving early recollections is Victor Lauriston. A Chatham journalist and historian, Lauriston laid out the early history of Lambton County in his 1949 book *Lambton County's Hundred Years: 1849/1949.* But his interest in the oil industry extended back many years. In 1924 Lauriston wrote an article for *Maclean's* magazine, "The Town of World Travellers," in which the story of the foreign drillers was first brought to light to a national audience. Over the years he also produced articles for several newspapers on the Lambton oil business.

Hermann F. Spoerker: The managing director of Oil & Gas Tek International, in Leoben, Austria, is a great admirer of William McGarvey and hunted down details of McGarvey and his company.

(For other writers of events or people involved in Ontario's early oil days, see the authors of the various publications referred to below.)

Libraries:

Lambton County Library: In this library in Wyoming, Ontario, the Lambton Room contains letters, newspaper articles, brief reminiscences, and other donated materials, as well as census and genealogy records. Among its collection are the files of the late George Smith of Sarnia, whose love of history has assured future historians a wealth of material that would otherwise have been lost forever. The Lambton Room also contains a private letter from Thomas Sterry Hunt of the Geological Survey.

Few editions of the old *Oil Springs Chronicle* and *Oil City Derrick* newspapers survive, however excerpts remain in the files of the Lambton Room. Also among its collection are early oil production records obtained from the Government of Ontario; letters chronicling the dispute between Colonel Harkness and the Pennsylvania oil man, Ernest C. Miller; and details of the life of Charles Nelson Tripp, including land transaction records and court documents that follow his descent into poverty.

The library also has on microfilm early editions of Sarnia's *Observer* and the Petrolia newspapers mentioned in this book.

Weldon Library: At the University of Western Ontario in London, Ontario, the Weldon contains many historical and out-of-print books on the history of oil, its discovery, uses and the people involved.

London Public Library: This library contains the earliest copies, on microfilm, of the *London Free Press and Daily Western Advertiser*, and reprints of historic atlases of Ontario counties.

Hamilton Public Library: The story of James Miller Williams can be found in the library's Special Collections room. Death notices in the *Hamilton Evening Times* and the *Hamilton Spectator*, and the *Dictionary of Hamilton Biography* are particularly helpful. The scrapbook, "Historic Houses in Hamilton," volume 5, provides the history of his home, Mapleside.

Newspapers:
Newspapers published contemporary to the events contain letters and articles describing incidents and telling of the true-life stories of heroism and adventure. Besides the *Oil Springs Chronicle* and the *Oil City Derrick*, these items have been culled from: London's *Free Press*, Petrolia's *Advertiser*, the *Petrolea Topic* (amalgamated in 1917 to form the *Advertiser-Topic*), Sarnia's *Observer* (also known in earlier years as the *Canadian Observer* and the *Sarnia Observer and Lambton Advertiser*), Toronto's *Daily Globe* (now the *Globe and Mail,*) the former Toronto *Evening Telegram*, the former *London Advertiser*, the *Windsor Star* and an early Chatham newspaper, the *Planet*. Some of those newspapers are on file at the Lambton County Library, the London and Chatham public libraries, and the Weldon Library at the University of Western Ontario in London. As well as the clippings noted earlier that were obtained from the museums and county library, some clippings have also been provided by family members.

Magazines and periodicals:
Maclean's magazine published Victor Lauriston's work, "The Town of World Travellers," in May 1924. Various articles were also published by the *Imperial Oil*

Review, including in volume 14, "Petrolia: Cradle of Oil Drillers" (August/September 1930); in volume 5, "Imperial Oil Pioneer Dies" (May 1921); and in volume 49, "The Amazing Jake Englehart" (September 1955).

Ontario History volume LXXXV, number 1 (March 1993) offers "The 'Mysterious' Jacob Englehart and the Early Ontario Petroleum Industry."

The May 1934 edition of the *Anglo-Persian Oil Company Limited* magazine provided information on the life of Duncan McNaughton.

Western Ontario Historical Notes of September 1960 contains an article by Edward Phelps on the inauguration of the Oil Museum of Canada.

Three German-language publications provided material on William H. McGarvey, and John S. Bergheim, and their Galician-Carpathian Petroleum Company Ltd.: *Zeitschrift des Internationalen Vereines der Bohringenieure und Bohrtechniker*, *Petroleum*, and *Chemiker- Und Techniker-Zeitung*. Also, the publication, *Die Grob-Industrie Osterreichs 1898*, by Verlag Leopold Weib. These were provided courtesy of the Technisches Museum fuer Industrie und Gewerbe in Vienna, Austria.

Pamphlets and booklets:

Various pamphlets were helpful both for developing the broad framework of the story, and filling in details of the early history of petroleum in Oil Springs and Petrolia. Foremost among them are *Road to Destiny: A History of Highway 21*, by Charles Whipp; and *Canada's Tale of Toil & Oil* by Patricia McGee, which describes pieces of equipment that are illustrated by artist George P. Rickard. Also J.H. Johnston's pamphlet, *Recollections of Oil Drilling at Oil Springs Ontario*, recounts early stories of the oil pioneers.

Modern-day Hard Oiler Phil Morningstar collaborated with Wanda Pratt and the Oil Museum of Canada in producing the pamphlet, *Early Development of Oil Technology*, which was helpful in describing the methods and equipment utilized in the historic fields.

Books and theses:
Lambton:

Descriptions of Lambton, its people and its communities can be found in Victor Lauriston's *Lambton County's Hundred Years, 1849-1949* (Sarnia: Haines Frontier Printing Co., 1949), and *Belden's Lambton County Atlas of 1880* (Toronto: H. Billing Co., 1880), later republished under the name *Belden's Illustrated Historical Atlas of the County of Lambton, Ontario, 1880* (Sarnia: Edward Phelps, 1973.)

Lauriston's book, while not sourced, is an excellent outline of oil's place in the county's history and experiences of the foreign drillers. *Belden's* also provides an economic picture of the region up to 1880, describes an early refinery, and is the first known chronicling of the story of the notorious Harry Prince.

The Commemorative Biographical Record, (Toronto: J.H. Beers & Company, 1906), is a good source of family profiles from the early oil years. It includes John D. Noble's address to the first petroleum congress in Paris, in 1900.

The most complete general look at the story of oil within Lambton County can be found in *Rivers of Oil* by Hope Morritt (Kingston: Quarry Press Inc., 1993).

Petrolia: 1866-1966 by Charles Whipp and Edward Phelps (Petrolia: Petrolia *Advertiser-Topic,* 1966), offers a broad history of that town and many of its early characters who were Hard Oilers.

Sarnia, Gateway to Bluewaterland, by Edward Phelps (Burlington: Windsor Publications Inc., 1987), describes that city during the same period, including the Fenian "threat."

London librarian and historian Edward Phelps offers the definitive account of the life and times of John Henry Fairbank in his unpublished MA thesis, "John Henry Fairbank of Petrolia: A Canadian Entrepreneur," (London: University of Western Ontario, 1965). The thesis also contains details of many of the people with whom Fairbank came into contact, and his business dealings.

Canadian Economic Development, by A.W. Currie (Toronto: T. Nelson & Sons. Ltd., 1942), discusses the use of petroleum as locomotive fuel.

More on the life of Fairbank's sometimes-competitor, sometimes-partner — Jacob "Jake" Englehart — can be found in *Jake Englehart* by Michael Barnes (Cobalt: Highway Book Shop).

The Gazetteer and Director of the Counties of Kent, Lambton and Essex (Toronto: McEvoy & Company,1866) contains a description of the early Petrolia.

General:

For an explanation of how petroleum is formed, the references, *Grolier Multimedia Encyclopedia* (Novato, Ca.: Grolier, 1997) and *The Canadian Encyclopedia* (Toronto: McClelland & Stewart, 1995) — both on CD — offer a sound grounding. In Fritjof Capra's *The Web of Life* (New York: Anchor Books Doubleday, 1996), the author discusses the latest scientific views on the creation of life which include the hydrocarbon soup that formed petroleum.

The Canadian Encyclopedia also is helpful in identifying the work of the much underrated Abraham Gesner, as well as the early years of the Canadian Geological Survey; its first director, William Edmond Logan; and his adventuresome staff. *Grolier's* also provides a description of Austria, its art and architecture, the province of Galicia, and Ferdinand Graf von Zeppelin.

The history of petroleum seepages and petroleum's early uses are well explained in *Dusters and Gushers: The Canadian Oil and Gas Industry,* by consulting editor James D. Hilborn (Toronto: Pitt Publishing, 1968); *Petroleum: Prehistoric to Petrochemicals, by G.A. Purdy (Toronto: Copp Clark, 1957);* and in *The Wildcatters,* by Samuel W. Tait, Jr. (Princeton: Princeton University Press, 1946.) *Prehistoric to Petrochemicals* also is a good outline of the history of petroleum in Canada, its discovery, the technology, and the founding of Imperial Oil.

The Physiography of Southern Ontario by L.J. Chapman and D.F. Putnam (Toronto: University of Toronto Press, 1951), describes how the province's historic oil region looks, and how it came to be that way.

The Story of Oil, by Walter Sheldon Tower (New York: D. Appleton &

Co., 1909) describes the medicinal uses petroleum was put to in early American society.

The Dictionary of Hamilton Biography, volume 1, edited by Thomas Melville Bailey (Hamilton: 1981), contains information about the life and times of James Miller Williams. Also see the *Wentworth County Historical Atlas* , J.M. Williams & Company (Toronto: H.R. Page, 1875.)

Petroleum In Canada, by Victor Ross (Toronto: Southam Press, 1917) talks about the early foreign drillers and their technology.

The Early and Later History of Petroleum, by J.T. Henry (New York: Augustus M. Kelley, 1970), is an early description of oil in Canada and the United States. First published in 1873, it contains a description of Hugh Nixon Shaw's gusher, written just a few years after the event.

The Illustrated Historical Atlas of the County of Middlesex (Toronto: H.R. Page & Co., 1878), describes London's place in the petroleum business. Other general history descriptions of that city from the period are in *London 200: An Illustrated History*, by Orlo Miller (London: London Chamber of Commerce, 1992), and *The Forest City: An Illustrated History of London, Ontario*, by Frederick H. Armstrong (Windsor Publications, 1986).

A more general description of early life in the province can be found in *Aspects of Nineteenth Century Ontario*, edited by F.H. Armstrong, H.A. Stevenson and J.D. Wilson (Toronto: University of Toronto Press, 1974).

The Times Atlas of World History, edited by Geoffrey Barraclough (Maplewood, N.J.: Hammond Incorporated, 1978), provided insight into the First World War, politics and changing boundaries that occurred around the world, influencing and affecting the work of those who searched for, drilled and refined oil.

The politics of pre-First World War Europe and its impact on the search for oil in Canada and the Middle East are made clearer by reading letters contained in *Winston S. Churchill*, by Randolph S. Churchill, companion volume II, Part 3 (London: Butler & Tanner Ltd., 1969); *The World Crisis*, by Winston Churchill (New York: C.Scribner's Sons, 1923-29); *Fear God and Dread Nought: The Correspondence of Admiral of the Fleet Lord Fisher of Kilverstone*, vol. VII, edited by Arthur J. Marder (London: Cape, 1956); and *First Sea Lord* by Richard Hough (London: Severn House, 1969).

Oil's discovery and development in the Middle East is detailed in *Adventure In Oil* by Henry Longhurst (London: Sidgwick and Jackson Ltd., 1959), and *Oil in the Middle East* by Stephen Hemsley Longrigg (London: Oxford University Press, 1961). Winston Churchill wrote the foreword for *Adventure In Oil*.

Oil's story in other parts of the world is told in *Oil in the Soviet Union* by Heinrich Hassmann (Princeton: Princeton University Press, 1953), and *The Petroleum Resources of Indonesia* by Ooi Jim Bee (Kuala Lumpur: Oxford University Press, 1982).

Canadian Men and Women of the Time edited by Henry James Morgan (Toronto: William Briggs, 1898, 1912), lists some of the business accomplishments of William McGarvey.

Hard Oiler!

Oil Finding by Cunningham Craig (London: Edward Arnold, 1912), the book picked up by foreign driller Duncan McIntyre, contained an introduction from famed British petroleum advisor Sir Boverton Redwood, and represented the growing realization that geology should play a significant role in exploration. The success of John E. Crosbie in Oklahoma, after he left Lambton and the foreign fields, is told in *Then Came Oil* by C.B. Glasscock (Indianapolis: Bobbs-Merrill Company, 1938).

This is a partial list of Lambton County foreign drillers and the fields in which they served. It has been compiled from information provided by foreign drillers W.W. McRae and John Sinclair, and from Dorothy Stevenson of Petrolia, as well as newspaper accounts and diaries. Many names appear more than once, as frequently Lambton drillers worked in several foreign fields.

Algeria: Frank Egan, John Webb

Alsace-Loraine: Gilbert Crosbie, William Mairs, Sam Phillips, Angus Sutherland, Charles Wallen, Edwin Wallen

Arabia: John Browder, Seth Keith, Thomas Knapp, John McCort, Alex Watson

Argentina: John Blackwell, R. Blackwell, A. Calvert, David Holmes, Thomas McCort, James McLister, Scotty Miller

Australia: C. Anderson, William Beadle, Rach Beamer, Charles Beldon, J. Bell, Charles Bennett, John Bennett, William Blackwell, W. Booth, James Boyd, Alex Brown, J.T. Brown, James Brown, John Brown, Russel Brown, G. B. Bryson, D. Cameron, Hugh Cameron, James Chalmers, William Courtney, William Crawford, Garfield Crawford, F. Crawford, E. Drader, H. Drader, F. England, George Fair, Richard Fair, Thomas Fair, George Forsyth, A. Foyne, John Gleason, John Harold, William Harold, Ben Hayden, F. Holbrook, James Hoskin, W. Huston, T. Ivenson, Arthur Johnson, F.W. Johnson, George Johnson, James Johnson, Robb Johnson, Sam Johnson, Wallace Johnson, William Johnson, Irvin Joyce, Lath Keith, Elmer Kerby, Pat Laner, W. Lindsay, James Loughead, George Lougheed, W.G. MacKenzie, William MacKenzie, David Martin, John Martin, Joseph Martin, C. McCaig, R. McCaig, Frank McCann, George McCann, A. McKilop, J. McLellan, Henry LcLister, George McMillan, James McMillan, Sam McNeil, Angus Morrison, George Morrison, James Morrison, Hector Morrison, Joseph Newton, W. Pauling, Joseph Porter, Max Porter, Archie Ralston, S. Ralston, W. Rose, Thomas Sanson, A. Schooley, Pat Shannon, Arthur Simmons, Charles Simmons, John Simmons, A. Simpson, Duncan Sinclair, George Slack, T. Sparham, Lew Stevenson, Frederick Tichborne, James Tichborne, Jonathan Tichborne, R. Tichborne, Joseph Thompson, A. Tomlinson, Alvah Townsend, James Vance, Val Vance, O. Vanderwater, Chalmers Waddel, J. Waddel, John Waddel, Richard Wade, Sandy Wallen, George Williams, Charles Williamson, J.W. Willoughby, John Wills, John Woodley, W. Woodley

Bavaria (Germany): Ernie Booth, James Booth

Borneo (Indonesia): D. Aikens, F. Babcock, George Bell, J. Bennett, John Blackwell, J. Blake, James Blake, W. Blake, George Body, E. Booth, J.G. Boyd,

George Brake, W. Brake, J. Brooks, Harry Brown, J. Brown, S. Brown, George Bryson, J.E. Buchanan, Mike Burns, H. Cable, T. Coleman, J. Collins, J. Cunningham, J. Esson, John Garrison, W. Gibson, F. Gillespie, William Gillespie, Archie Growder, G. Haley, F. Denderson, Billie Hill, B. Isbister, T. Ivenson, Thomas Ivenson, Sid Judson, Ed Julian, Charlie Keck, J. Keene, Manny Keith, M.J. Kelly, R.W. Laird, J. Lambert, Charles Macalpine, F. McCann, James McCrie, W. McKowen, James McMillan, W.W. McRae, Scotty Miller, J. Osborne, T. Paul, S. Phillips, Alex Robertson, W. Laurie, James Rawson, William Rawson, Fred Saunders, Wallace Saunders, J. Sauvey, Fred Simmons, Gus Slack, George N. Smith, John Stokes, James Templeton, Alvah Townsend, H. Tuttle, Frank Wade, A. Webb, Fred Webb, A. Wolsey, M.J. Woodward, F. Zimmer, J. Zimmer

British Borneo (Sarawak, now Malaysia): James Blake, James Brookes, Gilbert Brown, James Brown, A. Brownlee, R. Calvert, T. Collins, A. Coyne, Fred Draper, William Gillespie, R. Heal, J. Keene, Charles Macalpine, James Francis Marshant, E. McCort, Duncan McIntyre, L. McMillan, James F. Nesbit, Stewart Nesbit, J. Patterson, R. Rainsberry, James Rawson, Bloss Sutherland, A. Webb, Fred Webb, J. Zimmer, Alex Robertson

Brazil: Kenneth Anderson, Alexander McAlister, Hector Morrison, Frank Racher

British New Guinea: George Bryson, E. Kerby

Burma/India: W. Beach, W. Bell, David Boyle, Arthur Brown, H. Brown, J. Brown, S. Brown, George Bryson, Joseph Burton, Miles Coleman, Thomas Collins, W. Courtney, John Doig, Sam Donald, Robert Dunlop, J. Eaglesham, John Flett, W.S.D. Fraser, John M. Garrison, W. Gibson, Sam Gillis, W. Gillis, A. Gilson, John Growder, J. Harold, A. Holmes, David Holmes, Eric Hussey, J. Hussey, Eli Josh, Thomas Josh, S. Keith, A. Lambert, J. Mallott, H. Marchant, W. McCarron, Thomas McCort, A. McDougall, Robert McCrie, James McGill, Joseph McGill, Ted McGowan, Bill McMillan, G. Miller, Del Mullin, Frank Nichol, Thomas Pare, Harry Park, Clare Perkins, R. Rainsberry, Ed Slack, Reube Slack, Tinswood Slack, Ed Thompson, James Thompson, Joseph Thompson, W. Thompson, R.A. Townsend, Hum Tracy, R. Vansickle, W. Welsh, George Willet

Celebes Island (Indonesia): John Brooks, Thomas Knapp

Ceram Island (Indonesia): George Bryson, Arthur Lambert, W.J. McKowen, Robert Parker, Fred Webb, Pat Wilcox

Colombia: J. Bagnol, John Braybrook George Bryson, H. Bryson, A. Burns, Cliff Collins, Matt Collins, G. Currie, F. Douglas, D. Holmes, D. Matheson,

Karl. S. Metcalfe, A. Mewburn, George Miller, R. Miller, Del Mullin, Bert Strait, Fred Webb, A. Wilson, A. Wolsey

Crete: James Blake, W. Blake, W. Zimmer

Cuba: Alex Robertson

Egypt: Sam Babcock, F. Beresford, J. Blackwell, James Blake, William Blake, W. Bowles, R. Brooks, J. Brown, A. Brownless, H. Cable, A. Calvert, J. Collins, Mat Collins, T. Collins, George Eady, Fred Edward, G. Ferguson, W. Gibson, John Growder, G. Haley, Bloss Josh, John Josh, J. Josh Jr., Sid Judson, J. Keene, Manny Keith, S. Kersey, Tom Knapp, W. Lambert, F. Lawson, J. McCort, T. McCort, Thomas Paul, George Peat, A. Randall, R. Rawson, James Sanson, Tinswood Slack, F. Stinson, George Sulman, R. Vansickle, William Victean, Frank Wade, T. Wardell, Alex Watson, James Wilson

England: James Blake, Gown Growder, James McLister

Equador: Sam Brown, J. Eaglesham, W.D. Hinman, Spot McArthur, W. McCutcheon, James McLister, George Rawlings

Galicia (Austria): S. Babcock, James Booth, W. Booth, W. Bowles, J.E. Boyd, J. Bradley, James Brown, James Browning, A. Burns, George Burns, H. Cable, George Childs, John Connolly, George Craig, Gilbert Crosbie, S. Daniels, F. Drader, Andy Fair, Fraser Gifditt, James Fowler, Wellington Harding, Robert Hill, Josh Houston, F. Jefferies, C. Johnson, D. Johnson, Nelson Keith, Charles Keith, L. Keith, S. Keith, W. Keith, R.W. Laird, J. Lambert, Carl MacIntosh, George MacIntosh, John MacIntosh, H. MacIntosh, John Markle, J. Martin, W. McCutcheon, Fred McGarvey, William H. McGarvey, James McGill, Thomas McGill, Blondie McLean, Thomas McLean, William McMillan, J. Mervin, Charles Nicholas, Ernie Nicholas, George Normandy, W. Pauling, Cecil Perkins, Cyrus Perkins, J. Eli Perkins, Jacob Perkins, Sam Ralston, James Rowe, Buzz Scott, Elgie Scott, Malcolm Scott, Pat Shannon, W. Shaw, Ed Simms, Neal Sinclair, D. Slack, R.E. Slack, Reuben Slack, William Slack, Tinswood Slack, Howard Smith, Charles Snyder, Alfred Stotts, Gerald Stotts, Walt Stotts, George Tanner, W. Thompson, R. Tierenen, Charles Wallen, Edwin Wallen, Sandy Wallen, James Wolsey, Jean Vansickle, Rhes Vansickle, H. Voght, Quin Zimmer, Joseph H. Zimmerman, W. Zimmerman

Germany: G. Craig, James Fowler, J.E. Perkins, Neal Sinclair, G. Sniders, George Tanner

Ireland: James Booth, William Christner, John Growder

Italy: J. Andison, Ken Andison, N. Andison, George Fair, R. Jackson, J. Doig, Roddy McDermid, L. Ribbing, Carlo Ribighini, Duncan Sinclair, Neal Sinclair, R.E. Slack, Nate Wade, R. Wade

Ivory Coast (French West Africa): A. Anderson, W. Beach, W. Booth, Mike Burns, Gilbert Crosbie, F. Drader, Henry Drader, W. Gibson, Josh Houston, J. Keene, E. Kelly, Jacob Perkins, N. Tomlinson, D. Vansickle, A. Wolsey

Java (Indonesia): J.C. Buchanan, W. Covert, A. Gibson, A. Haley, Thomas Invenson, Yank Johnson, Sid Johnson, A. Lambert, Pat Lenna, Spot McArthur, W.J. McKowen, Duncan McNaughton, T. Paul, Josh Porter, Malcolm Scott, Fred Simmons, Flo Snively, William Thompson, Thomas Vansickle, Charles Wallen, Si Zimmerman

Madagascar: Albert Huggard, David Porter, M.L. Yeager

Mesopotamia and Persia: W. Andison, S. Babcock, H. Battice, Len Beadle, F. Berger, Bert Blackwell, C. Blackwell, J. Blackwell, E. Booth, W. Booth, William Brandon, George Brown, Harry Brown, W. Brown, J. Buchanan, J. Bruton, William Cole, J. Collins, T. Collins, Bert Cox, F. Crawford, A. Currie, T. Deacon, H. Dickinson, J. Dodge, J. Donald, James Douglas, W. Drope, George Eady, Fred Edward, M. Evoy, C. Ferns, J. Fisher, A. Gibson, J. Goeck, W. Jack Graham, G. Gregory, A. Gudgeon, S. Haley, J. Hall, W. Harris, H. Hedden, J. Heferndon, E. Hillis, D. Holmes, M. Holmes, Ted Holmes, J. Houses, E. Houston, Thomas Ivenson, V. Invenson, A. Johnson, B. Josh, E. Josh, John Judson, Charles Keith, E. Kells, G. Gerby, W. Kerr, J. Kidd, Tom Knapp, A. Lambert, J. Lambert, W. Lambert, A. Landhue, Pat Lennon, Harry Lucas, Duncan McIntyre, Fred McCann, George McCall, J. McCort, R. McCrie, J. McDermid, A. McDougald, T. McGowan, A. McKillop, J. Mckilpatric, M. McLeod, Duncan McNaugton, Hugh McPherson, C. McWilliams, Lorne Metcalfe, J. Miller, M. Moore, T. Pare, W. Parker, Ray Patterson, T. Paul, Peck Perkins, R. Perkins, Sam Phillips, Spun Phillips, George Porter, E. Powers, Ace Robertson, James Sanson, Mac Simpson, Tinsdale Slack, F. Smith, H. Smith, H. Snider, James Stevens, Lew Stevenson, E. Stokes, George Tanner, William Tomlinson, Hum Tracey, John Tracey, C. Warner, T. Warner, J.A. Williamson, W. Wills, W. Wilson, H. Winger, A. Wolsey, T. Wolsey, R. Yeager

Mexico: William Cole, Henry Gregory, Bill Hussey, Eric Hussey, Roy Robinson, Bloss Stevenson, A. Wolsey

New Caledonia (French South Pacific): Rach Beamer, Thomas Fair, William Houston, C. Locke, S. McNeil, Pat Shannon

Newfoundland: J. Brown, T. Collins, J. McAlister, James Wade

New Zealand: William Booth, E. Drader, George Fair, Richard Fair, Henry McLister, Ashton Simpson, Orm Vandewater

Palestine: J.E. Perkins, Josh Porter

Peru: G. Bennet, Ralph Bennett, T. Bennet, George Brake, Frank L. Braybrook, Ray Braybrook, William A. Braybrook, George Brown, A. Burns, Alf Burns, Joseph Burns, Jerry Currie, Jim Dean, Atwill Drope, Lorne Duncan, Bruce Dunlop, W. Gillis, Cliff Hacket, A. Harper, William Henderson, Dalton Hinman, Earl Houston, King Houston, H. Hussey, William Kitchen, George McDonald, Don MacGregor, Robert MacGregor, Tom McCort, John McLaren, Alex McLister, Wynne Merrill, George Miller, H. Morrison, H.T. Morrison, George Rawlings, J.A. Sutherland, G.H. Trangmar, T. Ward, Joe Wilkie, William White, J. Wilkin, James Wilson, J. Wolsey

Poland: Ernie Booth, James Booth, C. Sniders, W. Harding, W. Woodley

Romania: Ken Andison, James Boyd, G. Craig, W. Courtney, John Drope, A. Fair, G. Fair, Manney Keith, W. Keith, W. McMillan, A. Ralston, Neal Sinclair, C. Sniders, Charles Vansickle, R. Vansickle, William Woodley

Russia: Richard W. Boulton, W. Bowles, Gilbert Crosbie, Hank Lambert, Carl MacIntosh, Albert McGarvey, James McGarvey, Charles Wallen, Edwin Wallen, Thomas Wolsey, Joseph H. Zimmerman

Sachalin Island (Siberia, Russia): H. Anderson, Richard Bolton, Gilbert Crosbie, J. McGill, A. Winters, T. Wolsey

South Africa: Thomas Anderson, John Coryell, W. Coryell, R. Dunlop

Spain: J. Blake, M.L. Yeager, William Zimmerman

Sumatra (Indonesia): F. Babcock, S. Babcock, E. Balls, J. Bennet, J. Brooks, Harry Brown, James Brown, George Bruce, A. Calvert, T. Collins, George A. Colbourne, Craig G. Crawford, W. Crawford, J.W. Crosbie, John Crosbie, G. Eady, John Garrison, William Gillespie, A. Gibson, G. Gregory, John Hall, J. Holmes, Josh Hughson, F. Husband, E. Ivenson, Sid Judson, K. Keene, Tom Knapp, R.W. Laird, P. Laner, W. Laurie, F. Lawson, George Luxton, Charles Macalpine, S. McArthur, R.E. McCort, Duncan McIntyre, M.C. McKowen, James McMillan, Lorne McMillan, W.W. McRae, D. Milligan, Robert Parker, T. Paul, C. Perkins, D. Porter, Jim Rainsberry, R. Rawlings, J. Sauvey, A. Rouse, Reube Slack, Tim Slack, W. Smith, John Stafford, Bloss Sutherland, John Tracey, James Tichborne, James Vansickle, Jean Vansickle, R. Vansickle, E. Volway, James Volway, T.C. Waddell, Charles Wallen, Edwin Wallen, Fred Wallen, Fred Webb, Leo Wilson, Edward Winnett, M.L. Yeager, R. Yeager

Hard Oiler!

Tarakan Island (Borneo, Indonesia): James Boyd, George Craig, Buzz Isbister, W.J. McKowen, Frank McCann, W.W. McRae, George Peat, Jonathan Sauvey

United States: Bill Hussey, Hiram A. Marshant, James F. Marshant, Laurence Oliver

Venezuela: A. Brownlee, James Boyd, A. Calvert, Bill Cole, W. Culver, Archie Currie, George Glover, Ray Gregory, Dave Harris, Ted Harris, W.H. Harris, A. Holmes, Eric Hussey, Herb Hussey, T. Invenson, Bloss Josh, Eli Josh, John Josh, Thomas Josh, John Judson, W. Kay, John Keene, W. Kitchen, Dot Lambert, W. Lambert, C.E. Lindquist, W. Manross, H. Marchant, James Francis Marshant, R.E. McCort, James McMillan, Doc Mott, Laurence Oliver, Henry Patterson, Con Peat, George Peat, Frank Racher, R. Rawson, Ray Gregory, Ivan Russel, James Sanson, George N. Smith, James Stevens, Lew Stevenson, James Wade, G. Williams, A. Wolsey, O. Wolsey, Frank Yerks, Fred Zimmer

West Indies (includes Trinidad and Barbados): G. Adams, H.H. Anderson, W. Bowles, George Brown, Harry Brown, James Brown, John Brown, J. Chenney, William Cole, George Craig, R. Craise, Ray Gregory, Bill Harris, Ted Harris, Eric Hussey, W. Kitchen, A. Lambert, John McCort, Thomas McCort, Dick Miller, Duncan McNaughton, Laurence Oliver, Thomas Paul, Con Peat, George Peat, James Peat, Frank Racher, M. Thompson, Noble Ward, F. Wicks, J. Wilkin, David Wright, Frank Yerks, Fred Zimmer, Charles Wallen

Notes

Chapter 1: Out of a Swamp

1. Tower, Walter Sheldon, *The Story of Oil*. [New York: D. Appleton & Co., 1909.]
2. Lucas family history as recounted by Fay Bertrand, Vancouver, B.C., 14 June 1998.
3. *Illustrated Atlas of the Dominion of Canada*. [Toronto: H.Belden & Co., 1880.]
4. See earlier reference to Tower.
5. Details of Gesner's life and his work with petroleum are from *The Canadian Encyclopedia Plus*, multimedia reference work on CD-ROM. [Toronto: McClelland & Stewart Inc., 1995.]
6. Purdy, G.A., *Petroleum: Prehistoric to Petrochemicals*. [Toronto: Copp Clark Publishing Co., 1957.]
7. Harkness, R.B., "Ontario's Part in the Petroleum Industry," *Canadian Oil and Gas Industries* magazine, February/March 1951.
8. Ibid.
9. Elford, Jean Turnbull, *Canada West's Last Frontier: A History of Lambton*. [Sarnia: Lambton Historical Society, 1982.]
10. Harkness, "Ontario's Part."

Chapter 2: The First of the Hard Oilers

11. Stories of the origins of the term circulate widely in Petrolia and Oil Springs. These two versions are part of the folklore of central Lambton County, handed down among many of the families whose roots date back to the early days of oil.
12. Author's interview with Bertha Gleeson, 4 March 1998, Petrolia, ON. All references to Gleeson are from this or subsequent interview of 25 June 1998.
13. Obituary, the *Daily Globe*, Toronto, 2 November 1866.
14. Harkness, "Ontario's Part."
15. Ibid.
16. Charter of the International Mining and Manufacturing Company from Biography and Genealogy file, Charles Nelson Tripp, Box 2: Oil History [11A-KB Tripp], Lambton Room, Lambton County Library, Wyoming, ON.
17. Tripp file, Lambton Room.
18. Author's interview with Donald Wilde, 25 February 1998. Subsequent references to Wilde are also from this interview.

19. Purdy.
20. Tripp file, Lambton Room. Historians Edward Phelps and George Smith have collected evidence of judgements against Tripp and the sale of lands which indicate the depth of his financial problems.
21. Purdy.
22. Tripp file, Lambton Room.
23. Unless otherwise noted, all materials about James Miller Williams are from the *Dictionary of Hamilton Biography*, Vol. 1, edited by Thomas Melville Bailey [Hamilton: 1981]; and the "Historic Houses in Hamilton" scrapbook, Vol. 5, both from the Hamilton Public Library, Hamilton, ON.
24. Purdy.
25. Harkness, "Ontario's Part."
26. Purdy.
27. Merchant, F.W./Miller, Mrs. James, correspondence, Oil Museum of Canada, Oil Springs file, Oil Springs, ON.
28. The name *"Observer"* has appeared in several forms in Sarnia over the years. Besides the *Canadian Observer*, there was the *Conservative Observer*, launched in 1853, and the *Lambton Observer and Western Advertiser*. Today, the *Sarnia Observer* continues to publish. To avoid confusion, further references will be to the *Observer*.
29. Talman quotes records from the Lambton County registry office showing Williams acquired the west gum bed in Enniskillen Township in 1856, and that by 23 September 1859 — just 27 days after the Drake well struck oil, "the Enniskillen industry was mature enough to produce complaints by consumers over the high prices." Talman letters file, Oil Museum of Canada.
30. Harkness, R.B./Miller, Ernest C., correspondence, various dates, 1960, in Harkness correspondence file, Box 11[1], 11A-A, Lambton Room.
31. *Observer*, Sarnia, ON., 30 December 1858.
32. Tait, Samuel W. Jr., *The Wildcatters*. [Princeton: Princeton University Press, 1946.]
33. Wilde, Donald.
34. Tripp file, Lambton Room.
35. The newspaper from which the obituary was taken is not known, but the clipping is photocopied in Tripp's file at the Lambton Room.
36. Merchant/Miller correspondence.
37. Ibid.
38. *Belden's Lambton County Atlas of 1880* [Toronto: H. Billing Co., 1880], later republished under the name *Belden's Illustrated Historical Atlas of the County of Lambton, Ontario, 1880* [Sarnia: Edward Phelps, 1973].

Chapter 3: The Man Who Made Boom-Town Boom

39. Obituary, the *Daily Globe*, Toronto, 20 February 1863.
40. Unless otherwise noted, description and details of Hugh Nixon Shaw's life culled from biographical sketches in Shaw files at Oil Museum of Canada; and Petrolia Discovery's "Biographical Sketches" ["Sketches" is a scrapbook compiled by Petrolia Discovery staff from various sources, including members of Hard Oiler families]; Shaw biography file, Lambton Room, Box 4 [61]; Shaw Oil Well file, Lambton Room [11EC-L]; and the recollections of Frank W. Merchant from Merchant/Miller correspondence.
41. Harkness/Miller correspondence.
42. Wilde, Donald.

43. Lauriston, Victor, *Lambton County's Hundred Years, 1849-1949.* [Sarnia: Haines Frontier Printing Co., 1949.]

44. "The Oil Wells of Enniskillen," the *Free Press*, London, ON., 14 February 1862. Unless otherwise noted, all details of Shaw's gusher are from this source. [At the time the newspaper was called the *London Free Press and Daily Western Advertiser*, however for the sake of clarity it will be *Free Press* in all additional references.]

45. Henry, J.T., *The Early and Late History of Petroleum.* [New York: Augustus M. Kelley, 1970; original publication 1873.]

46. Johnston, J.H., *Recollections of Oil Drilling at Oil Springs Ontario,* booklet, provided by Oil Museum of Canada, Oil Springs, ON.

47. Morritt, Hope, *Rivers of Oil.* [Kingston: Quarry Press Inc., 1993.]

48. *Belden's Atlas.*

49. Hunt, Thomas Sterry, letter, Oil Springs file, Oil Museum of Canada.

50. *Belden's Atlas;* and Charles Whipp, *Road to Destiny: A History of Highway 21,* booklet, provided by Oil Museum of Canada.

51. Ibid.

52. Gale, Annie Adamson, "Tweedsmuir History of Oil Springs," scrapbook compiled by Women's Institute of Oil Springs, Oil Museum of Canada. All references to Mrs. Gales are from this source.

53. Whipp, *Road to Destiny.*

54. Pricing information contained within this publication comes from various sources, including Purdy; Edward Phelps's unpublished MA thesis, "John Henry Fairbank of Petrolia: A Canadian Entrepreneur" [London, ON.: University of Western Ontario, 1965]; *Belden's Atlas;* and an exhibit displayed at the Oil Museum of Canada.

55. Lauriston.

56. Lambton Room, Oil History, Box 1.

57. "Tweedsmuir History of Oil Springs."

58. Author's interview with Charles Whipp, London, ON., 26 March 1998.

59. Unless otherwise noted, description of Oil Springs that follows taken from *Belden's Atlas* and "Tweedsmuir History."

60. Description of racial incident from "Disgraceful Riot at Oil Springs," *Observer*, 20 March 1863; and "Racial War Waged in Early Sixties," *Advertiser-Topic*, 30 January 1936. (The newspaper that today is known as the *Petrolia Topic* has undergone several name and ownership changes. The *Petroleum Advertiser*, founded in 1869, later became the *Petrolia Advertiser.* The *Petrolea* (note spelling) *Topic* was founded in 1879. The two amalgamated in 1917 and for many years the newspaper was known as the *Advertiser-Topic.* At the time of publication of this book in 1998, it was the *Petrolia Topic.* Further references will use the names *Advertiser, Topic* and *Advertiser-Topic,* depending on the date and publication.)

61. Following description of Oil Springs hotel conditions taken from letters, recollections in Oil Springs files of Oil Museum of Canada.

62. Lambton Room, Oil Springs file, Oil History, Box 1.

63. Ibid.

64. Oil Museum of Canada display on Shaw well.

65. *Belden's.*

66. Ibid.

67. *Illustrated Historical Atlas of the County of Middlesex, 1878.* [Toronto: H.R. Page & Co., 1878.]

68. Armstrong, Frederick, *The Forest City: An Illustrated History of London, Ontario.* [London: Windsor Publications, 1986.]

69. Armstrong; Purdy; Ben S. Scott, *Western Ontario Historical Notes,* VI, 3/4 [September-December 1948]. Armstrong says 1862, while Purdy suggests 1863. Purdy says it was a partnership between Spencer and Waterman, while Armstrong credits Spencer. Scott says Spencer and Waterman built the first "substantial" oil refinery in London in 1863.

70. *Belden's.*

71. Ibid.

72. Obituary, John H. Rowe, *Observer,* 15 November 1939.

73. Unless otherwise noted, historical oil production information is obtained from Government of Ontario records in the R.B. Harkness file, Box 1, Oil History [11A-A to 11A-F], Lambton Room.

Chapter 4: John Henry Fairbank: Putting Down Roots

74. Phelps, Fairbank thesis. Unless otherwise noted, all information about the Fairbank family and their business affairs is from this source.

75. Ibid.

76. See earlier note on pricing information.

77. Description of early refining methods from author's interview with Charles Fairbank, 19 December 1997, Oil Springs; *Belden's Atlas;* Purdy; and Johnston.

78. *Illustrated Atlas of Middlesex.*

79. Unless otherwise stated, details of Petrolia's early years from Charles Whipp and Edward Phelps, *Petrolia: 1866-1966.* [Petrolia: *Petrolia Advertiser-Topic*, 1966]; and *Belden's Atlas.*

80. *Gazetteer and Directory of the Counties of Kent, Lambton, and Essex, 1866-67.* [Toronto: McEvoy & Co., 1866.]

81. Details of John Noble's life from *The Commemorative Biographical Record* [Toronto: J.H. Beers & Co., 1906]; and "Biographical Sketches."

82. Display, Drake Well Museum, Titusville, PA.

83. Author's interview with Charles Fairbank, 19 December 1997.

84. *Commemorative Biographical Record.*

85. Details of producers' and refiners' cooperatives and cartels in this chapter from: Phelps, Fairbank thesis; Whip and Phelps, *Petrolia;* and Purdy.

86. Bradley, Murray, videotaped interview with Charles Fairbank, 1994. Courtesy Maureen Bradley, 19 January 1998, London, ON.

87. "Biographical Sketches."

88. Author's interview with Charles Fairbank.

89. All references in this chapter to R.I. Bradley are obtained from Bradley family documents and clippings, provided by Maureen Bradley, London, ON.

90. Henry, J.T., *The Early and Late History of Petroleum* [New York: Augustus M. Kelley, 1970; original publication 1873.]

91. Phelps, Fairbank thesis.

92. Ibid.

93. Ibid.

94. *Observer,* Sarnia, 28 November 1873.

95. The account is from a handwritten note in the Lambton Room files of Sarnia historian George Smith, Box 2, Oil History. While unsigned, it is interesting as an eye-witness account of what the town looked like at that moment in time. The anonymous writer walked west from the railway station to the suburb known as Pithole, a place of rigs and shanties, the homes of the labourers employed at the area's wells.

96. *Advertiser,* 2 May 1879.
97. "Biographical Sketches."

Chapter 5: Rascals, Heroes, Blasts, and Blazes

98. Besides *Belden's,* the Harry Prince story was also recounted by Lauriston in an article published in the *Free Press* 4 September 1948. Lauriston included that same information in his book, *Lambton's Hundred Years,* published in 1949. Interestingly, an obituary in the *Advertiser,* published 11 October 1878, makes no reference to any irregularities in Prince's business affairs and the first such reference appears to have been in *Belden's,*two years after his death.
99. *Advertiser,* 11 October 1878.
100. "Biographical Sketches."
101. Lauriston.
102. Griffin, Selwyn P., "Petrolia, Cradle of Oil Drillers," *Imperial Oil Review,* vol. 14, August/September 1930.
103. MacGregor, Ken, letters, MacGregor file, Oil Museum of Canada.
104. "Biographical Sketches."
105. Ibid.
106. Whipp and Phelps. Details of the fire departments and their work in this section are all from this source.
107. Purdy.
108. *Advertiser,* 5 September 1884.
109. *Advertiser,* 29 June 1898. The full account of the incident is from this source.
110. Purdy.
111. *Advertiser,* 11 July 1879.
112. *Advertiser,* 3 October 1890.
113. Bradley, Murray, videotaped interview; and Bradley family materials provided by Maureen Bradley. All references to nitroglycerine and R.I. Bradley's experiences are from these sources unless otherwise noted.
114. *Advertiser,* 10 April 1891.
115. Author's interview with Dorothy and Charles Stephenson, 5 January 1998, Marthaville, ON.
116. "Biographical Sketches." The following references to Harrison Corey are also from this source.
117. The incident is recreated here from an account by Selwyn P. Griffin published in *Imperial Oil Review,* vol. 14, August/September 1930.
118. Bradley videotaped interview with Charles Fairbank, 1984, provided by Maureen Bradley.
119. Author's interview with Charles Whipp, 26 March 1998.
120. MacGregor correspondence, MacGregor file, Oil Museum of Canada.

Chapter 6: The Oil Barons

121. Phelps.
122. Descriptions of Petrolia life in this chapter are from Whipp and Phelps, unless otherwise noted.
123. *Advertiser,* 13 November 1885.
124. *Advertiser,* 28 December 1888, 4 January, and 8 February 1889.
125. Whipp and Phelps.

126. *Advertiser*, 22 October 1896.

127. *Advertiser*, 12 March 1896.

128. Phelps.

129. Ibid.

130. Ibid.

131. Whipp and Phelps.

132. Phelps. Unless otherwise noted, description of the Fairbank family and J.H. Fairbank's political career in this chapter are from this source.

133. Unless otherwise noted, details of Englehart's life and works are from *Imperial Oil Review* obituary, vol. 5, May 1921; "The Mysterious Jacob L. Englehart and the Early Ontario Petroleum Industry," *Ontario History*, 85 (1), March 1993; Michael Barnes, *Jake Englehart* [Cobalt: Highway Book Shop]; and Hope Morritt, *Rivers of Oil.*

134. *Advertiser*, 5 July 1878.

135. Author's interview with former Petrolia Discovery manager Marlynn Jolliffe, 17 January 1998, Toronto.

136. Phelps.

137. Jolliffe.

138. Author's interview with Charles Whipp, 26 March 1998.

139. From McGarvey family records provided by Pete McGarvey, Orillia, ON.

140. Unless otherwise noted, details of Ribighini's life from Lauriston; "Biographical Sketches" from Petrolia Discovery; and *Advertiser* obituary, 22 July 1897.

141. Currie, A.W., *Canadian Economic Development* [Toronto: T. Nelson & Sons. Ltd., 1942.]

142. "Biographical Sketches."

143. Ibid.

144. Government of Ontario records, Harkness file, Box II(1) Oil History, 11A-A, Lambton Room

Chapter 7: This Business of Oil

145. Drake Well Museum display.

146. Unless otherwise noted, description of early drilling methods and development of the Candian Rig are from J.H. Johnston's pamphlet, *Recollections of Oil Drilling at Oil Springs Ontario: Early Development of Oil Technology*, by Wanda Pratt and Phil Morningstar [Petrolia: Oil Museum of Canada, 1987]; R.B. Harkness's file at the Lambton Room; and John D. Noble's speech to the 1900 Petroleum Congress in Paris, reprinted in *Commemorative Biographical Record.*

147. Drake Well Museum display.

148. Author's interview with Murray Brown, CEO, Bluewater Energy Quest, oil and natural gas exploration company, 12 January 1998, Petrolia, ON.

149. History of the Oil Well Supply Company from Murray Bradley, through videotaped interview, 1994, with Charles Fairbank; and Bradley family materials provided by Maureen Bradley.

150. Pratt and Morningstar, *Early Development of Oil Technology.*

151. Author's interview with Charles Fairbank, 19 December 1997.

152. Description of the traditional refining method and refineries from *Belden's Atlas*; Noble's Paris lecture; and Purdy.

153. Producer and refiner cooperatives and catels are described in *Advertiser* newspaper articles of various dates through the 1870s to '90s; Phelps's Fairbank thesis; Purdy; Whipp and Phelps; and a display at the Oil Museum of Canada.

154. *Advertiser,* 8 February 1878.
155. Charles Fairbank interview.
156. An excellent discussion and explanation of the economics of Canada's early oil industry can be found in "The Mysterious Jacob L. Englehart," noted earlier.
157. Purdy.
158. Unless otherwise noted, details of Imperial's development in this chapter are from Purdy.
159. *Advertiser,* 27 June 1898.
160. Purdy.
161. Ford, R.W., *A History of the Chemical Industry in Lambton County,* booklet. [Sarnia: Dow Chemical Canada Inc., 1964.]

Chapter 8: The Travellers

162. Sinclair, John, "Some Early History," *Advertiser-Topic,* 28 February 1924. In a letter to the newspaper, Sinclair, himself a foreign driller and frequently a recruiter for overseas employers, recalled the first group of Lambton Hard Oilers who went abroad.
163. Lamentably, editions of the *Advertiser* from 1872 and 1873 are no longer extant. However, Hope Morritt, author of *Rivers of Oil,* told the author in 1998 that while researching her book, she had an interview with Helen Corey in Petrolia on 17 September 1992. (Mrs. Corey died in 1997.) "She said that her parents were at the railway station when the (first) foreign drillers left. It was a very emotional moment because people thought they might never see these guys again — it was like going to the moon. The band played the old Scottish song, 'Will Ye No Come Back Again.' (Helen) was married to Harrison Corey, whose grandfather was (also) Harrison Corey," the nitroglycerine manufacturer.
164. Bertha Gleeson recalled a story told by a foreign driller about his experience with a port-of-New York agent. The man told the agent he was returning to Toronto and the agent didn't know where that was. When the man said he was going on to Petrolia, the agent's face lit up in recognition and replied that they received at least one person a week going to or from that community.
165. Bee, Ooi Jim, *The Petroleum Resources of Indonesia* [Kuala Lumpur: Oxford University Press, 1982.]
166. *Advertiser-Topic,* 11 March 1926.
167. A copy of Gillespie's contract can be found in Appendix II of this book. The original is in Gillespie's file at the Oil Museum of Canada.
168. Fairbank interview, 19 December 1997.
169. Letter from W.O. Kupsch, professor, University of Saskatchewan department of Geological Sciences, Saskatoon, 15 May 1986, from file of William H. McGarvey, Oil Museum of Canada.
170. Sinclair, John, letter to *Advertiser-Topic,* 28 February 1924. More than four decades after the fact, Sinclair is mistaken in his recollection that the men were sent to Italy in 1880. An article in the *Advertiser,* 18 April 1879, recounts the event. An article, "Petrolia's Sons Abroad," published by the *Topic* on 2 May 1890, notes that "a little over ten years ago, Mr. Neil Sinclair ... left Petrolia for Italy, and engaged with a company there to bore for oil."
171. Griffin, *Imperial Oil Review.*
172. Obituary of John S. Bergheim in the German-language periodical, *Petroleum,* no. 1, 1912. All German-language periodicals are provided by Technisches Museum of Vienna, Austria.

173. Morgan, Henry James, *Canadian Men and Women of the Time* [Toronto: William Briggs, 1898 and 1912.]

174. Gillespie, William, correspondence, provided by Kathleen Gillespie, Petrolia, ON.

175. *Advertiser*, 11 December 1874.

176. All references to Millicent Woods and John McIntyre are from author's interview, 7 January 1998, Sarnia, ON.

177. All references to Dorothy and Charles Stevenson are from author's interview, 5 Jaunary 1998, Marthaville, ON.

178. All references to Margaret Gregory Smith are from author's interview, 5 January 1998, Petrolia, ON.

179. Author's interview with Murray Brown, 12 January 1998, Petrolia, ON.

180. Ross, Victor, *Petroleum in Canada* [Toronto: Southam Press, 1917.]

181. Details of Laurence Oliver's experiences as a foreign driller are taken from author's interview, 27 February 1998, Petrolia, ON.; and taped interview of Oliver by Charles Whipp, 1984, on file at Petrolia Discovery.

Chapter 9: The Petroleum King of Austria

182. *Advertiser*, obituary of Helena McGarvey, 21 December 1898.

183. Unless otherwise noted, details of McGarvey's life and family come from family records and recollections provided by Pete McGarvey of Orillia, ON.; and Lauriston, "Town of World Travellers," *Maclean's* magazine, 1 May 1924.

184. McGarvey family file, Biographies and Geneological records, Lambton Room.

185. Griffin.

186. Ibid.

187. Kupsch; Lauriston, "Town of World Travellers."

188. Whipp and Phelps.

189. Bergheim probably arrived in Petrolia in 1881. An article in the *Observer*, 16 March 1917, says it was '81. Bergheim's obituary in the German-language periodical, *Petroleum*, says Bergheim and McGarvey met in 1881. An article about their company, "Galizische Karpathen-Petroleum-Actien-Gesellschaft," in *Die Grob-Industrie Osterreichs 1898*, says they began drilling in Galicia in 1884, although in fact it was earlier — probably in late 1882. [Note that the relevant sections of *Petroleum* and *Die Grob-Industrie Osterreichs 1898* are provided courtesy Christian Hannesschlager at the Technisches Museum of Vienna, Austria.]

190. "Galizische Karpathen-Petroleum-Actien-Gesellschaft," from *Die Grob-Industrie Osterreichs 1898*, provided by Christian Hannesschlager, Technisches Museum fuer Industrie und Gewerbe, Vienna, Austria.

191. Lauriston, "Petrolia Boy Who Became Oil King: Billy McGarvey Discovered the Great Galician Fields," *Advertiser-Topic*, 16 June 1921.

192. *Advertiser-Topic*, 16 February 1939.

193. Records of McGarvey, MacIntosh and Perkins families, provided by: Pete McGarvey, Orillia, ON.; Jane Day, Bury St. Edmunds, Britain; and Lorna Mays, Mississauga, ON.

194. *Advertiser*, 23 May 1884.

195. *Advertiser*, 6 August 1884.

196 *Advertiser*, 6 July 1886.

197 Memoirs of Frieda Erika Von Espenhan, provided by Lorna Mays, Mississauga, ON.

198. *Advertiser*, 23 May 1890.

199. Description of Canadian foreign drillers' living conditions and a typical Galician

wedding from Von Espenhan memoirs.

200. Wedding description from *Advertiser*, 19 December 1895.

201. McGarvey family file, Biographies and Geneological Records, Lambton Room.

202. At the time, McGarvey's name was frequently spelled "*Mac*Garvey" — he was known as "Mac" by friends — however current family members prefer the spelling used throughout this book.

203. Dr. Hermann F. Spoerker, managing director, Oil & Gas Tek International, Leoben, Austria.

204. William H. McGarvey obituary, *Zeitschrift des Internationalen Vereines der Bohringenieure und Bohrtechniker*, no. 24, 15 December 1914; and *Die Grob-Industrie Osterreichs 1898*.

205. Bergheim obituary, *Petroleum* periodical.

206. Lauriston, "Petrolia Boy."

207. William H. McGarvey obituary, the *Evening Telegram*, (Toronto), 8 December 1914; and obituary from *Zeitschrift* periodical.

208. *Petroleum* periodical, no. 16, 1908.

209. Details of the anniversary party from *Advertiser*, 19 August 1892.

210. Bergheim obituary.

211. Letter, Edward McGarvey, London, ON., to nephew James McGarvey, Alliston, ON., 6 March 1897. Provided by Pete McGarvey, Orillia, ON.

212. Obituary, *Advertiser*, 21 December 1898; and McGarvey file, Biographies and Genealogy, Lambton Room.

213. Griffin.

214. McGarvey obituary, *Evening Telegram*.

215. Bergheim obituary, *Petroleum*.

216. "Diesel power," *Grolier Multimedia Encyclopedia*.

217. *Fear God and Dread Nought: The Correspondence of Admiral of the Fleet Lord Fisher of Kilverstone*, vol. VII, edited by Arthur J. Marder. [London: Cape, 1956.]

218. A description of world politics and historical developments at the turn of the century is culled from *The Times Atlas of World History*, edited by Geoffrey Barraclough [Maplewood, N.J.: Hammond Incorporated, 1978.]

219. Bernardi, General Friederich von, *Germany and the Next War.* [Toronto: McClelland, Goodchild, and Stewart, 1914.]

220. *Evening Telegram*, 24 February 1911.

221. Von Espenhan.

222. Bergheim obituary.

223. *Maclean's* article reprinted in *Advertiser-Topic*, 16 June 1921.

224. *London Free Press*, 8 December 1914.

Chapter 10: Escape from Destruction

225. Details of the experiences of the MacIntosh family are from the memoirs of Frieda Erika Von Espenhan MacIntosh, and her son, Ralph MacIntosh, provided by Lorna Mays, Mississauga, ON.

226. Unless otherwise noted, details of the experiences of the Wallen family are from an interview with Florence Wallen, published in the *Free Press,* 15 February 1919; and from the memoirs of Charles Wallen Jr., provided by Mrs. Mary Wallen, Grand Bend, ON.

227. Lauriston, "Town of World Travellers."

228. *Advertiser*, 16 July 1886.

229. *Times Atlas of World History.*

230. Lauriston, "Town of World Travellers."

231. Perkins family file, Biographies and Genealogy, Lambton Room.

232. Lauriston, "Town of World Travellers."

Chapter 11: The Persian Solution

233. Tower.

234. Ibid.

235. Phelps.

236. Unless otherwise noted, details of early oil exploration in the Middle East are from Henry Longhurst, *Adventure in Oil* [London: Sidgwick and Jackson, 1959]. The book's foreword was written by Winston Churchill.

237. Obituary, *Anglo-Persian Oil Co. Ltd.* magazine, vol. X, no. 3, May 1934 [London: Britannia House], Courtesy Oil Museum of Canada, McNaughton file.

238. Churchill, Randolph S., *Winston S. Churchill,* companion vol. II, Part 3, 1911-1914 [London: Heinemann, 1966.]

239. Ibid.

240. Longhurst.

241. *Atlas of World History.*

242. "Biographical Sketches."

243. Ibid.

244. Author's interview with Murray Brown.

245. Ibid.

246. Slack family file, Oil Museum; and Oil Museum display. McRie's name is also listed on the *Titanic's* manifest of those who perished with the ship.

247. "Biographical Sketches."

Chapter 12: Expedition to Sumatra

248. Unless otherwise noted, details of the life of Edward Winnett are from Winnett's diary, on file at the Oil Museum of Canada, and from the Winnett family history provided by Marion Winnett Berdan, Petrolia, ON.

249. Miller, Orlo, *London 200: An Illustrated History* [London: London Chamber of Commerce, 1992.]

250. Ibid.

251. Tower.

252. Longrigg, Stephen Hemsley, *Oil in the Middle East* [London: Oxford University Press, 1961.]

253. Ibid.

254. *Advertiser,* 7 October 1897.

255. Ibid, 11 March 1926.

Chapter 13: They Sought Adventure

256. Description of William Gillespie's life from Gillespie file, Oil Museum of Canada; "Biographical Sketches;" Lauriston, "Bill Gillespie Comes Home," *London Advertiser,* 28 August 1926; and letters, possessions and recollections from Gillespie's daughter, Kathleen Gillespie, Petrolia, ON.

257. Lauriston, "Bill Gillespie Comes Home;" and letter from Mark J. Mloszewski,

Kingston, ON., in Gillespie file, Oil Museum of Canada.

258. Frederick Saunders biography file, Oil Museum of Canada, including a 1940 interview with the *Windsor Star* and a letter from M. Milo, manager of La Corona refinery, Tampico, Mexico, 17 October 1922.

259 From taped interview with Dorothy Stevenson, 4 June 1984, on file at Petrolia Discovery; and author's interview with Dorothy Stevenson.

260. From author's interview with Jean Mearce, 21 January 1998, Corunna, ON.

261. Fred Webb file, Foreign Drillers, Oil Museum of Canada.

262. *Advertiser-Topic*, 2 November 1922.

263. Taped interview with Laurence Oliver, 1984, on file with Petrolia Discovery.

264. Author's interview with Laurence Oliver, 27 February 1998, Petrolia, ON.

265. Ranney file, Oil Museum of Canada.

266. Taped interview with Arnold Thompson, 16 April 1984, on file at Petrolia Discovery.

267. *Advertiser-Topic*, 27 December 1923.

268. MacIntosh family records, provided by Lorna Mays.

269. Taped interview with Bob Brown, June 1984, on file at Petrolia Discovery.

270. *Commemorative Biographical Record.*

271. Glasscock, C.B., *Then Came Oil* [Indianapolis: Bobbs-Merrill Company, 1938].

272. Details of Duncan McIntyre's life and experiences as a foreign driller from family records provided by John McIntyre and Millicent Woods, 7 January 1998, Sarnia, ON.; and *Observer*, 21 July 1915, 27 June 1918, and 8 May 1930; and 1985 notes from George Smith, McIntyre family file, Biographies and Genealogy, Lambton Room.

273. *Advertiser-Topic*, 22 February 1923.

274. Author's interview with Margaret Smith.

275. *Advertiser*, 17 August 1898.

276. Ibid, 29 March 1899.

277. Ibid, 8 March 1899.

278. Ibid.

279. Lauriston, "Town of World Travellers."

Chapter 14: Farewell to the Barons

280. Whipp and Phelps.

281. Phelps.

282. *Advertiser*, 12 March 1896.

283. Ibid, 14 February 1914.

284. *Free Press*, 7 December 1914.

285. *Advertiser-Topic*, 7 April 1921 (obituary), 14 April 1921 (report of funeral); and *Imperial Oil Review* obituary, "Imperial Oil Pioneer Dies," May 1921.

286. Author's interview with Komoka, ON.-based geologist and consultant Bob Cochrane, 19 March 1998, Komoka, ON.

Chapter 15: Looking Ahead

287. Author's interview with Fairbank.

288. "Biographical Sketches," Petrolia Discovery.

289. Author's interview with Charles Whipp.

290. Author's interview with Terry Carter, Oil, Gas, and Salt Resources Library, 19 March 1998, London, ON.

Bibliography

Books

Armstrong, F.H., H.A. Stevenson, J.D. Wilson. *Aspects of Nineteenth Century Ontario.* Toronto: University of Toronto Press, 1974.

Armstrong, Frederick, *The Forest City: An Illustrated history of London, Ontario.* London: Windsor Publications, 1986.

Arnold, Ralph, George A. Macready and Thomas W. Barrington, *The First Big Oil Hunt.* New York: Vantage Press, 1960.

Bailey, Thomas Melville, editor, *The Dictionary of Hamilton Biography,* Vol. 1 Hamilton: 1981.

Barnardi, General Friederich von, *Germany and the Next War.* Toronto: McClelland, Goodchild, and Stewart, 1914.

Barnes, Michael, *Jake Englehart.* Cobalt: Highway Book Shop.

Bee, Ooi Jim, *The Petroleum Resources of Indonesia.* Kuala Lumpur: Oxford University Press, 1982.

Belden's Lambton County Atlas of 1880 Toronto: H. Billing Co., 1880; later republished under the name *Belden's Illustrated Historical Atlas of the County of Lambton, Ontario, 1880.* Sarnia: Edward Phelps, 1973.

Chapman, L.J., and D.F. Putnam, *The Physiography of Southern Ontario.* Toronto: University of Toronto Press, 1951.

Churchill, Randolph S., *Winston S. Churchill,* companion vol. II, Part 3, 1911-1914. London: Butler and Tanner Ltd, 1969.

Commemorative Biographical Record. Toronto: J.H.Beers, 1906.

Craig, E.H. Cunningham, *Oil Finding.* London: Edward Arnold, 1912.

Currie, A.W., Canadian Economic Development. Toronto: T. Nelson & Sons, 1942.

Elford, Jean Turnbull, *Canada West's Last Frontier: A History of Lambton.* Sarnia: Lambton Historical Society, 1982.

Fisher, John, *Fear God and Dread Nought: The Correspondence of Admiral of the Fleet Lord Fisher of Kilverston,* vol. VII, edited by Arthur J. Marder. London: Cape, 1956.

Gazetteer and Directory of the Counties of Kent, Lambton, and Essex, 1866-67. Toronto: McEvoy & Co., 1866.

Glasscock, C.B., *Then Came Oil.* Indianapolis: Bobbs-Merrill, 1938.

Hassman, Heinrich, *Oil in the Soviet Union.* Princeton: Princeton University Press, 1953.

Bibliography

Henry, J.T., *The Early and Late History of Petroleum.* New York: Augustus M. Kelley, 1970; original publication 1873.

Hilborn, James D., consulting editor, *Dusters and Gushers: The Canadian Oil and Gas Industry.* Toronto: Pitt Publishing , 1968.

Hough, Richard, *First Sea Lord: An Authorized Biography of Admiral Sir John Fisher.* London: Severn House,1969.

Illustrated Atlas of the Dominion of Canada. H.Belden & Co., 1880.

Illustrated Historical Atlas of the County of Middlesex, 1878. Toronto: H.R. Page & Co., 1878.

Lauriston, Victor, *Lambton County's Hundred Years, 1849-1949.* Sarnia: Haines Frontier Printing Co., 1949.

Longhurst, Henry, *Adventure in Oil.* London: Sidgwick and Jackson, 1959.

Longrigg, Stephen Hemsley, *Oil in the Middle East.* London: Oxford University Press, 1961.

Morgan, Henry James, *Canadian Men and Women of the Time.* Toronto: William Briggs, 1898 and 1912.

Morritt, Hope, *Rivers of Oil.* Kingston: Quarry Press, 1993.

Phelps, Edward, *Sarnia: Gateway to Bluewaterland.* Burlington: Windsor Publications,1987.

Purdy, G.A., *Petroleum: Prehistoric to Petrochemicals.* Toronto: Copp Clark, 1957.

Ross, Victor, *Petroleum in Canada.Wentworth County Historical Atlas,* Toronto: Southam Press, 1917.

Tait, Samuel W. Jr., *The Wildcatters.* Princeton: Princeton University Press, 1946.

Tower, Walter Sheldon, *The Story of Oil.* New York: D. Appleton & Co., 1909.

Wentworth County Historical Atlas. Toronto: H.R. Page, 1875.

Booklets, Pamphlets, Theses

Ford, R.W., *A History of the Chemical Industry in Lambton County.* Sarnia: Dow Chemical Canada, 1964.

Johnston, J.H., *Recollections of Oil Drilling at Oil Springs Ontario.* Provided by Oil Museum of Canada, Oil Springs, ON.

Phelps, Edward, "John Henry Fairbank of Petrolia: A Canadian Entrepreneur," MA thesis. London: University of Western Ontario, 1965.

Pratt, Wanda, and Phil Morningstar, *Early Development of Oil Technology.* Petrolia: Oil Museum of Canada, 1987.

Whipp, Charles, *Road to Destiny: A History of Highway 21.* Provided by Oil Museum of Canada, Oil Springs, ON.

Whipp, Charles, and Edward Phelps, *Petrolia: 1866-1966.* Petrolia: Petrolia Advertiser-Topic, 1966.

Newspapers

Advertiser, Petrolia, ON. Also *Topic,* and *Advertiser-Topic,* Petrolia, ON.

Daily Globe, Toronto.

Evening Telegram, Toronto.

Free Press, London, ON.

London Advertiser, London, ON.

261

Observer, Sarnia, ON.
Windsor Star, Windsor, ON.

Periodicals

Anglo-Persian Oil Co. Ltd. Magazine, vol. X, no.3, May 1934. London: Britannia House, 1934.
Griffin, Selwyn P., "Petrolia, Cradle of Oil Drillers," *Imperial Oil Review,* vol. 14, August/September 1930.
Harkness, R.B., "Ontario's Part in the Petroleum Industry," *Canadian Oil and Gas Industries* magazine, February/March 1951.
"Imperial Oil Pioneer Dies," *Imperial Oil Review,* May 1921.
Lauriston, Victor, "Town of World Travellers," *Maclean's* magazine, 1 May 1924.
"Mysterious Jake Englehart and the Early Ontario Petroleum Industry, The," *Ontario History,* 85 (1), March 1993.
"Obituary of Jake Englehart," *Imperial Oil Review,* Vol. 5, May 1921.
Scott, Ben S., *Western Ontario Historical Notes,* VI, 3/4 September/December 1948.

References

Canadian Encyclopedia Plus, The, multimedia reference work on CD-ROM. Toronto: McClelland & Stewart Inc., 1995.
Grolier Multimedia Encyclopedia. Novato, CA.: Grolier, 1997.
Times Atlas of World History, edited by Geoffrey Barraclough. Maplewood, N.J.: Hammond, 1978.

Diaries and Scrapbooks

"Biographical Sketches," compiled by Petrolia Discovery museum, Petrolia, ON.
Espenhan, Frieda Erika von, memoirs. Provided by Lorna Mays, Mississauga, ON.
MacIntosh, Ralph, excerpts from memoirs. Provided by Lorna Mays, Mississauga, ON.
Winnett, Edward, diary. Provided by Oil Museum of Canada, Oil Springs, ON.
Women's Institute of Oil Springs, "Tweedsmuir History of Oil Springs." Provided by Oil Museum of Canada, Oil Springs, ON.

Other

As well as the above sources, excerpts from several German-language publications were provided courtesy Christian Hannesschlager at the Technisch*es Museum of Vienna, Austria.* They are: the periodicals, *Petroleum,* and *Zeitschrift des Internationalen Vereines der Bohringenieure und Bohrtechniker, no.* 24; and the book, *Die Grob-Industrie Osterreichs 1898,* which contains the chapter titled "Galizische Karpathen-Petroleum-Actien-Gesellschaft."

Index